INQUIRY-BASED
LESSONS
IN WORLD HISTORY

EARLY HUMANS TO GLOBAL EXPANSION

INQUIRY-BASED
LESSONS
IN WORLD HISTORY

VOLUME 1   **GRADES 7–10**

Jana Kirchner, Ph.D., &
Andrew McMichael, Ph.D.

PRUFROCK PRESS INC.
WACO, TEXAS

Printed in the United States of America.

At the time of this book's publication, all facts and figures cited are the most current available; all telephone numbers, addresses, and website URLs are accurate and active; all publications, organizations, websites, and other resources exist as described in this book; and all have been verified. The author and Prufrock Press make no warranty or guarantee concerning the information and materials given out by organizations or content found at websites, and we are not responsible for any changes that occur after this book's publication. If you find an error or believe that a resource listed here is not as described, please contact Prufrock Press.

Prufrock Press Inc.
P.O. Box 8813
Waco, TX 76714-8813
Phone: (800) 998-2208
Fax: (800) 240-0333
http://www.prufrock.com

TABLE OF CONTENTS

INTRODUCTION

WHY WRITE THIS BOOK?

"How do I find primary sources that go along with my textbook?"

"Where do I locate political cartoons and maps that are appropriate for middle and high school students?"

"I want to use primary sources, but I don't have time to find good ones that fit in my units."

"I know I need to integrate literacy skills, but I don't know how with all of this content to teach."

These are common questions in any history classroom, and for more than 15 years we have worked to help teachers answer these and more. In the course of designing and implementing three U.S. Department of Education Teaching American History (TAH) grants, as well as working with teachers in their classrooms, we developed standards-based history lessons that model U.S. and world history using inquiry and discovery, with primary sources and essential questions to drive learning. This book, like *Inquiry-Based Lessons in U.S. History: Decoding the Past* (Kirchner & McMichael, 2015), is the culmination of those professional development sessions, planning and coaching conferences with teachers, and site visits to help implement inquiry-based, primary source lessons with students.

We have targeted the lessons in this book to middle and high school students, with the idea that world history is taught as a stand-alone course in those grades, and lesson plan supplements in the middle and high school courses must reach a number of audiences and cover a wide range of time periods and places. These lessons can easily be adapted for gifted students as supplemental history lessons in pull-out programs or for homeschooled students studying world history.

THE GENERAL APPROACH

World history is a lot to tackle in a year. Teachers have just learned students' names and adjusted the seating arrangement in the (for now) best way possible, and it seems like the countdown to test time has already begun. The subject spans thousands of years and the entire globe, so organizing a set of lesson plans in a way that makes sense can be overwhelming. There is no "right" method. In this book, we have done two things to help teachers organize lesson plans in the most pedagogically effective and efficient way. First, this book has a truly global focus meant to help teachers and students discover topical links in cultures around the world. Second, clear chapter titles and a generalized, sometimes-overlapping chronology are designed to help teachers quickly find what they need and to facilitate yearlong lesson planning.

Learning is enhanced when students see links between topics that might not seem related, and when those links are repeated or emphasized. For example, a student who engages with a lesson on Neanderthal and early human art is more likely to remember that material if the lesson is linked and reinforced during a later lesson that includes artwork. To that end, the lessons in this volume reinforce common themes, including art, religion, technology, culture, government, economics, and geography. In turn, teachers will find it easier to reinforce their own social studies themes throughout the year.

INQUIRY IN SOCIAL STUDIES: THE COLLEGE, CAREER, AND CIVIC LIFE (C3) FRAMEWORK

At the time of publication, the national focus in social studies is on the College, Career, and Civic Life (C3) Framework (National Council for the Social Studies [NCSS], 2013). Developed by a team of social studies professionals, curriculum specialists, K–12 teachers, social studies organizations, and university professors from across the United States, the C3 Framework has been referred to as a "watershed moment for social studies education in America" (Herczog, 2013, p. vii). The C3 Framework is based on the following guiding principles about high-quality social studies instruction:

- Social studies prepares the nation's young people for college, careers, and civic life.
- Inquiry is at the heart of social studies.
- Social studies involves interdisciplinary applications and welcomes integration of the arts and humanities.
- Social studies is composed of deep and enduring understandings, concepts, and skills from the disciplines. Social studies emphasizes skills and practices as preparation for democratic decision-making.
- Social studies education should have direct and explicit connections to the Common Core State Standards for English Language Arts and Literacy in History/Social Studies. (Herczog, 2013, p. viii)

The foundation of the C3 Framework is its focus on the inquiry arc using a four-square model (NCSS, 2013):

- Dimension 1: Developing questions and planning inquiries.
- Dimension 2: Applying disciplinary concepts and tools.
- Dimension 3: Evaluating sources and using evidence.
- Dimension 4: Communicating conclusions and taking informed action.

Dimension 1 focuses on creating compelling and supporting questions to frame a unit or lesson and then determining helpful sources to answer that question. This dimension guided the lesson plan organization for this book. It is important to note that the lessons in this book are short, one- to two-period lessons that use supporting questions (using C3 Framework language) rather than the general overarching unit questions that the C3 Framework refers to as compelling questions.

The organizing questions in this book are teacher-generated. However, allowing students to generate their own questions is an effective inquiry strategy. In several lessons in the book, we showcase Rothstein and Santana's (2011) Question Formulation Technique, an easy-to-implement strategy for teaching students how to generate good questions to focus their learning for a lesson or unit. For more detailed information about the Question Formulation Technique, visit the Right Question Institute's website and educator network (https://rightquestion.org).

Dimension 2 of the C3 Framework targets the four content areas of civics, economics, geography, and history as "lenses students use in their inquiries" (NCSS, 2013, p. 29). This book teaches students to read and think like historians as they explore the story of world history through a variety of primary and secondary sources.

Dimension 3, evaluating sources and evidence, includes gathering and evaluating sources for main ideas, point of view, context, and purpose, and using this analysis to develop claims. Each lesson in the book requires students to read and analyze sources as evidence they will use to answer an organizing question.

Dimension 4 involves students communicating and critiquing conclusions. Although the lessons in this book require students to develop a hypothesis and share it with the class, teachers have the flexibility to plan how students should communicate these conclusions (i.e., the product for the lesson). The "Make a Hypothesis" section of each lesson could be implemented as a whole-group discussion, a student presentation, or an individual writing assessment. The key is having students answer the organizing question by citing evidence from multiple sources.

To implement these dimensions, teachers need to develop a classroom that is based on inquiry. Wineburg, Martin, and Monte-Sano (2013) expressed the importance of historical inquiry for 21st-century learners in this authentic way:

> In an age where "I found it on the Internet" masquerades as knowledge, history serves as a vital counterweight to intellectual sloppiness. When a video uploaded from a cell phone in Tehran reaches San Francisco in half a second, history reminds us to start with basic questions: Who sent it? Can it be trusted? What angle did the Flip Video miss? (p. ix)

The teacher is no longer the provider of knowledge, but rather the facilitator of historical thinking. Gerwin and Zevin (2011) described the teacher's role in teaching history through inquiry as follows:

> First of all, encourage students to learn how to draw their own conclusions, and defend themselves against criticisms from other "detectives." Each participant, in effect, becomes a partner, a team member, in an investigation to which all have a chance to contribute. And contributions, including your own, must be defended and supported by evidence, sources, references, and reasons. You can join in with more suggestions, questions, and pointers, but this must be done carefully so as not to destroy students' sense of independent inquiry. (p. 21)

The strategies and sources used in lessons in this book can help teachers create this type of inquiry-based learning in their classrooms.

INTEGRATING HISTORY AND LITERACY STANDARDS

Although the C3 foundational principles and the dimensions of the inquiry arc are embedded in every lesson in this book, we chose to use world history (grades 5–12) content standards from the National Center for History in the Schools (NCHS, 1996) as the source for specific content standards. At the time of this book's publication, individual states are developing social studies standards targeting the C3 Framework. The NCHS standards provide a common, national set of history standards that are often referenced in the social studies field.

Each chapter also includes the targeted Common Core State Standards (CCSS; National Governors Association Center for Best Practices & Council of Chief State School Officers, 2010) for Literacy in History/Social Studies appropriate for middle school (grades 6–8) and high school (grades 9–10). Historical inquiry and literacy standards require students to assemble information and draw conclusions from a variety of primary and secondary sources. In describing this reading process, Wineburg et al. (2013) noted that "historians have developed powerful ways of reading that allow them to see patterns, make sense of contradictions, and formulate reasoned interpretations" (p. ix). With this focus on disciplinary literacy, or reading and thinking like a historian, the lessons in this book integrate multiple primary sources, including letters, journals, political cartoons, artwork, interviews, posters, pamphlets, and maps, to encourage students to conduct historical inquiry using original documents. A few of the lessons include optional secondary sources that can easily be integrated into the lessons. The concept of thinking like a historian frames the way the lessons are created; each lesson challenges students to examine a historical question, analyze the evidence, create a hypothesis, and use the specific evidence to support the hypothesis.

USING THE BOOK

In our experience over many years of working on both content and pedagogy, teachers usually agree on the importance of inquiry and integrating historical thinking skills. However, they often are not sure how to integrate skills with content standards, what this integration might look like in their specific content area or grade level, or where to find quality sources to use with students. This book contains sample lessons showing how to do just those things.

We designed the lesson plans to align with the scope and sequence of typical middle school and high school world history courses so that teachers can use them in several ways. First, teachers can use the lessons individually, tailoring them to state standards and existing classroom curricula. Second, the lessons are structured so that they can be used in a complementary fashion at appropriate places within the larger unit topic. Finally, teachers can swap out primary sources in each lesson with sources that they might already be using in their classrooms.

The book is divided into four chronological eras of three or four chapters. Each chapter begins with a short section detailing the historical context to provide teachers with a reference point for the primary source materials in the lesson plans, followed by the NCHS world history standards and Common Core Literacy in History/Social Studies standards targeted in the lessons. Following the introduction, each chapter contains inquiry lessons, beginning with an organizing question to frame the lesson and the teaching strategies employed in the lesson. Each lesson also either contains handouts with excerpts from documents used in the lesson or lists the primary and/or secondary source materials with web links. When appropriate for the lesson content, we have added section breaks and paragraph breaks to the primary sources. Depending on the ability of the students, teachers can use the entire primary source or choose their own excerpts.

The lessons each follow a similar structure focused on students doing inquiry, or thinking and reading like a historian. We developed individual lessons based on these phases: Lesson Hook, Organizing Question, Examine the Sources, and Make a Hypothesis. Each part of the lesson includes detailed instructions for planning and implementation, as well as commonly used literacy strategies. Background information and tips for implementing these literacy strategies are available from many online sources.

SEARCH TIPS FOR FINDING OTHER RESOURCES

Finding useful primary sources can often be a challenge for teachers who are short on time and resources. Google is a good place to start, but it is important to know that a search engine like Google generally returns a broader range of results than a teacher might want. "Operands" such as a plus (+) or minus (-) sign will narrow a search by forcing the engine to include or exclude specific terms. In Figure 1, for example, Googling the phrase "Qing Dynasty" generates results that include encyclopedia definitions from Wikipedia and Britannica. The search terms shown in Figure 2 remove those websites, narrowing the results somewhat, while the search terms in Figure 3 help focus the search on a particular event in the history of the Qing Dynasty. The search terms in Figure 4 redirect the search, using quotes, to websites that include teaching resources about the Qing Dynasty.

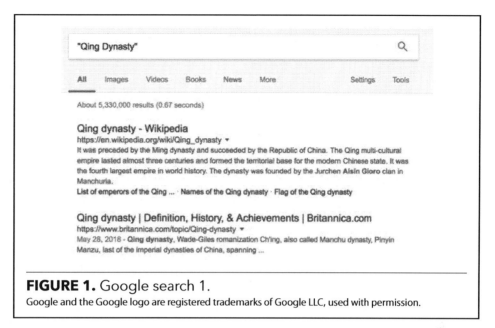

FIGURE 1. Google search 1.
Google and the Google logo are registered trademarks of Google LLC, used with permission.

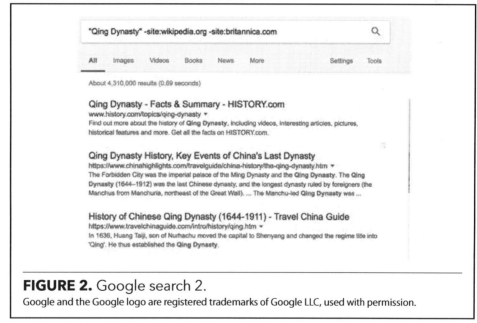

FIGURE 2. Google search 2.
Google and the Google logo are registered trademarks of Google LLC, used with permission.

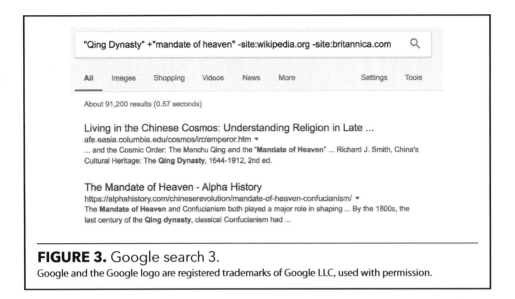

FIGURE 3. Google search 3.
Google and the Google logo are registered trademarks of Google LLC, used with permission.

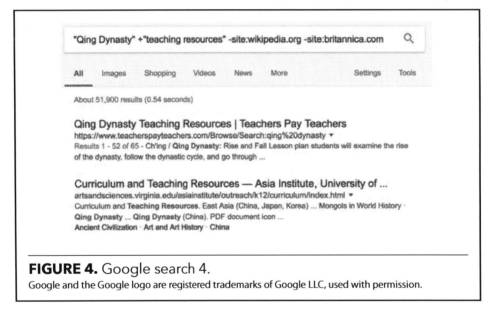

FIGURE 4. Google search 4.
Google and the Google logo are registered trademarks of Google LLC, used with permission.

Many resource-focused websites employ their own search engines, but these can be confusing and inefficient. In most cases, simply using Google to directly search through an archive is easiest. For example, the Library of Congress's search engine is sometimes difficult to use, so a teacher might turn to Google instead. A Google search for "World War II" initially returns more than 500 million results across the Internet. Adding "+site:loc.gov," as shown in Figure 5, directs the search to the Library of Congress's archives, produces fewer results by focusing it considerably, and includes teacher resources in the results.

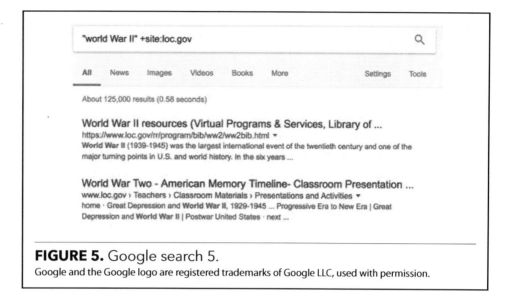

FIGURE 5. Google search 5.

Google and the Google logo are registered trademarks of Google LLC, used with permission.

Some excellent websites with primary sources include:

- The Library of Congress (https://www.loc.gov),
- The National Archives (https://www.archives.gov),
- The Internet Archive's Prelinger Archives (https://www.archive.org/details/prelinger),
- The Internet History Sourcebooks Project (https://sourcebooks.fordham.edu),
- Finding World History (http://chnm.gmu.edu/worldhistorysources/whmfinding.php),
- West Sound Academy (http://libguides.westsoundacademy.org/primary_sources/world_history),
- Newton Gresham Library (https://shsulibraryguides.org/worldprimary),
- List of Reading Like a Historian Lessons at Stanford University (https://sheg.stanford.edu/list-reading-historian-lessons), and
- The Avalon Project (http://avalon.law.yale.edu).

The following introductory lesson demonstrates a way of getting both students and teachers to think like historians. The lesson can serve as an introduction for students at the beginning of the semester, or as a refresher partway through the year.

INTRODUCTORY LESSON

HOW DO HISTORIANS AND ARCHAEOLOGISTS KNOW ABOUT THE PAST?

BACKGROUND INFORMATION FOR TEACHERS

How do we know when something is true? This question has occupied philosophers since before the dawn of written history. For humans, some truths are very obvious (e.g., the sun always rises on one side of the horizon and always sets on the other). From hard-won experience, early humans knew many things about their world. They knew that lions were dangerous and that certain plants were safe to eat while others were not. They learned from experience how to tell those plants apart.

Early philosophers speculated about how the natural world worked and about their histories. More than 2,000 years ago in the Mediterranean, the Greek philosopher Aristotle worked to learn more about the universe through observation, deduction, and logical speculation. Greeks dissected animals to discover how internal organs worked. "Natural philosophers," followers of a branch of study that included mathematics and the sciences, used logic and observation to "know" things about the world. This led to some important discoveries that paved the way for scientific advances, but scientists today know that some of these conclusions were inaccurate. For example, although some Greek astronomers posited that the sun was at the center of the solar system, others, through observation of the motion of the sun across the sky, believed that the sun, moon, planets, and stars moved around the Earth in perfectly circular motions. When Aristotle dissected eels, he noticed that they didn't have reproductive systems that he could see. His conclusion was that they spontaneously generated from mud.

The "way of knowing" changed during the scientific revolution in the Western world. During that time, European scientists began to use *empiricism*, or the use of evidence usually gathered through research and experiment to reach a conclusion. Scientists developed a scientific method in which knowledge is gained by proposing a hypothesis—more simply, an explanation for something—that can be shown as true or false through an experiment or by simple observation. From experiments or observations, researchers then develop a theory, which is an explanation for something that has already been tested and verified through experiments or observation. Virtually every way of knowing in the world employs this method.

Like scientists, historians and archaeologists gather evidence to develop hypotheses and then theories for "why things were the way they were." In these fields, a hypothesis is usually a one-sentence answer to a question. For example, the question of "What happened to the settlers at Jamestown?" might be answered with the hypothesis that "they were killed by local Native Americans." The question "Why did the Emperor stop the Ming treasure voyages of Zheng He?" might prompt the hypothesis that "the voyages were too expensive for the Ming emperors to bear." For evidence, historians and archaeologists use primary and secondary sources, and if there is enough testable evidence, they can form a theory—an explanation that, given all of the best available evidence, answers the question.

This "way of knowing"—asking a question, gathering evidence, and then presenting a hypothesis—is a simple explanation for how we know about the past. That past, and the way of knowing about the past, can help us better understand the present and shape our future.

ORGANIZING QUESTION

How do historians and archaeologists know about the past?

STRATEGIES USED

Role-Play, List/Group/Label

MATERIALS NEEDED

1. Handout 0.1: Archaeology Cards (cut up in advance and placed in an envelope for each group)
2. Artifacts: 4–5 student backpacks (*Note*: If you are unable to use students' backpacks, collect examples of objects around the room [e.g., stapler, pencil, eraser, or similar items] or show pictures of random objects that might be found in a local mall.)
3. 1–2 images of any archaeology dig
4. Sticky notes

LESSON PLAN

Lesson Hook: Divide students into groups of 4–5, making sure to have an even number of groups. Ask each group to go to an area of the room and choose one group member's backpack to empty on a desk. Ask students to also choose one writer for their group. Explain that archaeologists uncover objects that they frequently don't understand; they have to describe these items impartially, and in great detail, so that other researchers can better understand the artifacts. In this hook, the task is to describe the objects from the backpack in as much detail as possible without naming the objects or saying what they are used for. For example, a stapler should not be described as something that holds paper together. Students should stick to a strict physical description. They may number the items and list descriptors under each item. Once each group has made a list of the items (artifacts) in each backpack, have students repack the backpacks.

Next, ask students to trade their lists with another group. The new group should read the list of descriptors and try to guess what the objects are, based on the descriptive words. Ask students what was easy or challenging about this activity. Mention that they might have already known what the items were because most students have similar items in their backpacks.

The Organizing Question: Explain to students that they are going to analyze some clues about a culture to help them understand the organizing question: *How do historians and archaeologists know about the past?*

Examine the Sources: *Role-Play*—Display images of an archaeology dig and ask students what they know about archaeology or the job of an archaeologist. Explain that they are going to work with their groups to think like an archaeologist or historian and try to learn information about a society, using only clues found at an archaeological dig.

List/Group/Label—Distribute Handout 0.1: Archaeology Cards. Explain the following task and stress that there are no right or wrong categories:

> You are part of an archaeology team that has just discovered a tablet of words. Your task is to look for patterns in the words and group them in some way. Create a label for each of your groups (e.g., jobs, family, trade).

Make a Hypothesis: When students finish creating their word groups with labels, ask each group to make a hypothesis about the time (i.e., century) and place in which this culture existed. Students should be prepared to give several examples of evidence to support their group's hypothesis, using any of the clues from their organized categories.

As students complete this activity, have a student from each group write the time and place on a sticky note, and then share what is on the note. Write the list of time periods and places on the board. Students will probably offer examples from multiple countries or continents and many different time periods. Ask students what they notice about the differences in their hypotheses about time and place, even though all of the groups had the same clues. Discuss what was easy or difficult about this task, ask if they had any clue "outliers" that just didn't fit, and compare that to the challenges historians and archaeologists have in interpreting evidence from the past.

Note: Students will want to know what the correct answer is for time and place, but there is no correct answer. The purpose is to get them to understand the role of historians and archaeologists in interpreting the past. If used as an introduction to the class, this activity is a good way to teach students about the artifacts, primary sources, and secondary sources that they will be using for the rest of the year. It is also a good way to teach them that sometimes we just do not know, and might never know, the answers to some very important historical questions.

Optional Extension: Google the phrase *unknown historical objects* and look at the lists of mysterious objects that scientists have (so far) been unable to identify. Have your students generate some hypotheses about the origins of these objects.

HANDOUT 0.1
ARCHAEOLOGY CARDS

Teacher directions: Cut out the items below to create a deck of cards for one student group.

TOWN	ROAD	TENT	WITCH
CHEAP	CAMEL	CATTLE	HEALER
MULE	DAUGHTER	DRY SEASON	FARM
FURNACE	SCHOOL	WHEAT	COLD
UMBRELLA	MUSIC	GHOST	FAMILY
LAW	MOUNTAIN	BRASS	COPPER
HARVEST	TAX	SON	TOWER
SALT	PAPER	WAR	CANOE
GOD	HOUSE	SLAVE	CHEESE
YAMS	SPIDER	BOOK	GOAT
TEACHER	BLACKSMITH	IVORY	TEMPLE
BARBER	HORSE	MONEY	COTTON

Inquiry-Based Lessons in World History, Volume 1 © Prufrock Press Inc.

15,000-1045 BCE

PART I

EARLY HUMANS

CHAPTER 1

THE NEOLITHIC ERA AND EARLY SETTLEMENTS

If we don't have a common heritage to share, something to get excited about, then what are we living for?

—Sarah Parcak, American anthropologist

HISTORICAL CONTEXT:
WHAT DO I NEED TO KNOW?

The question of what makes humans "human" has vexed philosophers and scientists for millennia. Early ideas focused on what made humans different from animals; we have language, we make tools, and we have a conceptual understanding of death. Scientists now know that different animals also understand and do these things, and that what it means to be human is complex and has evolved over time. Our very earliest ancestors evolved from even earlier primates. Of all of the recent human ancestors, none captures the imagination so much as *Homo neanderthalensis*, who lived from around 450,000 to 38,000 years ago. Early depictions portrayed the Neanderthals (pronounced *nee-ann-der-tals*) as brutish, knuckle-dragging, unintelligent beasts. More recent evidence indicates that they had much larger brains than modern humans and controlled fire, made sophisticated stone tools, created art, and hunted. They may have buried their dead in symbolic rituals and adorned their bodies with jewelry.

They interbred with *Homo sapiens* often enough that non-African humans carry as much as 2% Neanderthal DNA.

Groups of modern humans organized into settlements as early as 300,000 years ago, but it was not until more than 60,000 years ago that a Neanderthal stenciled the outline of his or her hand on a cave wall in Spain. Scientists can determine a range of possible dates by measuring the decay of radiocarbon and calcium carbonate. More complex artwork began more than 30,000 years ago. Surviving creations appear in caves in France, Spain, Indonesia, South Africa, Australia, and elsewhere. Common subjects included the outlines of human hands and local game animals, while pictures of people were much less common. Whether early humans created cave art for religious purposes, for entertainment, to record their history, or for some other purpose, we will never know.

Larger human settlements coincided with the rise of animal domestication and agriculture. People seem to have begun by domesticating dogs for hunting, and then sheep, goats, and cattle for agriculture, which could replace hunting. Humans learned how to grow wheat and barley, and then beans. The process began sometime after 12,000 years ago in Western Asia in the warmer, damper climate that followed the last Ice Age. Small agricultural settlements were increasingly common after 9,000 years ago. Thus was born the farming village, which is probably the place that most people called home after the spread of agriculture around the world. However, the security of village life brought new problems. The concentrated population in these settlements bred disease, and the cultivation of pieces of land over time led to territoriality and war.

In an agricultural society like that of the modern world, it takes fewer people to produce food than in hunter-gatherer societies, and agricultural societies tend to be about 25% larger than hunter-gatherer societies. Farming changed everything for humans, and no innovation in human history, with the exception of fire, did more to alter the course of human development than what is called the Agricultural or Neolithic Revolution. With an increased number of people who did not have to work to produce food for the group, these societies could have people specialize in non-food-producing activities. Some spent their time protecting their food or villages against outsiders (in an organized army), while others worked as full-time metallurgists. Some spent their time attempting to divine the nature of their gods and goddesses, and indeed the first indications of organized religion appeared at the same time as farming villages. Still others worked to improve farming methods, developing a way to haul crops from faraway fields (on wheels), more efficient ways to store grain over the winter (in clay pots), and, most importantly, a way to track (using writing, and then mathematics) how much food the village, city, or city-state had on hand to get through the winter. According to recent research (Blasi et al., 2019), humans' increased consumption of bread, a much softer food that requires fewer muscles to chew, probably also led to changes in the structure of the human jaw, allowing humans to pronounce "f" and "v" sounds.

Indeed, the development of agriculture—the Neolithic Revolution—changed human speech and gave birth to stratified societies, technological changes, and social and cultural organization that radically altered what it meant to be human.

STANDARDS ADDRESSED IN THE CHAPTER

NCHS World History Content Standards, Grades 5–12:

- **Era 1—Standard 1A:** The student understands early hominid development in Africa.
- **Era 1—Standard 2A:** The student understands how and why humans established settled communities and experimented with agriculture.
- **Era 1—Standard 2B:** The student understands how agricultural societies developed around the world.

CCSS for Literacy in History/Social Studies, Grades 6–8 and 9–10:

- **6–8:** Determine the central ideas or information of a primary or secondary source; Integrate visual information (e.g., in charts, graphs, photographs, videos, or maps) with other information in print and digital texts.
- **9–10:** Determine the central ideas or information of a primary or secondary source; Cite specific textual evidence to support analysis of primary and secondary sources, attending to such features as the date and origin of the information; Analyze in detail a series of events described in a text; Determine whether earlier events caused later ones or simply preceded them.

LESSON 1

ORGANIZING QUESTION

What can cave paintings tell us about life in the Stone Age?

STRATEGIES USED

I Notice/I Wonder, Think Aloud, Clue Stations

MATERIALS NEEDED

1. Handout 1.1: I Notice/I Wonder Clue Sheet
2. Video: The Bradshaw Foundation's "Lascaux Cave Paintings—An Introduction," available at http://www.bradshawfoundation.com/lascaux/index.php
3. Flashlights (one per group, if you choose to dim the lights for this activity)
4. The following cave paintings taped underneath desks or displayed around the room before class starts, labeled by number:
   - ✓ Photograph: *Red Cow and First Chinese Horse* from Lascaux Cave, France, available at http://www.bradshawfoundation.com/lascaux/index.php
   - ✓ Photograph: *Red Hand and Mammoth* from Chauvet Cave, France, available at http://www.bradshawfoundation.com/chauvet/hand_mammoth.php
   - ✓ Photograph: *Large Horse Panel* from Chauvet Cave, France, available at http://www.bradshawfoundation.com/chauvet/large_horse_panel.php
   - ✓ Photograph: *Bison* from Chauvet Cave, France, available at http://www.bradshawfoundation.com/chauvet/bison.php
   - ✓ Any painting from the Australian Rock Art Archive, available at http://www.bradshawfoundation.com/bradshaws/bradshaw_paintings.php
   - ✓ Any painting from the African Rock Art Gallery, available at http://www.bradshawfoundation.com/coulson/index.php
   - ✓ Any painting from the Rock Art Archive of South Africa, available at http://www.bradshawfoundation.com/south_africa/south_africa_gallery.php

5. A textbook reading or article about life in the Stone Age and/or analyzing cave art

LESSON PLAN

Lesson Hook: *I Notice/I Wonder*—Distribute Handout 1.1: I Notice/I Wonder Clue Sheet and play the "Lascaux Cave Paintings—An Introduction" video. Explain to students that they should watch the video and write things they notice and wonder about on their clue sheet next to Clue #1. It might be necessary to play the video twice so that they can add more details. Discuss student responses and brainstorm the ways that historians and archaeologists learn about the past before written records existed.

The Organizing Question: Explain that students will act as archaeologists to examine more cave paintings to help them determine the answer to the organizing question: *What can cave paintings tell us about life in the Stone Age?*

Examine the Sources: *Think Aloud*—Display a large image of *Red Cow and First Chinese Horse* from Lascaux Cave in France. Model your thinking so that students can see how to analyze an image and collect their ideas on the clue sheet.

Clue Stations—Divide students into groups of 3–4, give each group a flashlight, and assign each of them a desk location with a painting taped underneath to start their "cave exploring." You may choose to dim the lights and use flashlights to simulate a cave environment. Explain to students that they will work with their group to analyze the cave paintings in each station of the room and record their observations and questions on their I Notice/I Wonder Clue Sheet. Allow students 2–3 minutes at each clue station (desk) to describe what they notice and wonder about from the paintings.

Make a Hypothesis: As students complete their observations, have them discuss with their groups what they noticed in the paintings and what they think these clues might tell them about life in the Stone Age. Have student groups write two hypotheses on the bottom of the clue sheet and prepare to cite evidence from the cave paintings that supports their hypotheses.

Ask students to share their hypotheses with supporting clue examples. Write the hypotheses on the board as the groups explain each one. Then, have students look for similarities and differences between groups' hypotheses. Next, ask them what was challenging about this activity and how those challenges might be similar to ones faced by archaeologists and historians.

Have students share their "I Wonder" topics and write those on the board. Once students have discussed their questions, assign a textbook reading or an article about life in the Stone Age and/or one analyzing cave art. After they read the secondary source, have them review their hypotheses to see if they proved or disproved them with the additional reading. Also ask students if any of their "I Wonder" questions were answered from their reading.

Optional Activity: If time permits, students could create their own cave painting that either reflects the content they have read or would communicate clues about the current culture and time period with a future generation. For fun, students could be challenged to paint without brushes, similarly to ancient societies, by using "found" materials in the classroom or on school grounds.

HANDOUT 1.1
I NOTICE/I WONDER CLUE SHEET

Directions: Examine the evidence or clues posted around the room. Write down what you notice and what you wonder about from each clue. Your group will use this information to make hypotheses that answer the organizing question.

ORGANIZING QUESTION: What can cave paintings tell us about life in the Stone Age?

	I Notice . . .	I Wonder . . .
Clue #1 _____		
Clue #2 _____		
Clue #3 _____		
Clue #4 _____		
Clue #5 _____		
Clue #6 _____		
Clue #7 _____		
Clue #8 _____		

Based on the clues/evidence you examined, what are your hypotheses about the organizing question?

LESSON 2

ORGANIZING QUESTION

How did the Agricultural Revolution change the structure and organization of human societies?

STRATEGIES USED

Map Analysis, Chunking Text, Gist

MATERIALS NEEDED

1. Map of the spread of agriculture in the Stone Age (*Note*: Most textbooks include this type of map, but you can also find images online.)
2. Encyclopedia article: "The Coming of Farming" by TimeMaps, available at https://www.timemaps.com/encyclopedia/farming (*Note*: Begin with the section "The Origins of Farming" and divide the article into 6–7 sections, one per group.)
3. Highlighters (one per group of students)

LESSON PLAN

Lesson Hook: Before class, write the word *revolution* on the board. As class begins, give students 2 minutes to individually brainstorm all of the things they can think of related to the word *revolution*. Ask students to share their ideas with the class and write them on the board. Use these examples to develop a good class definition of revolution with examples.

The Organizing Question: Explain to students that they will examine an agricultural type of revolution by analyzing a map and an article for clues to answer the organizing question: *How did the Agricultural Revolution change the structure and organization of human societies?*

Examine the Sources: *Map Analysis*—Display a map showing the spread of agriculture. Ask students to examine the map for one minute, looking for answers to these questions:
- What details do you notice?
- What parts of the world saw the earliest agriculture? What does this tell you about the Agricultural Revolution?
- What do you think some effects of the Agricultural Revolution might be?

Allow students to share their responses and write examples of the effects on the board to use later in the lesson.

Chunking Text and Gist—Divide the class into 6–7 groups and assign each group a chunk of the text "The Coming of Farming." Tell students that they will be reading a text and using the gist strategy; as one group member reads a paragraph of the text, a second group member should write in the margin the gist, or summary, of what it means, using five words or fewer. A third group member should use a highlighter to mark examples of evidence that might answer the organizing question. Complete one section with the whole class as an example of what students should do in the task. Groups should stop at the end of each paragraph to discuss their gist words and highlighted evidence. You can also allow students to rotate their roles after each paragraph so that all students are responsible for each role. As each group finishes its chunk, allow students to write one gist statement from their chunk of text on the board and share it with the class.

Make a Hypothesis: Ask students to use the ideas from the Lesson Hook, the map analysis, and the article to answer the organizing question. Compare their hypotheses with ideas they generated in the map analysis section of the lesson. End the lesson with a summary discussion or an exit slip assessment of how the Agricultural Revolution impacted humans' everyday lives. Make sure that students cite evidence from sources to support their hypotheses.

Optional Extension: The article "The Coming of Farming" makes several statements about human history during the Agricultural Revolution. Students can highlight sentences and try to determine what kind of evidence historians and archaeologists used to arrive at those conclusions. For example, the statement that "Neolithic villages would have been structured along clan lines" (TimeMaps, n.d., para. 37) might raise questions about how we know that information, which can link to the Introductory Lesson.

LESSON 3

ORGANIZING QUESTION

How did the Agricultural Revolution lead to the rise of complex societies?

STRATEGIES USED

Picture Analysis, Creating a Timeline

MATERIALS NEEDED

1. Handout 1.2: Human Civilization Cards (cut up and shuffled in advance for each group of students)
2. Images of hunter-gatherer villages

LESSON PLAN

Lesson Hook: *Picture Analysis*—Display images of hunter-gatherers and ask students what type of work people do in a hunter-gatherer society. Students should explain their reasoning using details from the pictures.

The Organizing Question: Explain to students that they are going to examine some events to find an answer to the organizing question: *How did the Agricultural Revolution lead to the rise of complex societies?*

Examine the Sources: *Creating a Timeline*—Divide students into groups of 3–4 and give each group a complete set of Human Civilization Cards (cut out from Handout 1.2 and shuffled out of order). Their task is to put the events in order and write a few sentences defending why they organized the timeline events as they did. It might be helpful to tell students that the idea for this lesson comes from the video game *Civilization*, which some students might have played. That game requires sequential progress for students to be successful. Have each group share its timeline and discuss any differences between the groups.

Note: Although some events will go in a specific order (e.g., the Agricultural Revolution has to come first, followed by more food and greater population), others may not. For instance, the need to store more food should be followed by technology to solve that issue, but students might argue that technology (such as pottery bowls) could have been developed "accidentally" or for other purposes and then applied later when the need for more storage arose. Similarly, farming techniques could have developed at many different points in the timeline. The key is for students to defend their choices. See Figure 6 for reference.

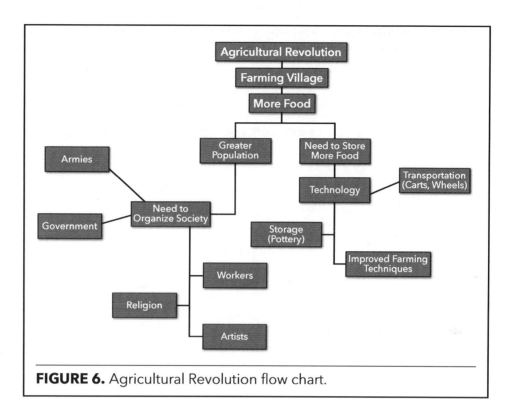

FIGURE 6. Agricultural Revolution flow chart.

Make a Hypothesis: Ask students to answer the organizing question using examples from the hunter-gatherer pictures and the timelines they created. You may choose to have students work individually or with their groups to create an answer.

HANDOUT 1.2
HUMAN CIVILIZATION CARDS

Teacher directions: Cut out the events below to create a deck of cards for one student group. Shuffle the cards so that the events are out of order.

AGRICULTURAL REVOLUTION	FARMING VILLAGE	MORE FOOD
GREATER POPULATION	NEED TO STORE MORE FOOD	TECHNOLOGY
STORAGE	TRANSPORTATION	IMPROVED FARMING TECHNIQUES
NEED TO ORGANIZE SOCIETY	GOVERNMENT	RELIGION
ARMIES TO DEFEND FOOD/VILLAGE	SPECIALIZATION OF THE LABOR FORCE	PRIESTS
FARMERS	MILITARY	ELITES
CREATIVE ART	WRITING	PHILOSOPHY

 Inquiry-Based Lessons in World History, Volume 1 © Prufrock Press Inc.

CHAPTER 2
RISE OF CIVILIZATIONS IN THE MEDITERRANEAN

(EGYPT AND MESOPOTAMIA)

The Nile, forever new and old,
Among the living and the dead,
Its mighty, mystic stream has rolled.

—Henry Wadsworth Longfellow

HISTORICAL CONTEXT: WHAT DO I NEED TO KNOW?

Agriculture came to Mesopotamia (modern-day Iraq) around 5000 BCE. The soft soil allowed for the development of wooden plows, but agriculture would not have been possible without technology. The Tigris and Euphrates rivers flooded irregularly and spread broadly over the plains without warning. In order to farm, people in the area put their technological energy into creating sophisticated systems of dams, dikes, and irrigation to control the water, transforming the area into rich farmland. However, the lack of key raw materials, such as minerals and timber, meant that Mesopotamia had to depend on foreign trade. When human beings trade goods, they also trade ideas, which can lead to turbulent change.

Change also came through war. Neighboring peoples who envied the Mesopotamians' rich cities frequently attacked. Defense and management of the complex society created a need for cooperation and central direction. Mesopotamia consisted of numerous city-states (i.e., independent political units made up of villages controlled by a city). Religion developed along with the various small cities that grew in Mesopotamia. A world of many cities, Mesopotamia was also a world of many gods, and most religions were polytheistic, following many gods, or henotheistic, believing in many gods but focusing worship on only one. Mesopotamians believed that one of the roles of mortals was to provide sacrifices to their gods. Temples and the priest class came to control many of the economic resources of the cities through ownership of land, herds, and the people who worked them.

Cuneiform writing, or representative pictures pressed into clay tablets, allowed people of different languages to communicate with each other by using pictures and then abstract symbols to represent common words. More importantly, in Mesopotamia the Babylonian king Hammurabi developed the first comprehensive laws in the West that attempted to establish a system of justice. The laws covered the conduct of physicians, boat builders, veterinarians, and various professions, and prescribed punishment depending on the social status of the victim and the perpetrator. The code of laws showed a stratified society broken into elites, the mass of the population, and slaves, and it gave legal rights to all. Much of the code tried to protect women and children from unfair treatment.

The Babylonians also developed the most sophisticated mathematical system prior to the 15th century CE, including multiplication tables, squares and square roots, cubes and cube roots, and other calculations. Although the Egyptians were the first to divide the day into 24 hours, the Babylonians used their mathematical system to divide hours into 60 minutes, minutes into 60 seconds, and a circle into 360 degrees. Although the Mesopotamian peoples put most of their technological energy into controlling the Tigris and Euphrates, advancing mathematics, and improving their armies, they also built some of the earliest massive buildings in the world outside of Europe and Egypt, including the Ziggurat of Ur, an administrative and temple complex completed around 2100 BCE.

Unlike the Tigris-Euphrates river system, the Nile floods regularly, at predictable times, and with a predictable spread. Because most of Egypt is desert, with only about 5% habitable by humans, the Nile River shaped its civilization. Life in the Nile Valley was relatively easy. Every summer the Nile flooded in a predictable manner, fertilizing the land with rich runoff water. The Nile's waters spread so broadly, moreover, that it took little human effort to irrigate most of the available farmland in the Nile Valley. The Nile's annual floods were regular and rarely damaging. As a result, Egyptian agriculture was one of the most productive in the ancient world. Egypt was also difficult to reach by outside invaders. The Nile Valley was cut off by deserts in the east and west, by rapids to the south, and by the Mediterranean Sea to the north.

Life in both Egypt and Mesopotamia was governed, in some ways, by the flooding of the rivers, and people in both areas had creation myths that included receding floodwaters. Humans in every part of the world have flood myths of some kind, from the Inca, to the Hopi, Inuit, Greeks, Irish, Koreans, Norse, and more. In the Sumerians' *The Epic of Gilgamesh*, the main character, Utnapishtim, builds a large boat on which all of the animals of the world and a few select humans survive. Although it was written much earlier than the Hebrew Bible, *The Epic of Gilgamesh* mirrors the story in the Book of Genesis so closely that scholars think that they might have similar origins. Flood stories seem so ingrained in the human psyche that archaeologists have searched for and discovered evidence of ancient, torrential floods in many parts of the world.

STANDARDS ADDRESSED IN THE CHAPTER

NCHS World History Content Standards, Grades 5–12:
- **Era 2—Standard 1A:** The student understands how Mesopotamia, Egypt, and the Indus valley became centers of dense population, urbanization, and cultural innovation in the fourth and third millennia BCE.
- **Era 2—Standard 1B:** The student understands how commercial and cultural interactions contributed to change in the Tigris-Euphrates, Indus, and Nile regions.
- **Era 2—Standard 2B:** The student understands how new centers of agrarian society arose in the third and second millennia BCE.

CCSS for Literacy in History/Social Studies, Grades 6–8 and 9–10:
- **6–8:** Determine the central ideas or information of a primary or secondary source; Integrate visual information (e.g., in charts, graphs, photographs, videos, or maps) with other information in print and digital texts.
- **9–10:** Determine the central ideas or information of a primary or secondary source; Cite specific textual evidence to support analysis of primary and secondary sources, attending to such features as the date and origin of the information.

LESSON 1

ORGANIZING QUESTION

What was life like for ancient Mesopotamians?

STRATEGIES USED

Carousel Brainstorming, Modeling

MATERIALS NEEDED

1. 4–5 images of places or things that are important in your students' lives (e.g., cell phone, video game, pizza delivery, mall, movie, church, basketball court, dance recital, school bus)

2. The following images displayed around the room (*Note*: Images may be found at several websites, including the British Museum and the University of Chicago's Oriental Institute's Mesopotamia Collection.):
   ✓ Photograph: Charles Woolley's *Ziggurat of Ur*, available at http://www.mesopotamia.co.uk/ziggurats/explore/photob10.html
   ✓ Drawing: *Cart*, available at http://www.mesopotamia.co.uk/trade/explore/exp_set.html
   ✓ Artifact: *Cuneiform Tablet*, available at http://www.mesopotamia.co.uk/writing/home_set.html
   ✓ Map: *Babylonia and Assyria*, available at https://media1.britannica.com/eb-media/50/64950-004-C4DE78B5.jpg
   ✓ Artifact: *Four-Lugged Vessel*, available at https://oi.uchicago.edu/collections/highlights/highlights-collection-mesopotamia
   ✓ Artifact: *Four-Faced God and Goddess*, available at https://oi.uchicago.edu/collections/highlights/highlights-collection-mesopotamia
   ✓ Artifact: *Duck Weights*, available at https://oi.uchicago.edu/collections/highlights/highlights-collection-mesopotamia

3. One sheet of chart paper posted beside each image
4. One marker and two or three sticky notes per group
5. Timer

LESSON PLAN

Lesson Hook: Display 4–5 images of things or places that might be important to students (see Materials Needed for ideas.) Ask students to look "back" at these images from the hypothetical standpoint of historians 2,000 years in the future. Have them guess what the pictures might represent and what they might tell future historians about the culture we live in. Encourage students to think as creatively as possible and then discuss what might be challenging about interpreting pictures or artifacts from the past.

The Organizing Question: Explain to students that they will work with partners to analyze some pictures of artifacts from life in ancient Mesopotamia. They will use these visuals to answer the organizing question: *What was life like for ancient Mesopotamians?*

Examine the Sources: *Carousel Brainstorming*—Divide students into groups of 3–4 and give each group one marker and a few sticky notes. Have students circulate around the room examining the visuals for clues about life in ancient Mesopotamia. Place a piece of chart paper beside each visual and have students record examples of any of the following topics:

- details that they notice in the image,
- what the image might reflect about Mesopotamia, and/or
- what questions they have.

Students can also respond to an idea someone else wrote, thereby beginning a written conversation about the image.

Modeling—You might wish to model how this process works by analyzing one of the images and writing ideas with the whole class. Allow students a few minutes at each picture and have them circulate clockwise around the room. A timer can help keep this activity moving efficiently. Once students have returned to the visual where they began, have them read the comments and questions that were posted on the chart paper. Depending on time, have them circle two or three of the best comments and questions to share with the class.

Make a Hypothesis: With their groups, challenge students to write one or two hypotheses about the organizing question on sticky notes, using only evidence from the visuals. Allow groups to share their hypotheses and place their sticky notes on the board. As each group shares, look for common patterns or themes and cluster those sticky notes together on the board. Leave these hypotheses on the board during the rest of the Mesopotamia unit and challenge students to prove or disprove their hypotheses based on facts they learn in the unit.

LESSON 2

ORGANIZING QUESTION

Why was the Nile so important to ancient Egyptians?

STRATEGIES USED

Picture Analysis, Turn and Talk, Think Aloud, Annotating Text

MATERIALS NEEDED

1. Handout 2.1: Excerpts From "Hymn to the Nile" (ca. 2100 BCE)
2. Images of the following Egyptian tomb paintings:
   ✓ *Egypt Tomb Oarboat*, available at https://upload.wikimedia.org/wikipedia/commons/7/77/EgyptTombOarboat.jpg
   ✓ *Marsh Scene*, available at http://albertis-window.com/wp-content/uploads/2014/03/Marsh-Scene-Tomb-of-Menna-1924-facsimile-of-original-from-ca.-1400-1352-BC-Met-Museum.jpg
   ✓ *Detail From a New Kingdom Tomb Painting, Showing the Harvest Being Gathered*, available at http://www.bbc.co.uk/history/ancient/egyptians/human_gallery_06.shtml
   ✓ *Plowing Egyptian Farmer*, available at https://www.ancient.eu/article/933/daily-life-in-ancient-egypt

3. Highlighters (one per student)

LESSON PLAN

Lesson Hook: *Picture Analysis*—Project one of the Egyptian tomb paintings on the board. Ask students to take one minute to write down details they notice from the painting and share their responses. Then, share the other three paintings, giving students one minute to add details to their lists and share their ideas.

Turn and Talk—Once students have examined all four wall paintings, ask them to turn to a partner and discuss ideas about what the paintings reflect about life in ancient Egypt. Allow several pairs to share their ideas and write them on the board. Prompt them to discuss the Nile if it is not one of their responses.

The Organizing Question: Explain to students that, having examined some tomb paintings about Egyptian life, they will continue to look for clues in a primary source to help them answer the organizing question: *Why was the Nile so important to ancient Egyptians?*

Examine the Sources: First, explain some background about "Hymn to the Nile" to students. Next, divide the class into groups of 3–4 and distribute Handout 2.1: Excerpts From "Hymn to the Nile" (ca. 2100 BCE). Explain to students that they will work with their group members to read the document and to annotate (or highlight) any examples of evidence about how or why the Nile was important to the Egyptians.

Think Aloud/Annotating the Text—Read the first paragraph of the document with the whole class and model how to pick out main ideas or clues, how to interpret difficult words or phrases, and what to annotate that would help answer the organizing question. After modeling this process, explain to students that they should read and annotate one paragraph at a time, stopping to discuss their annotations with their group. They may also want to make notes or questions in the margin to help them remember important ideas and thoughts.

Make a Hypothesis: As students finish the reading and discussion, have them come to a consensus with their groups about the 3–4 pieces of evidence that are the most important for answering the organizing question. Challenge them to look for examples from "Hymn to the Nile" that corroborate details that they noticed in the Egyptian paintings, as well as ways the text and the paintings might differ. Depending on time, this lesson could end with a discussion or a written assessment of the organizing question, in which students give supporting evidence from pictures and the written text.

HANDOUT 2.1
EXCERPTS FROM "HYMN TO THE NILE" (CA. 2100 BCE)

Hail to thee, O Nile! Who manifests thyself over this land, and comes to give life to Egypt! Mysterious is thy issuing forth from the darkness, on this day whereon it is celebrated! Watering the orchards created by Re, to cause all the cattle to live, you give the earth to drink, inexhaustible one! Path that descends from the sky, loving the bread of Seb and the first-fruits of Nepera, You cause the workshops of Ptah to prosper!

Lord of the fish, during the inundation, no bird alights on the crops. You create the grain, you bring forth the barley, assuring perpetuity to the temples. If you cease your toil and your work, then all that exists is in anguish. If the gods suffer in heaven, then the faces of men waste away.

Then He torments the flocks of Egypt, and great and small are in agony. But all is changed for mankind when He comes; He is endowed with the qualities of Nun. If He shines, the earth is joyous, every stomach is full of rejoicing, every spine is happy, every jaw-bone crushes.

He brings the offerings, as chief of provisioning; He is the creator of all good things, as master of energy, full of sweetness in his choice. If offerings are made it is thanks to Him. He brings forth the herbage for the flocks, and sees that each god receives his sacrifices. All that depends on Him is a precious incense. He spreads himself over Egypt, filling the granaries, renewing the marts, watching over the goods of the unhappy. . . .

A festal song is raised for you on the harp, with the accompaniment of the hand. Your young men and your children acclaim you and prepare their (long) exercises. You are the august ornament of the earth, letting your bark advance before men, lifting up the heart of women in labor, and loving the multitude of the flocks.

When you shine in the royal city, the rich man is sated with good things, the poor man even disdains the lotus; all that is produced is of the choicest; all the plants exist for your children. If you have refused (to grant) nourishment, the dwelling is silent, devoid of all that is good, the country falls exhausted.

O inundation of the Nile, offerings are made unto you, men are immolated to you, great festivals are instituted for you. Birds are sacrificed to you, gazelles are taken for you in the mountain, pure flames are prepared for you. Sacrifice is mettle to every god as it is made to the Nile. The Nile has made its retreats in Southern Egypt, its name is not known beyond the Tuau. The god manifests not his forms, He baffles all conception.

Men exalt him like the cycle of the gods, they dread him who creates the heat, even him who has made his son the universal master in order to give prosperity to Egypt. Come prosper! Come prosper! O Nile, come prosper! O you who make men to live through his flocks and his flocks through his orchards! Come prosper, come, O Nile, come (and) prosper!

LESSON 3

ORGANIZING QUESTION

What can flood stories reveal about values in ancient cultures?

STRATEGIES USED

Close Reading, Annotation, Venn Diagram

MATERIALS NEEDED

1. Handout 2.2: Excerpts From the Flood Story in *The Epic of Gilgamesh* (ca. 2000 BCE)
2. Handout 2.3: Excerpts From the Flood Story in the Bible
3. Images:
   ✓ Relief: *Utnapishtim and the Babylonian Flood Story*, available at http://www.ancientpages.com/2016/01/28/utnapishtim-babylonian-flood-story
   ✓ Painting: Jan Brueghel's *The Flood With Noah's Ark*, available at http://www.janbrueghel.net/object/the-flood-with-noahs-ark-london

4. Chart paper and markers (per group of students)
5. Optional summaries of flood stories from other cultures:
   ✓ Mark Isaak's "Flood Stories From Around the World," available at http://www.talkorigins.org/faqs/flood-myths.html
   ✓ MythoReligio's "15 Flood Myths Similar to the Story of Noah," available at https://www.mythoreligio.com/15-flood-myths-similar-to-the-story-of-noah

LESSON PLAN

Lesson Hook: Display the relief of *Utnapishtim and the Babylonian Flood Story.* Ask students to describe any details that they notice and what they think is the topic of this work. Next, show Jan Brueghel's *The Flood With Noah's Ark* and have students describe the details they notice and compare/contrast them with the Utnapishtim version.

The Organizing Question: Explain to students that they will examine flood stories from two different ancient civilizations to answer the organizing question: *What can flood stories reveal about values in ancient cultures?*

Examine the Sources: *Close Reading/Annotation*—Explain to students that most world cultures have a flood story. Although there are some similarities among these stories, there are also unique cultural elements embedded in each one. Tell students that they are going to do a close reading of a flood story from either the Sumerian or Hebrew culture. Briefly explain *The Epic of Gilgamesh* and review the Sumerian and Hebrew cultures. In close readings, students will read the text twice to complete the following tasks:

- First read: Highlight key events and characters in the story.
- Second read: Circle any examples of clues to the culture in the story (e.g., building tools, rivers, or other components).

Give half of the class excerpts from the Gilgamesh story (Handout 2.2) and the other half excerpts from the Bible story (Handout 2.3). Have students work with a partner to close read their assigned text, annotating for the two tasks.

Venn Diagram—After students finish their close reading tasks, have them partner with a different student who read the other story. Ask them to share their key events, characters, and culture clues with their new partners. Then, give each group a piece of chart paper and markers, and ask them to draw a Venn diagram that compares and contrasts the two stories. Ask students to share the ideas in their Venn diagrams with the class.

Make a Hypothesis: Give each group a few minutes to develop a hypothesis that answers the organizing question. The end of the lesson can be a whole-group discussion or an individual writing assignment used as a formative assessment.

Optional Extension: Have students research flood stories from other cultures, comparing and contrasting them with the Egyptian and Sumerian stories, and look for evidence of cultural connections. The two websites listed in the Materials Needed section provide summaries of flood stories from countries around the world.

HANDOUT 2.2
EXCERPTS FROM THE FLOOD STORY IN
THE EPIC OF GILGAMESH (CA. 2000 BCE)

Utnapishtim then said unto Gilgamesh: "I will reveal unto thee, O Gilgamesh, the mysterious story, and the mystery of the gods I will tell thee. The city of Shuruppak, a city which, as thou knowest, is situated on the bank of the river Euphrates. That city was very old, as were the gods within it. Even the great gods, as many as there were, decided to bring about a deluge: their father, Anu; their counsellor, the warrior Enlil; their leader, Ninurta; their champion, the god Ennugi. . . .

"But Ea, the lord of unfathomable wisdom argued: 'Thou man of Shuruppak, son of Ubara-Tutu, build a house, construct a ship; forsake thy possessions, take heed of the living! Abandon thy goods, save living things, and bring living seed of every kind into the ship. As for the ship, which thou shalt build, let its proportions be well measured: Its breadth and its length shall bear proportion each to each, and into the sea then launch it.'

"I took heed, and said to Ea, my lord: 'I will do, my lord, as thou hast commanded; I will observe and will fulfil the command. . . .'

"On the fifth day I set in place her exterior; it was an acre in area; its sides were ten gar high; ten gar also was the extent of its deck; I added a front-roof to it and closed it in. I built it in six stories, thus making seven floors in all; the interior of each I divided again into nine partitions. Beaks for water within I cut out. I selected a punting-pole and added all that was necessary. Three šar of pitch I smeared on its outside; three šar of asphalt I used for the inside (so as to make it water-tight). Three šar of oil the men carried, carrying it in vessels. One šar of oil I kept out and used it for sacrifices, while the other two šar the boatman stowed away. I slaughtered oxen; I killed lambs day by day. Jugs of beer, of oil, and of sweet wine, like river water (i.e., freely) I gave the workmen to make a feast like that of the New-Year's Day. To the god Shamash my hands brought oil. The ship was completed. Launching it was heavy work, and I added tackling above and below, and after all was finished, the ship sank in the water to two thirds of its height.

"With all that I possessed I filled it; with all the silver I had I filled it; with all the gold I had I filled it; with living creatures of every kind I filled it. Then I embarked also all my family and my relatives, cattle of the field, beasts of the field, and the uprighteous people—all them I embarked. A time had Shamash appointed, (namely): 'When the rulers of darkness send at eventide a destructive rain, then enter into the ship and shut its door.' This very sign came to pass, and the rulers of darkness sent a destructive rain at eventide. I saw the approach of the storm, and I was afraid to witness the storm; I entered the ship and shut the door.

"I entrusted the guidance of the ship to Puzur-Amurri, the boatman, and also the great house, and the contents thereof. As soon as early dawn appeared, there rose up from the horizon a black cloud, within which the weather god (Adad) thundered, and the heralds Shullat and Hanish went before across mountain and plain. The gods of the abyss arose. Nergal, the great, tore loose the dams of the deep. There went Ninurta and he caused the banks to overflow; the Anunnaki lifted on high (their) torches, and with the brightness thereof they illuminated the universe. The storm brought on by Adad swept even up to the heavens and all light was turned into darkness as Adad shattered the land like a pot.

"It blew with violence one whole day, submerging the mountains. Like an onslaught in battle it rushed in on the people. Nor could brother look after brother. Nor were recognised the people from heaven. The gods even were afraid of the storm; they retreated and took refuge in the heaven of Anu. There the gods crouched down like dogs; on the inclosure of heaven they sat cowering. . . . Six days and nights the wind blew, and storm and tempest overwhelmed the country. When the seventh day drew nigh the tempest, the storm, the battle which they had waged like a great host began to moderate. The sea quieted down; hurricane and storm ceased. I looked out upon the sea and raised loud my voice, but all mankind had turned back into clay. Likewise the surrounding sea became as flat as a roof-top.

"I opened the air-hole and light fell upon my cheek. Dumbfounded I sank backward and sat weeping, while over my cheek flowed the tears. I looked in every direction, and behold, all was sea. I looked in vain for land, but twelve leagues distant there rose (out of the water) a strip of land. To Mount Niṣir the ship drifted. On Mount Niṣir the boat stuck fast and it did not slip away. The first day, the second day, Mount Niṣir held the ship fast, and did not let it slip away. The third day, the fourth day, Mount Niṣir held the ship fast, and did not let it slip away. The fifth day, the sixth day, Mount Niṣir held the ship, fast, and did not let it slip away. When the seventh day drew nigh I sent out a dove, and let her go. The dove flew hither and thither, but as there was no resting-place for her, she returned. Then I sent out a swallow, and let her go. The swallow flew hither and thither, but as there was no resting-place for her she also returned. Then I sent out a raven, and let her go. The raven flew away and saw the abatement of the waters. She settled down to feed, went away, and returned no more.

"Then I let everything go out unto the four winds, and I offered a sacrifice. I poured out a libation upon the peak of the mountain."

HANDOUT 2.3
EXCERPTS FROM THE FLOOD STORY IN THE BIBLE

GENESIS 6:9–9:16, NEW INTERNATIONAL VERSION

This is the account of Noah and his family. Noah was a righteous man, blameless among the people of his time, and he walked faithfully with God. Noah had three sons: Shem, Ham and Japheth.

Now the earth was corrupt in God's sight and was full of violence. God saw how corrupt the earth had become, for all the people on earth had corrupted their ways. So God said to Noah, "I am going to put an end to all people, for the earth is filled with violence because of them. I am surely going to destroy both them and the earth. So make yourself an ark of cypresswood; make rooms in it and coat it with pitch inside and out. This is how you are to build it: The ark is to be three hundred cubits long, fifty cubits wide and thirty cubits high. Make a roof for it, leaving below the roof an opening one cubit high all around. Put a door in the side of the ark and make lower, middle and upper decks. I am going to bring floodwaters on the earth to destroy all life under the heavens, every creature that has the breath of life in it. Everything on earth will perish. But I will establish my covenant with you, and you will enter the ark—you and your sons and your wife and your sons' wives with you. You are to bring into the ark two of all living creatures, male and female, to keep them alive with you. Two of every kind of bird, of every kind of animal and of every kind of creature that moves along the ground will come to you to be kept alive. You are to take every kind of food that is to be eaten and store it away as food for you and for them." Noah did everything just as God commanded him.

The Lord then said to Noah, "Go into the ark, you and your whole family, because I have found you righteous in this generation. Take with you seven pairs of every kind of clean animal, a male and its mate, and one pair of every kind of unclean animal, a male and its mate, and also seven pairs of every kind of bird, male and female, to keep their various kinds alive throughout the earth. Seven days from now I will send rain on the earth for forty days and forty nights, and I will wipe from the face of the earth every living creature I have made." And Noah did all that the Lord commanded him. . . .

In the six hundredth year of Noah's life, on the seventeenth day of the second month—on that day all the springs of the great deep burst forth, and the floodgates of the heavens were opened. And rain fell on the earth forty days and forty nights. . . .

For forty days the flood kept coming on the earth, and as the waters increased they lifted the ark high above the earth. The waters rose and increased greatly on the earth, and the ark floated on the surface of the water. They rose greatly on the earth, and all the high mountains under the entire heavens were covered. The waters rose and covered the mountains to a depth of more than fifteen cubits. Every living thing that moved on land perished—birds, livestock, wild animals, all the creatures that swarm over the earth, and all mankind. Everything on dry land that had the breath of life in its nostrils died. Every living thing on the face of the earth was wiped out; people and animals and the creatures that move along the ground and the birds were wiped from the earth. Only Noah was left, and those with him in the ark. The waters flooded the earth for a hundred and fifty days.

HANDOUT 2.3, CONTINUED

But God remembered Noah and all the wild animals and the livestock that were with him in the ark, and he sent a wind over the earth, and the waters receded. Now the springs of the deep and the floodgates of the heavens had been closed, and the rain had stopped falling from the sky. The water receded steadily from the earth. At the end of the hundred and fifty days the water had gone down, and on the seventeenth day of the seventh month the ark came to rest on the mountains of Ararat. The waters continued to recede until the tenth month, and on the first day of the tenth month the tops of the mountains became visible.

After forty days Noah opened a window he had made in the ark and sent out a raven, and it kept flying back and forth until the water had dried up from the earth. Then he sent out a dove to see if the water had receded from the surface of the ground. But the dove could find nowhere to perch because there was water over all the surface of the earth; so it returned to Noah in the ark. He reached out his hand and took the dove and brought it back to himself in the ark. He waited seven more days and again sent out the dove from the ark. When the dove returned to him in the evening, there in its beak was a freshly plucked olive leaf! Then Noah knew that the water had receded from the earth. He waited seven more days and sent the dove out again, but this time it did not return to him. . . .

Then God said to Noah, "Come out of the ark, you and your wife and your sons and their wives. Bring out every kind of living creature that is with you—the birds, the animals, and all the creatures that move along the ground—so they can multiply on the earth and be fruitful and increase in number on it. . . ."

Then Noah built an altar to the Lord and, taking some of all the clean animals and clean birds, he sacrificed burnt offerings on it. The Lord smelled the pleasing aroma and said in his heart: "Never again will I curse the ground because of humans, even though every inclination of the human heart is evil from childhood. And never again will I destroy all living creatures, as I have done. . . ."

And God said, "This is the sign of the covenant I am making between me and you and every living creature with you, a covenant for all generations to come: I have set my rainbow in the clouds, and it will be the sign of the covenant between me and the earth. Whenever I bring clouds over the earth and the rainbow appears in the clouds, I will remember my covenant between me and you and all living creatures of every kind. Never again will the waters become a flood to destroy all life. Whenever the rainbow appears in the clouds, I will see it and remember the everlasting covenant between God and all living creatures of every kind on the earth."

CHAPTER 3
RISE OF CIVILIZATIONS IN ASIA

(CHINA AND INDIA)

India is the cradle of the human race, the birthplace of human speech, the mother of history, the grandmother of legend, and the great grand-mother of tradition. Our most valuable and most artistic materials in the history of man are treasured up in India only!

—Mark Twain

HISTORICAL CONTEXT: WHAT DO I NEED TO KNOW?

Civilizations in Asia arose in several places at once. As in the Mediterranean, the earliest civilizations coincided with the geography of the Neolithic Revolution. In the area that is now India, the earliest Bronze Age peoples in the Indus Valley created some of the first large cities in the world. Two of the earliest cities, Harappa and Mohenjo-daro, arose earlier than 2500 BCE along major river ways, and lent their names to the peoples associated with those two cities.

As in Egypt, Mesopotamia, and China, the Agricultural Revolution resulted in extra food and then an increased population—as many as 23,000 people in Harappa and up to 40,000 in Mohenjo-daro. Both were complex, well-fortified cities with multilayered government structures and centers for religious activities. Wheat, barley, peas, dates, melons, sesame, and cattle probably served as the major agricultural products. Despite their seemingly common origins in the Neolithic Revolution, the two cities were governed separately and had distinct cultures.

In both Harappa and Mohenjo-daro, craftspeople worked with copper, lead, tin, and bronze, and produced complex pottery with intricate designs. The Harappan peoples also polished stones called *carnelian* for use in jewelry, worked gold and shells, and practiced a kind of dentistry. Harappan cities were intricate, well-planned, and had complex irrigation, including drainage systems and public baths, as well as possibly heated baths in private homes, a central water supply, and a grid-style layout that indicates advanced city planning. Clay tablets from around 3300 BCE indicate an early, still-untranslated cuneiform-style writing system. Foodstuff, textiles, hardwood, and exotic animals seem to have been traded into Persia and Mesopotamia, and the Indus Valley in general used one of the earliest systems of standardized weights and measures.

Natural disasters, disease, and internal and external violence played roles in the gradual abandonment of major cities in the Indus Valley by 1500 BCE. A migration of Indo-Aryan peoples in the period from 2000–1000 BCE drastically changed the Indus Valley, Europe, and the Mediterranean. This Aryan (no relation to the later Nazi sense of "Aryan") influence is less the story of a single people than a migration of peoples with a common language—Indo-European. Today there are more than 1 billion who speak some descendent of the Indo-Aryan root language, including English, German, Greek, Celtic, and Latin and the Romance languages.

The period from 1500–500 BCE in the Indus Valley is known as the Vedic period, so-called for the Vedas, religious texts that provide most of the known information about the peoples living there during this time. Semi-nomadic Indo-Aryans in northern India formed agricultural villages and small tribes. The largest kingdom, the Kuru, was more like a collection of tribes than a single kingdom, and the period lacked any large cities. During this period (ca. 1000 BCE), cows became a prohibited food while horse sacrifice became more common. This period also saw the first emergence of the class system that remains in India today. Economically, the Vedic period was characterized by agriculture and herding, as well as a barter economy with no known coinage or even complex metalworking.

Despite archaeological excavations indicating an advanced civilization between 2100 and 1600 BCE, many historians regard the earliest known dynasty in China, the Xia, as mythological due to lack of written records and an oral tradition influenced by subsequent dynastic conflicts. The existence of the Shang Dynasty, which emerged around 1600 BCE, is firmly established by an abundant archaeological and written record. The archaeological evidence shows a coastal trade in sea shells, complex bronze-making and other metallurgy, monumental architecture, large shaft tombs, and extensive walled cities. Of greater significance is the system of writing known as oracle bone script, which formed the basis for Chinese writing.

The class structure of the Shang Dynasty was comprised of the king and nobles, a military class, craftspeople, and peasants. The king and nobles governed the kingdom with the help of local warlords and governors, collecting both taxes from subjects and tribute from nearby kingdoms. The king was the high priest of a religion devoted to a complex hierarchy of worship. At the top stood Shangdi, the supreme deity of the universe. After that came animistic spirits, including the spirits of the sun, the moon, the mountain, and others. Below those nature spirits came several levels of ancestors, all of whom, as in the Roman religions, could intervene in human lives via divination, offerings, and sacrifices.

Under the Zhou Dynasty, successor to the Shang, emperors formulated the idea of the "Mandate of Heaven" in which the right to rule was the product of the moral authority of the king or queen, and heaven imbued the ruling dynasty with both the right to rule and the obligation to protect the best interests of the kingdom as a whole. That mandate could be lost if the king or queen did not rule well. The Zhou also developed a system similar to what historians would later call *feudalism* to describe medieval Europe. In Zhou China, land was divided into fiefs that were passed from father to son in return for loyalty and service to the emperor. Under the Shang dynasty as well, the beginnings of long-lasting Chinese philosophical traditions emerged during the lifetimes of Confucius and Lao Tzu, founders of Confucianism and Taoism respectively.

STANDARDS ADDRESSED IN THE CHAPTER

NCHS World History Content Standards, Grades 5–12:

- **Era 2—Standard 1A:** The student understands how Mesopotamia, Egypt, and the Indus valley became centers of dense population, urbanization, and cultural innovation in the fourth and third millennia BCE.
- **Era 2—Standard 1B:** The student understands how commercial and cultural interactions contributed to change in the Tigris-Euphrates, Indus, and Nile regions.
- **Era 2—Standard 2A:** The student understands how civilization emerged in northern China in the second millennium BCE.

CCSS for Literacy in History/Social Studies, Grades 6–8 and 9–10:

- **6–8:** Determine the central ideas or information of a primary or secondary source; Integrate visual information (e.g., in charts, graphs, photographs, videos, or maps) with other information in print and digital texts.

- **9–10:** Determine the central ideas or information of a primary or secondary source; Cite specific textual evidence to support analysis of primary and secondary sources, attending to such features as the date and origin of the information.

LESSON 1

ORGANIZING QUESTION

What makes something a civilization?

STRATEGIES USED

Brainstorming, List/Group/Label, Discussion

MATERIALS NEEDED

1. Dictionary (per group of 2–3 students)
2. Small sticky notes (8–10 per student)
3. Computers or electronic devices for each group of students

LESSON PLAN

Lesson Hook: *Brainstorming*—Ask students to work with a partner to define the word *civilization* using a dictionary. The word is generally defined as "an advanced stage of development," but students should find this definition on their own. Ask them to use their sticky notes to list examples of things in their lives that fit the definition, such as "iPhone" or "cars." Have them place their sticky notes on the board.

The Organizing Question: Explain to students that they are going to work in small groups to find an answer to the organizing question: *What makes something a civilization?*

Examine the Sources: *List/Group/Label*—Once they have the sticky notes on the board, divide students into small groups and ask them to organize the list of notes into groups using common themes. For example, some students might have written "alphabet" or "writing," and these can be grouped together. Teachers will need to prompt students to help them organize their notes. Once students have organized the notes into groups, have them create labels that describe each group, such as "writing system" or "economy."

Next, in pairs or in groups of three, have students use computers to research "what makes something a civilization?" Ideally, each group will generate a list that has different characteristics because not all historians and social scientists agree on the term *civilization*. Write those categories on the board and, once again, ask students to reorganize the sticky notes, this time placing them into the categories from their research. For example, most lists will include "monumental architecture," "trade networks," and a "political structure." Ask students to compare and contrast their original categories with those they found in their research. Students should then discuss how their characteristics (groups and labels) do or do not fit into the dictionary definition, defending their choices. Continue to emphasize that there is no clear scientific consensus on what makes something a civilization.

Discussion—For the remainder of class, discuss what "places" could be categorized under a "civilization." Does the United States count? Your state? Your school or classroom? Why or why not? What are examples that can go in the categories? Does the United States have something in common with other countries that can together be described as a bigger civilization, like "Western Civilization"?

Make a Hypothesis: Have students create a hypothesis that answers the organizing question, using examples from their sticky notes, research, and discussions. This lesson should help students feel comfortable with the idea of no single right answer.

Optional Extension: As students study different groups and places during the course of the year, return to the idea of "civilization" and discuss whether or not the place they are studying would fit under that definition.

LESSON 2

ORGANIZING QUESTION

What was life like in the Harappan civilization in ancient India?

STRATEGIES USED

I Notice/I Wonder, Gallery Walk

MATERIALS NEEDED

1. Artifact: A picture of a seal with animal or religious motifs from Tarini Carr's "The Harappan Civilization," available at http://archaeologyon line.net/artifacts/harappa-mohenjodaro
2. The following images displayed around the room for a gallery walk:
   - ✓ Map: *Indus Valley Civilization, Mature Phase: 2600–1900 BCE,* available at http://www.ancient-origins.net/news-history-archaeology/ 5000-year-old-skeletons-harappan-civilization-excavated-india- 002920
   - ✓ Junhi Han's photos of Mohenjo-daro (Pakistan), available at http:// whc.unesco.org/en/list/138/gallery
   - ✓ Pascal Maitre's photo of Mohenjo-daro (Pakistan), available at http://whc.unesco.org/en/documents/108235
   - ✓ Two additional seals from Tarini Carr's "The Harappan Civili- zation," available at http://archaeologyonline.net/artifacts/harappa- mohenjodaro
   - ✓ Mamoon Mengal's "Indus Priest-King statue," available at https:// commons.wikimedia.org/wiki/File:Mohenjo-daro_Priesterk%C3% B6nig.jpeg

3. Chart paper placed beside each image in the gallery walk and divided into two columns: "I Notice" and "I Wonder"
4. Markers (1–2 per group)
5. Optional video: National Geographic's "History 101: Mohenjo Daro," available at https://www.nationalgeographic.com/archaeology-and-his tory/archaeology/mohenjo-daro
6. Optional article: John Roach's "Mohenjo Daro: 'Faceless' Indus Valley City Puzzles Archaeologists," available at https://www.nationalgeo graphic.com/archaeology-and-history/archaeology/mohenjo-daro

LESSON PLAN

Lesson Hook: *I Notice/I Wonder*—Display a picture of one of the seals found in Mohenjo-daro (see Materials Needed section). Ask students to draw a line down the middle of a sheet of paper and make an "I Notice" and an "I Wonder" column. Give students 2 minutes to write down any details they notice on the seal and what questions they have about it. Discuss their ideas and questions. Write some of the common questions on the board to use later in the lesson. End this section by asking students how archaeologists use artifacts as clues and what clues about the Harappan culture they might learn from the seal.

The Organizing Question: Explain to students that they will examine other images for information to help them make predictions and answer the organizing question: *What was life like in the Harappan civilization in ancient India?*

Examine the Sources: *Gallery Walk*—Organize students into groups of three, give each group a marker, and then assign each group to a station to begin the gallery walk. Have students examine a variety of images to make some predictions about the Harappan civilization in ancient India. Their task is to examine the image first, and then write on the chart paper what details they notice ("I Notice" column) and what questions they have ("I Wonder" column). Have students rotate clockwise, adding their comments and responding to others' written ideas. When they have returned to the image where they started, have them read all of the responses and report to the class some of the best ideas and questions. Write some of the best student questions on the board and use them for the rest of the lesson.

Make a Hypothesis: Have students work with their group to make a hypothesis that answers the organizing question. They should use evidence from the seal and the gallery walk images. End the lesson with a whole-group discussion and write the groups' hypotheses and supporting evidence on the board while students write them in their notes.

Optional Extension: Show National Geographic's "Mohenjo Daro 101" video and/or have students read the article "Mohenjo Daro: 'Faceless' Indus Valley City Puzzles Archaeologists." Have students write down ideas from the video or article that either support or refute their hypotheses or answer some of the questions the class generated from the gallery walk.

LESSON 3

ORGANIZING QUESTION

How did the Shang dynasty contribute to Chinese culture?

STRATEGIES USED

Analyzing Artifacts, Clue Stations

MATERIALS NEEDED

1. Artifact: Photograph of *Vessel* (ca. 1600–1046 BCE), available at https://www.metmuseum.org/toah/works-of-art/50.61.5
2. Map: *China 1500 BCE*, available at https://www.timemaps.com/history/china-1500bc
3. Images of the following artifacts displayed at clue stations around the room:
    ✓ Artifact: *Steam Pot With Zoomorph Pattern*, available at http://www.chinaonlinemuseum.com/bronzes-shang-shoumian-yan.php
    ✓ Artifact: *Wine Vessel With Three Goats,* available at http://www.chinaonlinemuseum.com/bronzes-shang-sanyang-zun.php
    ✓ Artifact: *Altar Set* (ca. 1046–771 BCE), available at https://www.metmuseum.org/toah/works-of-art/24.72.1-14
    ✓ Artifact: *Ivory Cup*, available at https://depts.washington.edu/chinaciv/archae/2fuhmain.htm
    ✓ Artifact: *Jade Tiger*, available at https://depts.washington.edu/chinaciv/archae/2fuhjade.htm
    ✓ Artifact: *Stone Ox*, available at https://depts.washington.edu/chinaciv/archae/2fuhjade.htm
    ✓ Artifact: *Shang Dynasty Inscribed Scapula* (ca. 1200 BCE), available at https://en.wikipedia.org/wiki/Oracle_bone#/media/File:Shang_dynasty_inscribed_scapula.jpg
    ✓ Artifact: *Replica of Oracle Turtle Shell With Ancient Chinese Oracle Scripts*, available at https://commons.wikimedia.org/wiki/File:Replica_of_oracle_turtle_shell_with_ancient_Chinese_oracle_scripts.jpg

4. Document Analysis Worksheet: Artifact (for Intermediate or Secondary Students), available at https://www.archives.gov/education/lessons/worksheets

LESSON PLAN

Lesson Hook: Display the *Vessel* photograph (ca. 1600–1046 BCE) without the accompanying facts visible. Ask students to look at it for a minute and write down as many details as possible that would help describe this artifact. Then display the details about the artifact. Discuss what clues about the culture students might learn from this artifact. Remind students about the role of an archaeologist in interpreting artifacts as evidence of ancient cultures.

The Organizing Question: Explain that students will think like archaeologists and examine artifacts from the Shang dynasty in China to determine the answer to the question: *How did the Shang dynasty contribute to Chinese culture?*

Examine the Sources: Display the *China 1500 BCE* map and explain that the Shang dynasty ruled China from 1750–1045 BCE.

Analyzing Artifacts—Review the Document Analysis Worksheet with students. Using the *Vessel* photograph from the Lesson Hook section, model for students how to use the guide to analyze an artifact (or a picture of one). Allow students to discuss the prompts on the analysis guide as they look at the picture of the vessel. Explain that there may be some details they do not know about their artifact.

Clue Stations—Divide the class into eight groups and assign each group a clue station with an artifact to examine. Give them time to complete the analysis guide for their artifact. (*Note*: Each of the websites in the Materials Needed section provides information about the artifacts if students need it. If some groups finish early, they can read about the discovery of the Shang tomb of Fu Hao and the artifacts discovered at https://depts.washington.edu/chinaciv/archae/2fuhmain.htm.)

When groups are finished, have them present the key points about their artifacts and what they might reveal about the Shang civilization. Display images of the artifacts as each group presents the ideas. Encourage students to write down main ideas about all of the artifacts to use for the hypothesis section of the lesson.

Make a Hypothesis: Have students return to their groups and make a hypothesis that answers the organizing question. They should use examples from at least four sources as evidence for their hypothesis about the contributions of the Shang dynasty. The organizing question could also be used as an individual writing prompt or exit slip.

2500 BCE-0

PART II

THE ANCIENT WORLD

CHAPTER 4

RISE OF RELIGIONS

One has to be humble if he desires to acquire knowledge.

—Rigveda

HISTORICAL CONTEXT: WHAT DO I NEED TO KNOW?

Religion, or the sense of a greater spiritual force, seems to have been part of the human experience for longer than humans have kept records. The earliest religions in the world were either animistic, with followers believing in spirits that inhabited everyday phenomena (e.g., lightning, trees, rivers), or polytheistic, with followers believing in many gods. Some groups, such as the Egyptians and early Israelites, were henotheistic, accepting the existence of multiple gods but worshipping only one of them. In Egypt this henotheism included a complex system of ancestor worship in which the pharaoh served as the gods' representative on Earth, responsible for ensuring what Egyptians called *Maat*, a kind of cosmic harmony between gods and humans. Ancestor worship and the role of the pharaoh led to the development of pyramids.

In the Indian subcontinent, the migration of Indo-Aryans around 1500 BCE brought new religious traditions. The Vedas contain the origins of Indian Hinduism and are the oldest religious texts still in existence outside of Egypt and

Sumeria. Hindus believe that these texts came from the creator-god Brahma, one of a trinity of gods that includes Vishnu, the preserver, and Shiva, the destroyer. The Vedas are categorized in four groups. The *Rigveda* contains more than 1,000 hymns in 10 sections known as *mandalas*, as well as appendices of "Brahmanas," or notes about the hymns, and two "Aranyakas," which discuss the philosophy behind the need and method of ritual sacrifices. The *Yajurveda* includes priestly recitations for use during sacred rituals. The *Samaveda* contains 1,875 verses of religious songs. Finally, the *Atharvaveda*, which was compiled later than the other three, details instructions for how to live everyday life, much in the same way that the Old Testament does for Christians or the Tanakh does for Jews.

The Vedas speak of humans as having fallen, or devolved, from a higher state of consciousness. In the Vedas, Puruṣa (pronounced "pur-u-sha") is a cosmic being responsible for creating all life after having been sacrificed by other gods. In time, Hindu understanding of Puruṣa evolved into more abstract terms— as the root of the universe, both indestructible and ever present. The creation story in the Vedas also established the Varna, or hereditary social system, as having come from four parts of the body of Puruṣa. That system divides India into Brahmins (priests and teachers), Kshatriyas (the military and ruling class), Vaishyas (farmers and traders), and Shudras (common laborers). The Dalits, or untouchables, were those who existed outside of the four main castes. The caste system persists in a less rigid form in India to this day.

Hinduism has no human founder, unlike Buddhism, which sprang from the life of Siddhārtha Gautama, the Buddha, who probably lived from 563–483 BCE. Just as Jesus began life as a Jew and then served as the foundation for a new religion, the Buddha began life as a Hindu, who, like other Hindus, believed in reincarnation. Observing the suffering of all life forms, the Buddha began a long period of meditation and, according to tradition, attained true enlightenment under a ficus tree. He then began to teach what he had discovered, including the Four Noble Truths: (1) existence is suffering, (2) suffering is caused by desire, (3) suffering can end through enlightenment, and (4) enlightenment can be obtained by following the Eightfold Path. In a period when Hindus revered those who led a monastic life of self-denial, the Eightfold Path (Right Understanding, Right Thought, Right Speech, Right Conduct, Right Livelihood, Right Effort, Right Mindfulness, Right Concentration) encompassed a moral code and way of living that would free followers from the cycle of birth, death, and reincarnation.

The Pali Canon, split into three parts and based on the teachings of the Buddha, are the central Hindu scriptures. The first, the *Vinaya Pitaka*, outlined the rules for communities of monks and nuns. The largest, the *Sutta Pitaka*, contained the teachings of the Buddha. Those two are often considered the more practical of the two "baskets" of teaching. Finally, the *Abhidhamma Pitaka* is a philosophical analysis of the Buddha's teachings, ostensibly laid out by the Buddha himself.

The origins of Judaism stretch back to the time of the Babylonians. Originally polytheistic, the very earliest Israelites worshiped Yahweh as one among many of the Canaanite gods. During the sixth and fifth centuries BCE, in the period known as the Babylonian Captivity, the Israelites and the Kingdom of Judah developed a monotheistic understanding and a belief in a covenant theology whereby God/Yahweh rewarded followers for a life of holiness. The earliest covenant, believed by both Christians and Jews, was formed between God and Noah, whereby God promised not to destroy humanity by a flood. Second Temple Judaism—the period between the destruction of Jerusalem by the Babylonians in 586 BCE and the destruction of the Second Temple in Jerusalem in 70 CE—is considered the formative period in the evolution of Jewish theology and, like Christianity and Islam, originated with the prophet Abraham. During this period, a wide array of Jewish philosophies, texts, and movements developed. By the period immediately preceding the destruction of the second temple by the Romans, however, two main schools had emerged.

Under Roman rule, the high priest in Jerusalem and the members of the Sanhedrin, or council, avoided politics and concerned themselves only with religious matters. In the first century BCE, two schools of Jewish thought emerged with different views regarding written and oral tradition, and with different outlooks on the law and how to worship. One group, the wealthy Sadducees, were prominent in the Sanhedrin and dedicated themselves to the Temple cult. They recognized the written Torah as the final, authoritative word and resisted new ideas that threatened traditions. Many of them came from the elite of Jewish society and thus supported the balance of power that had been established between Jews and Romans in Judea.

The other group, the Pharisees, were opponents of the Sadducees. The Pharisees focused on the spiritual needs of ordinary people. Pharisees believed that law was central to Judaism but argued that it could be interpreted flexibly, in light of the oral tradition. The Pharisees believed in the superiority of spiritual matters to political matters. They emphasized charity toward the poor, spoke in parables, and, unlike many Jews, accepted the idea of an afterlife and of the resurrection of the body. Pharisees also accepted the concept of a Messiah, who would bring a reign of divine justice to earth.

STANDARDS ADDRESSED IN THE CHAPTER

NCHS World History Content Standards, Grades 5–12:
- **Era 3—Standard 1B:** The student understands the emergence of Judaism and the historical significance of the Hebrew kingdoms.

- **Era 3—Standard 3D:** The student understands religious and cultural developments in India in the era of the Gangetic states and the Mauryan Empire.

CCSS for Literacy in History/Social Studies, Grades 6–8 and 9–10:
- **6–8:** Cite specific textual evidence to support analysis of primary and secondary sources; Determine the central ideas or information of a primary or secondary source; Analyze the relationship between a primary and secondary source on the same topic.
- **9–10:** Cite specific textual evidence to support analysis of primary and secondary sources, attending to such features as the date and origin of the information; Determine the central ideas or information of a primary or secondary source; Compare and contrast treatments of the same topic in several primary and secondary sources.

LESSON 1

ORGANIZING QUESTION

How are Hindu beliefs reflected in the hymn to the Puruṣa from the *Rigveda*?

STRATEGIES USED

Freewrite, Partner Read, Sketching Through the Text

MATERIALS NEEDED

1. Handout 4.1: Excerpts From Book 10 of the *Rigveda* About Puruṣa (ca. > 1100 BCE)
2. Optional sources for background information:
   - ✓ Any world history textbook chapter on Aryans and Hinduism
   - ✓ Article: Cristian Violatti's "The Vedas," available at https://www.ancient.eu/The_Vedas

LESSON PLAN

Note: It might help to teach the basic beliefs of Hinduism before using this lesson or use the lesson as the introduction to Hindu beliefs. See the Optional Extensions at the end of the lesson.

Lesson Hook: *Freewrite*—Ask students to write for 5 minutes about whether or not they think that the U.S. has social classes and why. Once students have collected their thoughts on paper, discuss this topic with the class. Encourage students to give specific examples to support their argument. Challenge them to look for connections between this topic and the rest of the lesson.

The Organizing Question: Explain to students that they are going to study Hinduism by analyzing a creation story from the Vedas, a collection of religious texts that form the foundation of the Hindu religion. They will work with partners to analyze the text and answer the organizing question: *How are beliefs of Hinduism reflected in the hymn to the Puruṣa from the* Rigveda?

Examine the Sources: First, depending on how much information the class has studied about the Aryans in India, it might help to provide students with some background about the Aryan culture and the texts (the Vedas and Upanishads) that became the basis of Hindu religious beliefs.

Partner Read and Sketching Through the Text—Distribute Handout 4.1: Excerpts From Book 10 of the *Rigveda* About Puruṣa (ca. > 1100 BCE). Explain to students that they will read a creation story and annotate main ideas as they read. Next, they will draw a picture that represents the key details in each section. Before dividing the class into groups, read Section 1 of the handout to the class. Model annotating for the main points, using context clues to understand challenging words, and analyzing what aspects of Hindu beliefs can be identified in the first section. Next ask students to think of a visual that would represent the main ideas from Section 1. Ask students to draw their visuals in the box below Section 1 on the handout.

Then, ask students to choose a partner and read through the text, one section at a time. As they read each section, they should annotate main ideas and decide on a visual to draw in the box below it. Allow time for all pairs to read and to draw their pictures. Once all pictures are drawn, have students summarize the text and share their visuals.

Make a Hypothesis: After several pairs have shared their drawings with the class, ask students to work with their partner to answer the organizing question.

Optional Extensions: Have students review their textbook or notes if they have been taught the beliefs of Hinduism. If this is new information for them, it could help to assign them a secondary source (a textbook section, video, or web article; see Materials Needed section) about the beliefs of Hinduism. While they read or watch a secondary source on the topic, they should look or listen for similar beliefs that they read in the Puruṣa hymn from the *Rigveda*.

The lesson could end with either a class discussion or a written assessment in which students answer the organizing question with specific evidence from the primary source and/or secondary sources. If time permits, ask students to connect what they learned about Hinduism to their ideas from the Lesson Hook section.

HANDOUT 4.1

EXCERPTS FROM BOOK 10 OF THE *RIGVEDA* ABOUT PURUṢA (CA. > 1100 BCE)

Directions: For each section of the text, read and annotate for main ideas. Then, draw a visual in the accompanying box to represent the main ideas.

SECTION 1

A thousand heads hath Puruṣa, a thousand eyes, a thousand feet.
On every side pervading earth he fills a space ten fingers wide.
This Puruṣa is all that yet hath been and all that is to be;
The Lord of Immortality which waxes greater still by food.
So mighty is his greatness; yea, greater than this is Puruṣa.
All creatures are one-fourth of him, three-fourths eternal life in heaven.

SECTION 2

As soon as he was born he spread eastward and westward o'er the earth.
When Gods prepared the sacrifice with Puruṣa as their offering,
Its oil was spring, the holy gift was autumn; summer was the wood. . . .

From that great general sacrifice the dripping fat was gathered up.
He formed the creatures of-the air, and animals both wild and tame. . . .

From it were horses born, from it all cattle with two rows of teeth:
From it were generated kine, from it the goats and sheep were born.

HANDOUT 4.1, CONTINUED

SECTION 3

When they divided Puruṣa how many portions did they make?
What do they call his mouth, his arms? What do they call his thighs and feet?
The Brahman was his mouth, of both his arms was the Rājanya made.
His thighs became the Vaiśya, from his feet the Śūdra was produced.

HANDOUT 4.1, CONTINUED

SECTION 4

The Moon was gendered from his mind, and from his eye the Sun had birth;
Indra and Agni from his mouth were born, and Vāyu from his breath.
Forth from his navel came mid-air the sky was fashioned from his head
Earth from his feet, and from his car the regions. Thus they formed the worlds.

LESSON 2

ORGANIZING QUESTION

What insights about Buddhist beliefs can be found in the *Sutta Pitaka*?

STRATEGIES USED

Inside/Outside Circle, Modeling, Modified Jigsaw

MATERIALS NEEDED

1. Handout 4.2: Excerpts From the *Sutta Pitaka* (ca. 400 BCE)
2. Index cards (one per student)
3. Timer

LESSON PLAN

Note: It can be helpful to teach the basic beliefs of Buddhism before using this lesson or use the lesson as the introduction, making predictions or inferences about Buddhist beliefs from the text. See the optional extension at the end of the lesson.

Lesson Hook: *Inside/Outside Circle*—Distribute index cards and ask students to spend 5 minutes jotting down their thoughts about the following questions on each side of the card:
- Side 1: What causes suffering in the world?
- Side 2: What does it take to be happy?

Next, have students stand and create two concentric circles, with the students in the inner circle facing the students in the outer circle. Each student should be facing a partner. Explain that they will have 2 minutes to share their thoughts about the first question with this partner. A timer can help keep this moving quickly. (*Note*: You can adjust the time if needed. You can also do this activity with two lines instead of circles if there are space constraints.) Once the timer goes off, only the outside circle of students should move one position clockwise. They should then have a discussion of the first question again with their new partners. Continue 3–4 times per question, based on the interest level of the students, and allow them to discuss both questions with multiple partners.

The Organizing Question: Explain to students that these types of challenging questions prompted Siddhartha Gautama to leave his home in search of answers and understanding. The answers he found became the basis of Buddhism. In this lesson they will read and analyze excerpts from his teachings to find an answer to the organizing question: *What insights about Buddhist beliefs can be found in the* Sutta Pitaka*?*

Examine the Sources: *Modeling*—Distribute Handout 4.2: Excerpts From the *Sutta Pitaka* (ca. 400 BCE). Explain to students that they will examine excerpts from the Buddha's teachings to infer some of the basic beliefs of Buddhism. Read the first two examples from Section 1 of Handout 4.2 to the class. Ask students to help determine the main idea from each piece of advice or comment. Then ask them what clues these might provide about Buddhist beliefs. Encourage students to write their annotations or notes in the margins of the text.

Modified Jigsaw—After modeling the first two points of Section 1 with the whole class, explain to students that they will use a modified jigsaw strategy to analyze the rest of the text.

- ■ Expert Groups: Divide the class into five numbered groups and assign each group a section of the text. Explain that students will become experts on their section. Their task is to read teachings from their assigned section and discuss the main ideas with group members. Remind them that each person will be responsible for teaching this section to others in the class in home groups. Encourage students to write notes and annotate main ideas in the margin of their handouts.
  - ☐ Group 1: The rest of Section 1
  - ☐ Group 2: Section 2
  - ☐ Group 3: Section 3
  - ☐ Group 4: Section 4
  - ☐ Group 5: Section 5

  After students complete their section discussion in expert groups, assign each student a letter (e.g., A–C or A–D, depending on the number of students in each group).
- ■ Home Groups: For the second part of the modified jigsaw, students will go to "home" or letter groups. All of the "A" students, "B" students, and "C" students, for instance, should sit together. In that home group, there will be an expert on each section of the text. Students should take turns sharing their section, including main ideas and what Buddhist beliefs they think are represented in those teachings. The other students in the group should write notes in the margins or annotate all sections of the text as they listen.

Make a Hypothesis: After all students in the home groups have shared their main ideas, have students write one or two hypotheses to answer the organizing question with multiple examples of evidence from the text. Either have students individually write their hypotheses and evidence as a formative assessment, or choose to have each group share the hypotheses and evidence in a class discussion. If time permits, return to the questions from the Lesson Hook section and have students discuss whether or not they found any advice that would add insight to their thinking from their Inside/Outside circle discussion.

Optional Extension: Have students review their textbook or notes about Buddhist beliefs. If this is new information for them, assign them a secondary source (a textbook section, video, or an online article) about the Buddha's teachings or Buddhists' beliefs. While they read or watch a secondary source on the topic, they should look or listen for similar beliefs that they read in the *Sutta Pitaka*.

HANDOUT 4.2
EXCERPTS FROM THE *SUTTA PITAKA* (CA. 400 BCE)

SECTION 1

VI:78 Do not associate with evil companions; do not seek the fellowship of the vile. Associate with the good friends; seek the fellowship of noble men.

VI:79 He who drinks deep the Dhamma lives happily with a tranquil mind. The wise man ever delights in the Dhamma made known by the Noble One (the Buddha).

VI:81 Just as a solid rock is not shaken by the storm, even so the wise are not affected by praise or blame.

VI:83 The good renounce (attachment for) everything. The virtuous do not prattle with a yearning for pleasures. The wise show no elation or depression when touched by happiness or sorrow.

VI:84 He is indeed virtuous, wise, and righteous who neither for his own sake nor for the sake of another (does any wrong), who does not crave for sons, wealth, or kingdom, and does not desire success by unjust means.

VI:87–88 Abandoning the dark way, let the wise man cultivate the bright path. Having gone from home to homelessness, let him yearn for that delight in detachment, so difficult to enjoy. Giving up sensual pleasures, with no attachment, let the wise man cleanse himself of defilements of the mind.

SECTION 2

I:12 Those who know the essential to be essential and the unessential to be unessential, dwelling in right thoughts, do arrive at the essential.

I:13 Just as rain breaks through an ill-thatched house, so passion penetrates an undeveloped mind.

I:14 Just as rain does not break through a well-thatched house, so passion never penetrates a well-developed mind.

I:19 Much though he recites the sacred texts, but acts not accordingly, that heedless man is like a cowherd who only counts the cows of others—he does not partake of the blessings of the holy life.

HANDOUT 4.2, CONTINUED

I:20 Little though he recites the sacred texts, but puts the Teaching into practice, forsaking lust, hatred, and delusion, with true wisdom and emancipated mind, clinging to nothing of this or any other world—he indeed partakes of the blessings of a holy life.

SECTION 3

VII:90 The fever of passion exists not for him who has completed the journey, who is sorrowless and wholly set free, and has broken all ties.

VII:91 The mindful ones exert themselves. They are not attached to any home; like swans that abandon the lake, they leave home after home behind.

VII:95 There is no more worldly existence for the wise one who, like the earth, resents nothing, who is firm as a high pillar and as pure as a deep pool free from mud.

VII:96 Calm is his thought, calm his speech, and calm his deed, who, truly knowing, is wholly freed, perfectly tranquil and wise.

SECTION 4

III:35 Wonderful, indeed, it is to subdue the mind, so difficult to subdue, ever swift, and seizing whatever it desires. A tamed mind brings happiness.

III:36 Let the discerning man guard the mind, so difficult to detect and extremely subtle, seizing whatever it desires. A guarded mind brings happiness.

III:38. Wisdom never becomes perfect in one whose mind is not steadfast, who knows not the Good Teaching and whose faith wavers.

III:42 Whatever harm an enemy may do to an enemy, or a hater to a hater, an ill-directed mind inflicts on oneself a greater harm.

III:43 Neither mother, father, nor any other relative can do one greater good than one's own well-directed mind.

SECTION 5

V:60 Long is the night to the sleepless; long is the league to the weary. Long is worldly existence to fools who know not the Sublime Truth.

V:61 Should a seeker not find a companion who is better or equal, let him resolutely pursue a solitary course; there is no fellowship with the fool.

V:64 Though all his life a fool associates with a wise man, he no more comprehends the Truth than a spoon tastes the flavor of the soup.

HANDOUT 4.2, CONTINUED

V:65 Though only for a moment a discerning person associates with a wise man, quickly he comprehends the Truth, just as the tongue tastes the flavor of the soup.

V:66 Fools of little wit are enemies unto themselves as they move about doing evil deeds, the fruits of which are bitter.

V:73 The fool seeks undeserved reputation, precedence among monks, authority over monasteries, and honor among householders.

LESSON 3

ORGANIZING QUESTION

What were the religious beliefs of the Israelites, and how did they compare/contrast with the beliefs of other civilizations during that time period?

STRATEGIES USED

Art Analysis, Annotating Text, Compare/Contrast

MATERIALS NEEDED

1. Handout 4.3: The Ten Commandments From the Bible
2. Handout 4.4: Venn Diagram Templates
3. Images:
   ✓ Painting: Rembrandt van Rijn's *Moses With the Ten Commandments*, available at https://commons.wikimedia.org/wiki/File:Rembrandt_-_Moses_with_the_Ten_Commandments_-_Google_Art_Project.jpg
   ✓ Painting: Gustave Doré's *Moses Showing the Ten Commandments*, available at https://commons.wikimedia.org/wiki/File:039.Moses_Comes_Down_from_Mount_Sinai.jpg
   ✓ Painting: Ferdinand Bol's *Moses Descends From Mount Sinai With the Ten Commandments*, available at https://commons.wikimedia.org/w/index.php?title=File:Ferdinand_Bol_-_Moses_descends_from_Mount_Siniai_with_the_Ten_Commandments_-_Google_Art_Project.jpg

4. Highlighters (one per student)
5. Textbooks, notes from previous units, or online sources about religion and culture in Mesopotamia, Egypt, and India

LESSON PLAN

Note: You may choose to do just the first part of this lesson and organizing question and return to the compare/contrast section at a later time after studying the religious beliefs of other cultures.

Lesson Hook: *Art Analysis*—Tell students that they are going to examine three pieces of art to determine clues about the lesson topic for the day. Prompt them to look for similarities and differences as they examine them. First display Rembrandt van Rijn's *Moses With the Ten Commandments*. Ask students to describe what details they notice and what message they think the artist was trying to convey. Then show Gustave Doré's *Moses Showing the Ten Commandments* and Ferdinand Bol's *Moses Descends From Mount Sinai With the Ten Commandments*, discussing key points for each one. Ask students what they see as similarities and differences in the paintings.

The Organizing Question: After discussing the three pieces of artwork, explain to students that they will analyze an excerpt from the Bible that will help them answer the organizing question: *What were the religious beliefs of the Israelites, and how did they compare/contrast with the beliefs of other civilizations during that time period?*

Examine the Sources: Depending on students' background knowledge or previous lessons in the unit, begin by showing the area of Canaan on a map and explaining background information on the Israelites, such as dates, key leaders, the Torah, and the beginnings of Judaism. Then distribute Handout 4.3: The Ten Commandments From the Bible.

Annotating Text—Explain to students that they will work with a partner to read the commandments and highlight important beliefs of the Jewish people. Once students are finished, have them share their annotations with the class.

Compare/Contrast—Next, organize students into four groups and assign each group one of the previously studied cultures: Mesopotamia, Egypt, and India. One culture will have more than one group assigned to it. Tell students that their task is to review their textbooks or notes, or research online to locate the religious and cultural beliefs of that civilization.

Make a Hypothesis: Once students have located and discussed religious and cultural beliefs of the Israelites and their assigned culture, have them work with their groups to create a two-circle Venn diagram showing similarities and differences. Another option is having groups share their findings and create three- or four-circle Venn diagrams that will compare and contrast multiple cultures and beliefs. See Handout 4.4 Venn Diagram Templates for several options. The complex Venn diagrams could be used as a homework assignment or as a way to differentiate for high-ability students (Roberts & Inman, 2015). End the lesson with students discussing or writing an answer to the organizing question.

HANDOUT 4.3

THE TEN COMMANDMENTS FROM THE BIBLE

EXODUS 20: 1–18, KING JAMES VERSION

And God spake all these words, saying,

I am the Lord thy God, which have brought thee out of the land of Egypt, out of the house of bondage.

Thou shalt have no other gods before me.

Thou shalt not make unto thee any graven image, or any likeness of anything that is in heaven above, or that is in the earth beneath, or that is in the water under the earth: Thou shalt not bow down thyself to them, nor serve them: for I the Lord thy God am a jealous God, visiting the iniquity of the fathers upon the children unto the third and fourth generation of them that hate me; And shewing mercy unto thousands of them that love me, and keep my commandments.

Thou shalt not take the name of the Lord thy God in vain; for the Lord will not hold him guiltless that taketh his name in vain.

Remember the sabbath day, to keep it holy. Six days shalt thou labour, and do all thy work: But the seventh day is the sabbath of the Lord thy God: in it thou shalt not do any work, thou, nor thy son, nor thy daughter, thy manservant, nor thy maidservant, nor thy cattle, nor thy stranger that is within thy gates: For in six days the Lord made heaven and earth, the sea, and all that in them is, and rested the seventh day: wherefore the Lord blessed the sabbath day, and hallowed it.

Honour thy father and thy mother: that thy days may be long upon the land which the Lord thy God giveth thee.

Thou shalt not kill.

Thou shalt not commit adultery.

Thou shalt not steal.

Thou shalt not bear false witness against thy neighbour.

Thou shalt not covet thy neighbour's house, thou shalt not covet thy neighbour's wife, nor his manservant, nor his maidservant, nor his ox, nor his ass, nor any thing that is thy neighbour's.

And all the people saw the thunderings, and the lightnings, and the noise of the trumpet, and the mountain smoking: and when the people saw it, they removed, and stood afar off.

HANDOUT 4.4
VENN DIAGRAM TEMPLATES

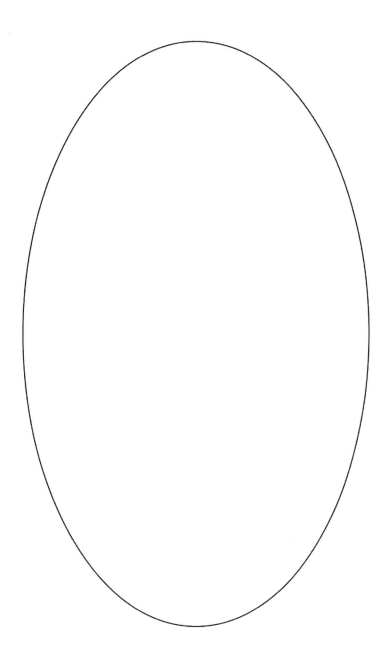

Venn (One Oval)

HANDOUT 4.4, CONTINUED

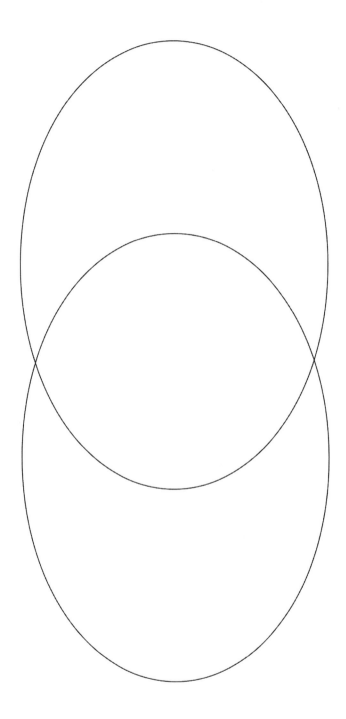

Venn (Two Ovals)

HANDOUT 4.4, CONTINUED

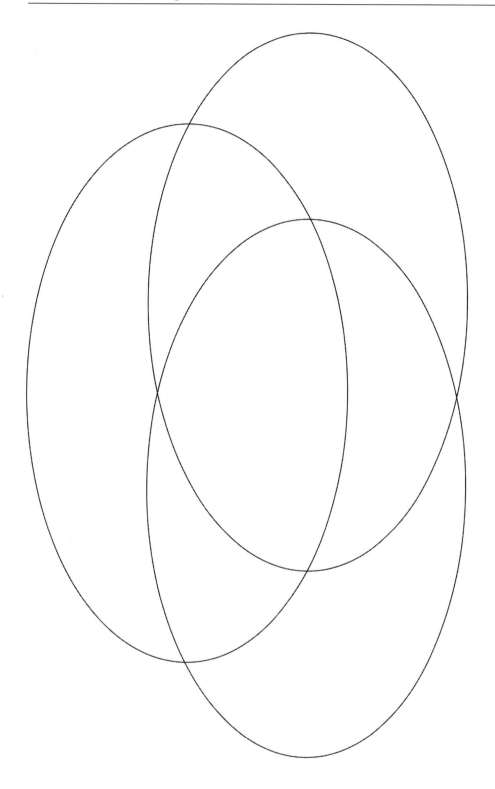

Venn (Three Ovals)

HANDOUT 4.4, CONTINUED

Venn Variation (Four Ovals)

From *Strategies for Differentiating Instruction: Best Practices for the Classroom* (3rd ed., pp. 222–225), by J. L. Roberts and T. F. Inman, 2015, Waco, TX: Prufrock Press. Copyright 2015 by Prufrock Press. Reprinted with permission.

CHAPTER 5
ACCOMPLISHMENTS AND ACHIEVEMENTS OF EARLY CIVILIZATIONS

Great things are done when men and mountains meet.

—William Blake

HISTORICAL CONTEXT: WHAT DO I NEED TO KNOW?

Classifying the sum total of human achievements in the period from 2500 BCE to around the birth of Jesus Christ would take more space than this volume allows. However, there are two particular "inventions" that historians and archaeologists mark as particularly important in the development of complex civilizations: the development of writing and the ability to create monumental architecture. Writing, in particular, was a transformative development in human history. The use of symbols—whether marks in clay or patterns of ink on paper—to convey meaning allowed for communication with people who spoke different languages. It provided a way of keeping accurate, permanent records of harvests and trade, greatly facilitating both activities. The earliest examples are cuneiform, hieroglyphics, and Chinese characters.

Historians divide ancient Egyptian history into Old (2686–2181 BCE), Middle (2055–1650 BCE), and New (1550–1069 BCE) Kingdom periods with "Intermediate" periods between them. Writing emerged in the earliest of these periods. Egyptian hieroglyphics were a complex combination of pictographs, symbols that represented syllabic sounds, and alphabetic symbols. Egyptian hieroglyphics were already in use by the time of the Old Kingdom, and it was during the Old Kingdom period that the great pyramids of Egypt, as well as the Great Sphinx, were built. Monumental architecture is often considered one marker of a great civilization and includes pyramids constructed by civilizations around the world, including the Aztecs, Mayans, Nubians, and others. It also includes great mounds such as in the Americas, large temples or churches, and large groups of stones. Scholars may never know the true purpose of some of these structures, such as Stonehenge or Easter Island, but the Egyptian pyramids are among the most famous and well-documented.

The earliest Egyptian pyramid that still exists is a tomb for the Pharaoh Djoser, who lived around 2660 BCE. Virtually all pyramids served as burial chambers for the Pharaoh, and the effort required to build these pyramids focused and transformed Egyptian society and economy. Artisans, engineers, stone masons, and laborers devoted considerable resources to constructing these tombs. Influenced by ancient Greeks' dislike of Egyptians, later peoples assumed that ordinary Egyptians and Jews resented laboring on the tombs. However, the pyramid builders were not slaves. In fact, they might have given their labor gladly, seeing it as an act of faith, just as people centuries later donated time and money to build medieval cathedrals. In all, the Egyptians built more than 100 pyramids in the period from 2686 BCE to 1650 BCE, after which the resources and centralized authority required to build such structures faded.

Cuneiform-style writing arose independently in several places. Sumerian cuneiform evolved from a system of clay cubes and spheres used to keep track of the ownership of groups of herd animals. Those tokens were marked with symbols to indicate the type and number of animals. From this, the Sumerians developed a formal system of writing as well as arithmetic. Eventually the tokens were replaced by tablets with writing meant to convey meaning on a wide range of subjects. By 2500 BCE, the pictures in cuneiform had changed to include symbols representing the Sumerian language.

Since pre-Shang times, Chinese fortune-tellers had based predictions on readings taken from bones or tortoise shells. A hole was drilled in a bone or shell, which was then heated over a fire. The bone or shell cracked, revealing patterns that the shaman used to make predictions. Over time, shamans began to paint designs on the shells before they were heated, and the designs and the cracks became part of the reading. In turn, the designs were gradually standardized and came to form the basis of Chinese writing. Like ancient hieroglyphics, early Chinese characters were pictographs, in which pictures are used to convey meaning. They evolved into increasingly complex ideographs, in which the picture conveys a concept. (*Note*: To demonstrate the difference between pictographs and ideographs to students, use this example: A picture of a stick figure man calls to mind "man" or "human" [pictograph], while stick figures of a man and a woman side-by-side, with a vertical line between them, generally gives people the idea of a "bathroom" [ideograph].)

The area controlled by the Shang was peopled by many cultures who spoke dozens, and perhaps hundreds, of mutually unintelligible languages. Standardized and sophisticated writing provided a common identity and bound people together. That identity began with elites but eventually filtered down to ordinary peasants and artisans. More than in any other society, writing became the key to Chinese identity and the growth of Chinese civilization.

STANDARDS ADDRESSED IN THE CHAPTER

NCHS World History Content Standards, Grades 5–12:

- **Era 2—Standard 1A:** The student understands how Mesopotamia, Egypt, and the Indus valley became centers of dense population, urbanization, and cultural innovation in the fourth and third millennia BCE.
- **Era 2—Standard 1:** The student understands how commercial and cultural interactions contributed to change in the Tigris-Euphrates, Indus, and Nile regions.
- **Eras 2 & 3—Standards 4A/5A:** The student understands major global trends from 4000 to 1000 BCE to 300 CE.

CCSS for Literacy in History/Social Studies, Grades 6–8 and 9–10:

- **6–8:** Cite specific textual evidence to support analysis of primary and secondary sources; Determine the central ideas or information of a primary or secondary source; Integrate visual information (e.g., in charts, graphs, photographs, videos, or maps) with other information in print and digital texts; Conduct short research projects to answer a question (including a self-generated question); Draw evidence from informational texts to support analysis, reflection, and research.
- **9–10:** Determine the central ideas or information of a primary or secondary source; Cite specific textual evidence to support analysis of primary and secondary sources, attending to such features as the date and origin of the information; Conduct short as well as more sustained research projects to answer a question (including a self-generated question) or solve a problem and narrow or broaden the inquiry when appropriate; Draw evidence from informational texts to support analysis, reflection, and research.

LESSON 1

ORGANIZING QUESTION

What do the pyramids reveal about Egyptian culture and beliefs?

Note: The organizing question for this lesson has been provided as a sample, but with the Question Formulation Technique (QFT; Rothstein & Santana, 2011), students will generate their own questions that will guide the lesson. Depending on the amount of time needed to research, this lesson may take two class periods. If the QFT strategy is new to you, visit the Right Question Institute's website (https://rightquestion.org) for more details, sample lessons, and resources.

STRATEGIES USED

Brainstorming, Question Formulation Technique, Student Research

MATERIALS NEEDED

1. Handout 5.1: Question Formulation Technique (QFT)
2. Images of the following pyramid structures:
   - ✓ Photograph: *Ancient Ziggurat at Ali Air Base, Iraq* (Mesopotamian), available at https://en.wikipedia.org/wiki/Ziggurat_of_Ur
   - ✓ Photograph: *Tikal Temple* (Mayan), available at https://en.wikipedia.org/wiki/Tikal
   - ✓ Photograph: *Nubian Pyramids*, available at https://en.wikipedia.org/wiki/Nubian_pyramids
   - ✓ Photograph: *Pyramids at Giza*, available at https://en.wikipedia.org/wiki/Egyptian_pyramids

3. World history textbooks or computers/devices for research
4. Optional articles for student research:
   - ✓ "How Were the Egyptian Pyramids Built?" by Owen Jarus, available at https://www.livescience.com/32616-how-were-the-egyptian-pyramids-built-.html
   - ✓ "The Egyptian Pyramid" by National Museum of American History, available at https://www.si.edu/spotlight/ancient-egypt/pyramid
   - ✓ "Standing Tall: Egypt's Great Pyramids" by José Miguel Parra, available at https://www.nationalgeographic.com/archaeology-and-history/magazine/2017/01-02/egypt-great-pyramids-giza-plateau

LESSON PLAN

Lesson Hook: *Brainstorming*—Ask students to brainstorm with a partner anything they know about pyramids. Allow students to share responses, and then tell them that they are going to examine pictures of pyramids from different places and time periods. Display the *Ancient Ziggurat at Ali Air Base, Iraq* photograph. Ask students to point out what they notice and what clues the photo might provide about the Mesopotamian culture. Then show the *Tikal Temple* and *Nubian Pyramids* photographs and ask the same questions about what students notice and what the pyramids reveal about the Mayan or Nubian cultures.

Question Formulation Technique—Next, explain to students that they are going to examine a Question Focus (QFocus) image for a Question Formulation Technique (Rothstein & Santana, 2011) lesson about Egypt. A QFocus is any type of prompt or stimulus used to encourage students to generate questions. For this lesson, a photograph of the Pyramids of Giza is the QFocus. Distribute Handout 5.1, which outlines the steps in the QFT, and remind students about the rules for producing questions. Display the *Pyramids at Giza* photograph and give students 1–2 minutes to write down as many questions as possible in their notes.

The Organizing Question: Once students have generated questions for the photograph, explain that they are going to work together to categorize and prioritize their questions with groups, choose their best questions, and research answers about the Egyptian pyramids.

Examine the Sources: Before students examine sources for information about Egyptian pyramids, have them complete the QFT process. Divide the class into groups of 3–4 students for the rest of the lesson.

- *Improving the questions*: Ask students to spend a few minutes sharing their own questions with others in their group. They should then label the questions as closed (C) or open (O), discuss the advantages and disadvantages of each type of question, and practice changing some questions from one type to another.
- *Prioritizing questions*: Ask students to come to a consensus in their groups about the two most important questions and write them on a sheet of paper in order to focus the research.
- *Next steps/student research*: Ask groups to develop a plan for how to answer the questions and what sources they might use. Allow groups time to use textbooks, computers, online articles, or other sources to research answers to their own important questions. When students are finished finding text-based answers to their questions, allow groups to share questions and the answers they found. Ask students to write

down questions and answers that were different from their group's so they learn more information about the pyramids of Egypt.

Make a Hypothesis: After all groups have shared questions and answers, ask students to write a response to the organizing question for this lesson (or choose one of the student-generated questions). Ask them to cite evidence in their answer from their own research and the findings of other groups.

HANDOUT 5.1
QUESTION FORMULATION TECHNIQUE (QFT)

Directions: Use the following steps to help generate your questions.

1. **QUESTION FOCUS (QFOCUS):**

   "A stimulus for jumpstarting student questions. It can be a short statement or a visual aid or aural aid in any medium or format that can stimulate student thinking that will be expressed through their questions" (Rothstein & Santana, 2011, p. 28).

2. **PRODUCE YOUR QUESTIONS:**

   ✓ Follow the rules.
   1. Ask as many questions as you can.
   2. Do not stop to discuss, answer, or judge.
   3. Record exactly as stated.
   4. Change statements into questions.

   ✓ Number your questions.

3. **IMPROVE YOUR QUESTIONS:**

   ✓ Categorize questions as Closed (C) or Open (O).
   » Closed: Answered with a "yes," "no," or one word
   » Open: Requires longer explanation

   ✓ Change questions from one type to another.

4. **PRIORITIZE YOUR QUESTIONS**

5. **SHARE AND DISCUSS NEXT STEPS**

6. **REFLECT**

Note: Adapted from *Make Just One Change: Teach Students to Ask Their Own Questions* (pp. 25–26), by D. Rothstein and L. Santana, 2011, Cambridge, MA: Harvard Education Press. Copyright 2011 by the President and Fellows of Harvard College. Adapted with permission.

LESSON 2

ORGANIZING QUESTION

How can writing systems provide clues about a particular culture or civilization?

STRATEGIES USED

Brainstorming, Picture Analysis, Student Research

MATERIALS NEEDED

1. Images:
   - ✓ Artifact: *Sumerian Cuneiform Clay Tablet With a List of Garden Plants*, available at http://www.britishmuseum.org/collectionim ages/AN00862/AN00862180_001_l.jpg?width=304
   - ✓ Artifact: *Oracle Bone From the Couling-Chalfant Collection* (ca. 1600–1050 BCE), available at https://www.bl.uk/collection-items/ chinese-oracle-bone
   - ✓ Artifact: *Egyptian Hieroglyphics at the British Museum in London*, available at https://commons.wikimedia.org/wiki/File:Egyptian_hie roglyphs_at_the_british_museum_in_London.jpg

2. Optional article: The British Museum's "Historic Writing," with background information on cuneiform, hieroglyphics, and oracle bones, available at http://www.britishmuseum.org/explore/themes/writing/hi storic_writing.aspx

LESSON PLAN

Lesson Hook: *Brainstorming*—Ask students to take 2 minutes to list all of the ways that they have used writing in any form during the last week. Have them share their lists. Ask them to brainstorm the purposes for and types of writing, as well as writing's impact on the modern world.

The Organizing Question: Explain to students that they will examine and research four ancient types of writing to determine an answer to the organizing question: *How can writing systems provide clues about a particular culture or civilization?*

Examine the Sources: *Picture Analysis*—For the first part of the lesson, place images of the written artifacts around the room. Ask students to look at each picture and brainstorm what they notice about the physical characteristics of the writing. Discuss their ideas as a class.

Student Research—Divide the class into six groups and give each group a type of writing: Sumerian cuneiform, Chinese oracle bones, or Egyptian hieroglyphics. Ask students to use their textbooks and/or online sources to find the following information about their assigned writing system:

- time period and location where the culture existed,
- how writing was used in the culture, and
- how writing was created (e.g., clay) and by whom (e.g., scribes, elites, etc.).

Allow students time in class to research these topics and prepare to present their findings at the end of class. Once each group finishes its research, have students think about what clues the writing system gives them about their culture. When all groups are finished, display pictures of each type of writing while each group shares the research about the writing system.

Make a Hypothesis: If necessary, this last section may be carried over to the beginning of the next class. After all groups present the information, regroup students so that each group has one expert on each culture. In their new groups, ask students to write down one or two hypotheses to answer the organizing question. Require them to use evidence from all three cultures to prove their hypotheses. This lesson can either close with a class discussion in which groups share the hypotheses or a writing assessment in which individual students answer the question with evidence.

CHAPTER 6

GOVERNMENTS IN THE ANCIENT WORLD

For the whole earth is the tomb of famous men; not only are they commemorated by columns and inscriptions in their own country, but in foreign lands there dwells also an unwritten memorial of them, graven not on stone but in the hearts of men.

—Pericles's Funeral Oration

HISTORICAL CONTEXT: WHAT DO I NEED TO KNOW?

Around 3100 BCE, the Nile Valley became a single unified kingdom of Egypt, with a capital city, perhaps at Memphis. Around this time, kingship, monumental architecture, and cuneiform writing arose. Divine kingship remained the cornerstone of Egyptian life (unlike for the Mesopotamians, who had warrior-kings). This structure brought about a large bureaucracy devoted to serving the divine king or queen. Originally the king lived in the royal city of Memphis in a structure called the *Great House*—"Per-ao" in the original language, or "pharaoh" in Hebrew. The first of these kings was Narmer, considered the first "dynastic" king and the founding king of the Egyptian dynastic system. Historians divide early Egyptian history into 31 dynastic periods spanning from about 3000 BCE until the conquest of Egypt by Alexander the Great in

332 BCE. During the Old and Middle Kingdoms from 2868–1786 BCE, during which the third to 12th dynasties reigned, great pyramid temple tombs were built for the kings, with a cult of the dead devoted to worshipping the present king's ancestors.

Although simple Mesopotamian cuneiform consisted of pictures that represent ideas or words, Egyptian hieroglyphics were more complex, containing representations of ideas, words, and syllables. For many centuries, historians and archaeologists were unable to translate Egyptian hieroglyphics. The discovery of the Rosetta Stone in 1799 CE changed that. The stone contained a decree from King Ptolemy V in 196 BCE, inscribed in Egyptian hieroglyphics and one other Egyptian script, as well as in Ancient Greek. After the translation of the Greek script, the other two translations followed by the mid-1800s CE, giving scholars the key to translating other Egyptian hieroglyphics. The Rosetta Stone is considered the key that unlocked the ability to understand ancient Egyptian civilization.

Unlike the Nile and Mesopotamia, Greece is barren, rocky, lies between the mountains and the sea, and is made up of small islands. Only 10% of the area is flat, and the climate is uncertain; rainfall varies greatly from year to year, threatening farmers with crop failure. Wheat, barley, and beans formed the staple crops, and Greeks produced grain, olives, and wine beginning in 3000 BCE. Beginning in the period from 800–500 BCE, Greeks abandoned monarchy and replaced it with governance by wealthy landowners (oligarchy). These aristocrats made laws and debated them, decided for war or peace, and settled disputes among the citizens. They created formal councils and assemblies (i.e., groups of the people to advise them) and even juries for courts. Along with this, they laid down rules for the selection of people to these bodies—essentially a constitution.

Two major forms of political organization developed: the ethnos and the polis. Most major Greek city-states, including Athens, were considered poleis. Villages were clustered around a citadel for protection, and many Greek city-states dedicated their citadels to an individual god or goddess (e.g., Athena for Athens). When the citadel sat on a tall hill, as it did in several Greek cities, it was known as an acropolis. Rapid population growth led to the fusion of towns and villages into larger, politically independent cities. Life in the polis was patrilineal with a household headed by a man.

In Athens, the polis was governed by a central government made up of an open assembly of all citizens and a council of 500. A citizen could propose laws and then stand in a central square and defend the need for the law to the assembly. If the assembly agreed, the law went to the council for approval. This system encouraged male Athenian citizens to participate in their democracy and practice their oration to defend their proposals. This led to the development of professionals called *sophists* who soon acquired a reputation as word-twisters more interested in winning an argument than seeking truth.

The polis in Sparta was an oligarchy located in the southern part of mainland Greece. Sparta was a closed society, suspicious of foreigners, secretive toward the outside world, and contemptuous of book learning. Around 650 BCE, a three-part class system emerged consisting of helots, perioikoi, and Spartiate. The helots were unfree laborers who worked the land and were owned by the whole community. The perioikoi were free but subordinate to the Spartiate, who were the only full citizens. Only men could be Spartiate because, as in Athens, they were the backbone of the army. Sparta was dependent on its army because there were so many helots to keep under control.

Far to the east, the Persian Empire—what is modern-day Iran—began in 550 BCE with Cyrus the Great, who united several nearby empires, including the Babylonians, under one banner establishing what was at the time the largest empire in history. He divided his empire into four states, under which regional administrative units called *satrapies* were administered by a governor, called a *satrap*. Aside from courts, tax collection, and other routine administrative matters, the satrap oversaw a general and a secretary who controlled the military and the official records respectively. Aside from the district armies, Cyrus himself created an army that included 10,000 "Immortals" who served as his personal guard.

A complicated succession brought Darius I, considered one of the greatest rulers of the ancient world, to power. When the ruler Cambyses II went insane and died from an infection, a pretender to the throne emerged. According to the Greek historian Herodotus in what is likely an apocryphal tale, Darius and six nobles discussed the type of government that would best serve the Persians: democracy, monarchy, or oligarchy. Darius convinced the nobles that monarchy would work best, although one of the nobles decided to opt out. To determine who would rule, the remaining six would sit on horses facing the sunrise. The first whose horse neighed would rule. Herodotus's story is that one of Darius's slaves secretly rubbed his hands on a broodmare and then, unseen, placed his hands to the nose of Darius's horse. When that horse then whinnied, and thunder and lightning followed, the nobles dismounted their horses and declared their fealty to Darius.

Persian innovations continued under Darius I, including an empire-wide postal system (the first known in history), empire-spanning roads, massive temples, a trade system that linked the Greek islands to India, and the Mausoleum at Halicarnassus, considered one of the Seven Wonders of the Ancient World.

STANDARDS ADDRESSED IN THE CHAPTER

NCHS World History Content Standards, Grades 5–12:

- **Era 3—Standard 2A:** The student understands the achievements and limitations of the democratic institutions that developed in Athens and other Aegean city-states.
- **Era 3—Standard 2C:** The student understands the development of the Persian (Achaemenid) empire and the consequences of its conflicts with the Greeks.
- **Era 3—Standard 3B:** The student understands the social and cultural effects that militarization and the emergence of new kingdoms had on peoples of Southwest Asia and Egypt in the second millennium BCE.

CCSS for Literacy in History/Social Studies, Grades 6–8 and 9–10:

- **6–8:** Determine the central ideas or information of a primary or secondary source; Integrate visual information with other information in print and digital texts; Identify aspects of a text that reveal an author's point of view or purpose; Determine the meaning of words and phrases as they are used in a text, including vocabulary specific to domains related to history/social studies.
- **9–10:** Determine the central ideas or information of a primary or secondary source; Cite specific textual evidence to support analysis of primary and secondary sources, attending to such features as the date and origin of the information; Determine the meaning of words and phrases as they are used in a text, including vocabulary describing political, social, or economic aspects of history/social science; Compare the point of view of two or more authors for how they treat the same or similar topics, including which details they include and emphasize in their respective accounts.

LESSON 1

ORGANIZING QUESTION

What characteristics did Egyptians consider important in an effective pharaoh?

STRATEGIES USED

Annotation, Sketching Through the Text

MATERIALS NEEDED

1. Handout 6.1: Excerpts From the Rosetta Stone Decree (196 BCE)
2. 2–3 images of the Rosetta Stone
3. Two pieces of chart paper, labeled "Sketching Through the Text—Rosetta Stone Decree" and divided into five sections (numbered 1–5), posted on opposite sides of the room
4. One marker per group

LESSON PLAN

Lesson Hook: Display two or three pictures of the Rosetta Stone. Ask students to point out details about the stone or the writing on it. Explain how the Rosetta Stone was discovered and why it was such an important find in translating Egyptian hieroglyphics.

The Organizing Question: Tell students that they are going to look closely at the markings on the Rosetta Stone to look for clues to the organizing question: *What characteristics did Egyptians consider important in an effective pharaoh?*

Examine the Sources: *Annotation/Sketching Through the Text*—Distribute Handout 6.1: Excerpts From the Rosetta Stone Decree (196 BCE). Give students a few minutes to read the historical background of the decree and answer any questions that they may have about the purpose and structure of the text. Explain to students that they will read a section of the decree and annotate main ideas from that section. Next, they will choose three pictures that represent the main points of their assigned section. Before dividing the class into groups, read the first section out loud and model annotating the paragraph for the main points, using context clues to understand challenging words, and analyzing what clues about Egyptian rulers can be found in Section 1. Then, ask students to think of three visuals that represent the main ideas of Section 1. Let two students draw those visuals in the first section of the "Sketching Through the Text—Rosetta Stone Decree" posters that you've placed in the classroom.

Next, divide the class in half and create four groups on each side of the room. (*Note*: For a small class, use only one poster and do not divide the class in half.) Assign each group one section of the text (Sections 2–5). Explain that they are to read their assigned section, annotate the main ideas, and then decide on three visuals to draw on the "Sketching Through the Text" poster paper. Allow time for all groups to draw their pictures. Once all pictures are drawn, have each group summarize its section and explain the drawings to the rest of the class. Encourage students to write the main ideas and make the drawings on their handouts. Once all groups have presented, read the concluding note on Handout 6.1 as a class.

Make a Hypothesis: Depending on time remaining, you may want to have students use their text annotations and pictures to write an answer to the organizing question that includes multiple examples from the decree. You might also conclude the lesson with a class discussion about the organizing question.

HANDOUT 6.1

EXCERPTS FROM THE ROSETTA STONE DECREE (196 BCE)

Historical background: The inscription on the Rosetta Stone is a copy of a decree passed by the General Council of Egyptian priests in Egypt in 196 BCE to celebrate the coronation of Ptolemy V. The beginning of the decree includes a list of titles for Ptolemy V and praises him for his love of the gods, his people, and his country. Excerpts below from the second section highlight the positive things he has done for Egypt.

SECTION 1

In the reign of the young one who has succeeded his father in the kingship, lord of diadems, most glorious, who has established Egypt and is pious towards the gods, triumphant over his enemies, who has restored the civilised life of men . . . a king like the Sun, great king of the Upper and Lower countries, offspring of the Gods. . . .

Decree: There being assembled the Chief Priests and Prophets and those who enter the inner shrine for the robing of the Gods, and the Fan-bearers and the Sacred Scribes and all the other priests from the temples throughout the land who have come to meet the king at Memphis. . . . they being assembled in the temple in Memphis this day declared.

SECTION 2

Whereas king Ptolemy, the ever-living . . . has been a benefactor both to the temples and to those who dwell in them, as well as all those who are his subjects, being a god sprung from a god and goddess . . . being benevolently disposed towards the gods, has dedicated to the temples revenues in money and corn and has undertaken much outlay to bring Egypt into prosperity, and to establish the temples, and has been generous with all his own means; and of the revenues and taxes levied in Egypt some he has wholly remitted and others he has lightened, in order that the people and all the others might be in prosperity during his reign.

SECTION 3

And whereas he has remitted the debts to the crown being many in number which they in Egypt and in the rest of the kingdom owed; and whereas those who were in prison and those who were under accusation for a long time, he has freed of the charges against them;

And whereas he has directed that the gods shall continue to enjoy the revenues of the temples and the yearly allowances given to them, both of corn and money, likewise also the revenue assigned to the gods from vine land and from gardens and the other properties which belonged to the gods in his father's time.

HANDOUT 6.1, CONTINUED

SECTION 4

And whereas he has directed that impressment for the navy shall no longer be employed, and of the tax in byssus cloth paid by the temples to the crown he has remitted two-thirds;

And whatever things were neglected in former times he has restored to their proper condition, having a care how the traditional duties shall be fittingly paid to the gods; and likewise has apportioned justice to all. . . .

And whereas he provided that cavalry and infantry forces and ships should be sent out against those who invaded Egypt by sea and by land, laying out great sums in money and corn in order that the temples and all those who are in the land might be in safety . . . when the Nile made a great rise in the eighth year (of his reign), which usually floods the plains, he prevented it, by damming at many points the outlets of the channels (spending upon this no small amount of money . . . and as to those who had led the rebels in the time of his father and who had disturbed the land and done wrong to the temples, he came to Memphis to avenge his father and his own kingship, and punished them all as they deserved.

SECTION 5

And he maintained the honours of the temples and of Egypt according to the laws; and he adorned the temple of Apis with rich work, spending upon it gold and silver and precious stones, no small amount; and whereas he has founded temples and shrines and altars, and has repaired those requiring it, having the spirit of a beneficent god in matters pertaining to religion. . . .

And he and his children shall retain the kingship for all time. With propitious fortune: It was resolved by the priests of all the temples in the land to increase greatly the existing honours of King Ptolemy.

Note: In the remaining part of the decree, the priests of Egypt explained how they planned to increase the ceremonies and honor given to Ptolemy in the temples by doing such things as putting statues and figures of him in the temples and honoring his birthday and coronation days each year.

LESSON 2

ORGANIZING QUESTION

How did Persians decide on the best type of government for their expanding empire?

STRATEGIES USED

Brainstorming, Think Aloud, Very Important Points (VIPs)

MATERIALS NEEDED

1. Handout 6.2: Excerpts From Herodotus's *The Histories* (ca. 440 BCE)
2. Images:
   - ✓ Map: *Persian Empire, 500 BCE*, available at https://mapcollection. files.wordpress.com/2012/09/persian-empire.jpg
   - ✓ Relief: *Darius in Persepolis*, available at https://en.wikipedia.org/ wiki/Darius_I#/media/File:Darius_In_Parse.JPG

LESSON PLAN

Note: This lesson is a good introduction to types of government (monarchy, democracy, and oligarchy) as well as to the rule of King Darius and his actions to control the Persian Empire.

Lesson Hook: *Brainstorming*—Display the map *Persian Empire, 500 BCE.* Ask students to brainstorm ideas on a sheet of paper for the best way to rule this empire. Prompt them to include ideas about type of government, economy, military, and other possible branches. After 5 minutes of brainstorming, have students share their ideas. Students will probably have different ideas about the best way to govern such a large empire. Write these on the board to refer to at the end of the lesson.

The Organizing Question: Explain to students that the Persians also disagreed about how best to govern their expanding empire in the sixth century BCE. Tell students that they will analyze a primary source to help them answer the organizing question: *How did Persians decide on the best type of government for their expanding empire?*

Examine the Sources: Before starting with the text, provide students with background about Herodotus and show the map of the Persian Empire again.

Think Aloud—Divide the class into groups of 3–4 and distribute Handout 6.2: Excerpts From Herodotus's *The Histories* (ca. 440 BCE). Each section contains the arguments about what type of government is best for Persia. Next, assign each group a section of the text to read and analyze. Explain that students will work with their group to read the text, annotate the main ideas, and look up definitions for difficult words. Model for students by reading the introduction and a few sentences of Section 1 to them, using context clues to decipher difficult words. Model your thinking for students by annotating the main ideas of Otanes.

Very Important Points (VIPs)—After working through a few sentences of the first section together, explain to students that they will choose three Very Important Points, or VIPs, that reflect the most important ideas from their assigned section. Model this for students by letting them help create a VIP statement for the first few sentences read out loud. Explain to students that they will work with their groups to complete the same process with their own assigned section of the text. Afterward, have each group share its VIP statements. The class should listen and write other groups' VIP statements in the margins of the document.

Now show the *Darius in Persepolis* relief and ask students to explain reasons why they think monarchy won the debate. Explain that Darius became king of Persia in 521 BCE and did many things to organize and control the empire.

Make a Hypothesis: Either in groups, in class discussion, or as an individual writing response, have students answer the organizing question with supporting details from all three sections of the text.

Optional Extension: Have students read or research the accomplishments of Darius and evaluate the effectiveness of his rule as king of Persia. Refer to the Lesson Hook section to compare/contrast students' ideas about the best way to govern and Darius's approach to ruling.

HANDOUT 6.2

EXCERPTS FROM HERODOTUS'S *THE HISTORIES* (CA. 440 BCE)

BOOK III: THE PERSIANS REJECT DEMOCRACY

When the tumult was abated, and five days had passed, the rebels . . . held a council on the whole state of affairs, at which words were uttered. . . .

SECTION 1

Otanes was for giving the government to the whole body of the Persian people. "I hold," he said, "that we must make an end of monarchy; there is no pleasure or advantage in it. You have seen to what lengths went the insolence of Cambyses, and you have borne your share of the insolence of the Magian. What right order is there to be found in monarchy, when the ruler can do what he will, nor be held to account for it? Give this power to the best man on earth, and it would stir him to unwonted thoughts. The advantage which he holds breeds insolence, and nature makes all men jealous. This double cause is the root of all evil in him; sated with power he will do many reckless deeds. . . .

For whereas an absolute ruler, as having all that heart can desire, should rightly be jealous of no man, yet it is contrariwise with him in his dealing with his countrymen; he is jealous of the safety of the good, and glad of the safety of the evil; and no man is so ready to believe calumny. Of all men he is the most inconsistent; accord him but just honour, and he is displeased that you make him not your first care; make him such, and he damns you for a flatterer. But I have yet worse to say of him than that; he turns the laws of the land upside down. . . . But the virtue of a multitude's rule lies first in its excellent name, which signifies equality before the law; and secondly, in that it does none of the things that a monarch does. All offices are assigned by lot, and the holders are accountable for what they do therein; and the general assembly arbitrates on all counsels. Therefore I declare my opinion, that we make an end of monarchy and increase the power of the multitude, seeing that all good lies in the many."

SECTION 2

Megabyzus' counsel was to make a ruling oligarchy. "I agree," said he, "to all that Otanes says against the rule of one; but when he bids you give the power to the multitude, his judgment falls short of the best. Nothing is more foolish and violent than a useless mob; to save ourselves from the insolence of a despot by changing it for the insolence of the unbridled commonalty—that were unbearable indeed. Whatever the despot does, he does with knowledge; but the people have not even that; how can they have knowledge, who have neither learnt nor for themselves seen what is best, but ever rush headlong and drive blindly onward, like a river in spate? Let those stand for democracy who wish ill to Persia; but let us choose a company of the best men and invest these with the power. For we ourselves shall be of that company; and where we have the best men, there 'tis like that we shall have the best counsels."

HANDOUT 6.2, CONTINUED

SECTION 3

Darius was the third to declare his opinion. "Methinks," said he, "Megabyzus speaks rightly concerning democracy, but not so concerning oligarchy. For the choice lying between these three, and each of them, democracy, oligarchy and monarchy being supposed to be the best of its kind, I hold that monarchy is by far the most excellent. Nothing can be found better than the rule of the one best man; his judgment being like to himself, he will govern the multitude with perfect wisdom, and best conceal plans made for the defeat of enemies. But in an oligarchy, the desire of many to do the state good service ofttimes engenders bitter enmity among them; for each one wishing to be chief of all and to make his counsels prevail, violent enmity is the outcome, enmity brings faction and faction bloodshed; and the end of bloodshed is monarchy; whereby it is shown that this fashion of government is the best.

Again, the rule of the commonalty must of necessity engender evil-mindedness; and when evil-mindedness in public matters is engendered, bad men are not divided by enmity but united by close friendship; for they that would do evil to the commonwealth conspire together to do it. This continues till someone rises to champion the people's cause and makes an end of such evil-doing. He therefore becomes the people's idol, and being their idol is made their monarch; so his case also proves that monarchy is the best government. But (to conclude the whole matter in one word) tell me, whence and by whose gift came our freedom—from the commonalty or an oligarchy or a single ruler? I hold therefore, that as the rule of one man gave us freedom, so that rule we should preserve; and, moreover, that we should not repeal the good laws of our fathers; that were ill done."

Having to judge between these three opinions, four of the seven declared for the last.

LESSON 3

ORGANIZING QUESTION

How does Pericles's "Funeral Oration" reflect the civic virtues of Athenians during their Golden Age?

STRATEGIES USED

Brainstorming, Annotation, Sketching Through the Text

MATERIALS NEEDED

1. Handout 6.3: Excerpts From Pericles's "Funeral Oration" (ca. 400 BCE)
2. Two pieces of chart paper, labeled "Sketching Through the Text—Pericles's Funeral Oration" and divided into seven sections (numbered 1–3 on the first poster and 4–7 on the second), posted on opposite sides of the room
3. Markers (one per small group)

LESSON PLAN

Lesson Hook: *Brainstorming*—Write the following prompt on the board and give students 5 minutes to write down as many ideas as they can in response:

"In Praise of the United States"—Pretend that you are responsible for giving a speech to highlight the virtues of the U.S. government and culture in order to focus people on positive aspects during an era of conflict. In 5 minutes, write down all of the possible things you might say to a crowd who will gather to hear your speech.

At the end of 5 minutes, allow students to share their responses. Write these ideas on the board to use as a compare/contrast at the end of the lesson. Ask students how the comments they wrote might be biased or missing some facts because of the purpose and audience for the speech.

The Organizing Question: Explain to students that they will look at the funeral speech given by Pericles during the Greek Peloponnesian War. They will read and analyze the speech for clues to answer the organizing question: *How does Pericles's "Funeral Oration" reflect the civic virtues of Athenians during their Golden Age?*

Examine the Sources: You might need to give the class some background about the "Age of Pericles" and the speech itself. Focus on the independent Greek city-states and the Peloponnesian War; Pericles's goal of making Athens a city-state that Greeks would be proud of with public buildings, art, philosophy, and democracy; the purpose of the speech; and Thucydides's recording and editing of the speech.

Annotation/Sketching Through the Text—Distribute Handout 6.3: Excerpts From Pericles's Funeral Oration (ca. 400 BCE) to the class. Explain to students that they will read a section of the speech and annotate main ideas from that section. Next, they will choose two pictures that represent the main points of their assigned section. Before dividing the class into groups, read the first section out loud to model annotating the paragraph for the main points, using context clues to understand challenging words, and analyzing what civic virtues were discussed in Section 1. Next, ask students to help you think of two visuals that would represent the main ideas of Section 1. Let a student draw those visuals in Section 1 of the "Sketching Through the Text" poster.

Next, divide the class into five groups and assign them each one section of the text (Sections 2–6; Section 7 will be used later). Explain that they are to read their assigned section, annotate the main ideas, and then decide on two visuals to draw on the "Sketching Through the Text" posters. Allow time for all groups to draw their pictures. Once all pictures are drawn, have each group summarize its section and explain the drawings to the rest of the class. Encourage students to write the main ideas and make the drawings on their handouts. After all of the groups have presented, read Section 7 together with the class and let students decide the last two pictures for the poster.

Make a Hypothesis: Depending on time remaining, you may want to have students use their text annotations and drawings to write an answer to the organizing question that includes multiple examples from the speech. Conclude the lesson with a class discussion of the organizing question. Make sure to discuss some potential biases Pericles might have had and whether or not students think his speech was accurate. If time permits, have students compare and contrast their ideas from the Lesson Hook section with the ideas and purpose of Pericles's speech.

HANDOUT 6.3

EXCERPTS FROM PERICLES'S "FUNERAL ORATION" (CA. 400 BCE)

FROM THUCYDIDES'S *HISTORY OF THE PELOPONNESIAN WAR*

SECTION 1

Most of those who have spoken here before me have commended the lawgiver who added this oration to our other funeral customs. It seemed to them a worthy thing that such an honor should be given at their burial to the dead who have fallen on the field of battle. But I should have preferred that, when men's deeds have been brave, they should be honored in deed only, and with such an honor as this public funeral, which you are now witnessing. Then the reputation of many would not have been imperiled on the eloquence or want of eloquence of one, and their virtues believed or not as he spoke well or ill. For it is difficult to say neither too little nor too much; and even moderation is apt not to give the impression of truthfulness. The friend of the dead who knows the facts is likely to think that the words of the speaker fall short of his knowledge and of his wishes; another who is not so well informed, when he hears of anything which surpasses his own powers, will be envious and will suspect exaggeration. Mankind are tolerant of the praises of others so long as each hearer thinks that he can do as well or nearly as well himself, but, when the speaker rises above him, jealousy is aroused and he begins to be incredulous. However, since our ancestors have set the seal of their approval upon the practice, I must obey, and to the utmost of my power shall endeavor to satisfy the wishes and beliefs of all who hear me.

SECTION 2

I will speak first of our ancestors, for it is right and seemly that now, when we are lamenting the dead, a tribute should be paid to their memory. There has never been a time when they did not inhabit this land, which by their valor they will have handed down from generation to generation, and we have received from them a free state. But if they were worthy of praise, still more were our fathers, who added to their inheritance, and after many a struggle transmitted to us their sons this great empire. And we ourselves assembled here today, who are still most of us in the vigor of life, have carried the work of improvement further, and have richly endowed our city with all things, so that she is sufficient for herself both in peace and war. Of the military exploits by which our various possessions were acquired, or of the energy with which we or our fathers drove back the tide of war, Hellenic or Barbarian, I will not speak; for the tale would be long and is familiar to you. But before I praise the dead, I should like to point out by what principles of action we rose to power, and under what institutions and through what manner of life our empire became great. For I conceive that such thoughts are not unsuited to the occasion, and that this numerous assembly of citizens and strangers may profitably listen to them.

HANDOUT 6.3, CONTINUED

SECTION 3

Our form of government does not enter into rivalry with the institutions of others. Our government does not copy our neighbors', but is an example to them. It is true that we are called a democracy, for the administration is in the hands of the many and not of the few. But while there exists equal justice to all and alike in their private disputes, the claim of excellence is also recognized; and when a citizen is in any way distinguished, he is preferred to the public service, not as a matter of privilege, but as the reward of merit. Neither is poverty an obstacle, but a man may benefit his country whatever the obscurity of his condition. There is no exclusiveness in our public life, and in our private business we are not suspicious of one another, nor angry with our neighbor if he does what he likes; we do not put on sour looks at him which, though harmless, are not pleasant. While we are thus unconstrained in our private business, a spirit of reverence pervades our public acts; we are prevented from doing wrong by respect for the authorities and for the laws, having a particular regard to those which are ordained for the protection of the injured as well as those unwritten laws which bring upon the transgressor of them the reprobation of the general sentiment.

SECTION 4

And we have not forgotten to provide for our weary spirits many relaxations from toil; we have regular games and sacrifices throughout the year; our homes are beautiful and elegant; and the delight which we daily feel in all these things helps to banish sorrow. Because of the greatness of our city the fruits of the whole earth flow in upon us; so that we enjoy the goods of other countries as freely as our own.

Then, again, our military training is in many respects superior to that of our adversaries. Our city is thrown open to the world, though and we never expel a foreigner and prevent him from seeing or learning anything of which the secret if revealed to an enemy might profit him. We rely not upon management or trickery, but upon our own hearts and hands. And in the matter of education, whereas they from early youth are always undergoing laborious exercises which are to make them brave, we live at ease, and yet are equally ready to face the perils which they face.

SECTION 5

If then we prefer to meet danger with a light heart but without laborious training, and with a courage which is gained by habit and not enforced by law, are we not greatly the better for it? Since we do not anticipate the pain, although, when the hour comes, we can be as brave as those who never allow themselves to rest; thus our city is equally admirable in peace and in war. For we are lovers of the beautiful in our tastes and our strength lies, in our opinion, not in deliberation and discussion, but that knowledge which is gained by discussion preparatory to action. For we have a peculiar power of thinking before we act, and of acting, too, whereas other men are courageous from ignorance but hesitate upon reflection. And they are surely to be esteemed the bravest spirits who, having the clearest sense both of the pains and pleasures

HANDOUT 6.3, CONTINUED

of life, do not on that account shrink from danger. In doing good, again, we are unlike others; we make our friends by conferring, not by receiving favors. Now he who confers a favor is the firmer friend, because he would rather by kindness keep alive the memory of an obligation; but the recipient is colder in his feelings, because he knows that in requiting another's generosity he will not be winning gratitude but only paying a debt. We alone do good to our neighbors not upon a calculation of interest, but in the confidence of freedom and in a frank and fearless spirit. To sum up: I say that Athens is the school of Hellas, and that the individual Athenian in his own person seems to have the power of adapting himself to the most varied forms of action with the utmost versatility and grace. This is no passing and idle word, but truth and fact; and the assertion is verified by the position to which these qualities have raised the state. For in the hour of trial Athens alone among her contemporaries is superior to the report of her. No enemy who comes against her is indignant at the reverses which he sustains at the hands of such a city; no subject complains that his masters are unworthy of him. And we shall assuredly not be without witnesses; there are mighty monuments of our power which will make us the wonder of this and of succeeding ages; we shall not need the praises of Homer or of any other panegyrist whose poetry may please for the moment, although his representation of the facts will not bear the light of day. For we have compelled every land and every sea to open a path for our valor, and have everywhere planted eternal memorials of our friendship and of our enmity. Such is the city for whose sake these men nobly fought and died; they could not bear the thought that she might be taken from them; and every one of us who survive should gladly toil on her behalf.

SECTION 6

Such was the end of these men; they were worthy of Athens, and the living need not desire to have a more heroic spirit, although they may pray for a less fatal issue. The value of such a spirit is not to be expressed in words. Any one can discourse to you for ever about the advantages of a brave defense, which you know already. But instead of listening to him I would have you day by day fix your eyes upon the greatness of Athens, until you become filled with the love of her; and when you are impressed by the spectacle of her glory, reflect that this empire has been acquired by men who knew their duty and had the courage to do it, who in the hour of conflict had the fear of dishonor always present to them, and who, if ever they failed in an enterprise, would not allow their virtues to be lost to their country, but freely gave their lives to her as the fairest offering which they could present at her feast. The sacrifice which they collectively made was individually repaid to them; for they received again each one for himself a praise which grows not old, and the noblest of all tombs, I speak not of that in which their remains are laid, but of that in which their glory survives, and is proclaimed always and on every fitting occasion both in word and deed. For the whole earth is the tomb of famous men; not only are they commemorated by columns and inscriptions in their own country, but in foreign lands there dwells also an unwritten memorial of them, graven not on stone but in the hearts of men. Make them your examples, and, esteeming courage to be freedom and freedom to be happiness, do not weigh too nicely the perils of war. The unfortunate who has no hope of a change for the better has less reason to throw away his life than the prosperous who, if he survive, is always liable to a change for

HANDOUT 6.3, CONTINUED

the worse, and to whom any accidental fall makes the most serious difference. To a man of spirit, cowardice and disaster coming together are far more bitter than death striking him unperceived at a time when he is full of courage and animated by the general hope.

SECTION 7

I have paid the required tribute, in obedience to the law, making use of such fitting words as I had. The tribute of deeds has been paid in part; for the dead have them in deeds, and it remains only that their children should be maintained at the public charge until they are grown up: this is the solid prize with which, as with a garland, Athens crowns her sons living and dead, after a struggle like theirs. For where the rewards of virtue are greatest, there the noblest citizens are enlisted in the service of the state. And now, when you have duly lamented, every one his own dead, you may depart.

CHAPTER 7
EVERYDAY LIFE IN THE ANCIENT WORLD

To guide a state great enough to possess a thousand war chariots: be attentive to affairs and trustworthy; regulate expenditures and treat persons as valuable; employ the people according to the proper season.
—Confucius, *Analects*

HISTORICAL CONTEXT: WHAT DO I NEED TO KNOW?

Around 1800 BCE, the Babylonian empire unified much of Mesopotamia. The society was both urban, with large cities, and agricultural, with small farming villages. The king was an absolute monarch, but ruled an extensive network of officials and judges and a priesthood. For most of the 1,200 years of the Babylonian kingdom, Babylonians recognized three main classes: the upper class, free people who were not in the upper class, and slaves.

A critical development was the Code of Hammurabi, the first known comprehensive set of laws in the West that attempted to establish a system of justice. The Code prescribed punishment depending on the social status of the victim and the perpetrator. Wealthy people, for example, would receive lighter punishment than those with lower social status who committed the same crimes. The Code gave legal rights to all and tried to protect women and children from unfair treatment. Women in Mesopotamia could initiate court cases, practice various trades, and hold public positions. Because the Code covered the conduct of physicians, boat builders, veterinarians, brewers, barkeepers, and a variety of other ordinary professions, it helps historians understand what life was like during the Babylonian period.

Most free marriages in this time period were arranged, but unlike in many areas, women in the Babylonian empire controlled their own dowries, and slaves had the right to gain freedom through self-purchase or by marrying a free person. The Babylonian empire maintained extensive trade networks, and the empire exported agricultural products, perfume, cosmetics, medicines, and finished goods made from imported metal and wood.

Greece—mostly Athens—is often seen as the home of democracy and is frequently compared to American democracy. However, Athenians understood themselves within a larger body politic, and Greek cities were not democracies in the modern sense. Many people, such as women, children, slaves, and male noncitizens, were excluded from political life. "Freedom" was a concept applied to an individual's actions within the community, not to the individual. Even with these limitations, the political life of the ancient Greeks was remarkably free—with citizens and leaders devoted to their city-states and the Greek way of life. Trying to understand how to live one's life was the domain of philosophers, of whom the major figures were Socrates, Plato, and Aristotle. Socrates believed that one became good by studying "the truth" and that no one who truly understood goodness would ever do evil. Socrates's favorite teaching technique was to lead people to realizations by asking meaningful questions, a technique called the *Socratic method* that is still used today. Socrates explored political theory and what it meant to be a good citizen.

Plato believed that the senses are misleading, and that although something called "truth" exists, it is attainable only by training the mind to overcome commonsense evidence. Unlike Socrates, Plato believed in the idea of absolute good and evil. Aristotle agreed with Plato about this, but unlike Plato he considered the senses to be important guides. Change, he believed, was not an illusion but an important phenomenon. According to Aristotle, every organism grows toward a particular end and everything in the universe has a purpose. Behind the cosmos was a principle that Aristotle called "the unmoved mover," the supreme cause of existence, a belief that made him popular with medieval Christians.

The two main forms of Greek drama—comedy and tragedy—began in religious festivals honoring the god Dionysus but quickly became a way to comment on public life. Ancient drama was written in a form that today would be called poetry, and it highlighted the relation of the individual to the community. In the fifth century BCE, a play consisted of three actors, who played all of the individual speaking parts, and a group of performers, called a chorus, that spoke in unison. Plays were performed in an open-air theater on a hillside of the Acropolis. Enormously popular, drama spread all over Greece. (Note that "theater" refers to a location where plays take place, while "theatre" refers to the art form.)

In drama, tragedy is when a good person comes to a bad fate because either he or she took a virtue too far or had to choose between two contradictory right paths of action. Each playwright submitted a trilogy of plays on a central theme, plus a comedy meant to break the tension afterward. The point of watching tragedy was that, in the words of the playwright Aeschylus, "suffering teaches." Comedy, too, was invented in Athens. Like tragedy, comedy offered a moral commentary on the defects of Athenian life. Comedies, which were independent plays rather than trilogies, were performed both at the Dionysia and at separate festivals.

Perhaps no philosopher is more closely associated with, symbolic of, and quoted to represent China than Confucius. Confucius (551–479 BCE) lived at the end of the Zhou Dynasty, and his philosophy spread during the subsequent Warring States period, a 250-year span of history during which seven kingdoms competed for control. It would be hard to overstate the impact of Confucius on Chinese culture and, indeed, world culture. With a focus on harmony— internally within the family, and between rulers and the people—Confucianism serves as a religious philosophy, a way of living, and a guideline for governance. The "Five Classics," probably written by Confucius, include guidelines for ethical behavior, important rituals, poetry, speeches, a method of divining the future, a description of the basic understanding of the universe, and a contemporary history of the Zhou empire.

Confucianism has no central god. Instead it outlines a path to righteous living as well as an understanding of a natural order in the universe in which humans are inseparable from nature and heaven. Unlike leaders of many schools of thought or religions, Confucius believed that humans were fundamentally good, but that they needed education and discipline to attain perfection through self-improvement. To achieve this, he believed humans should practice six virtues—ren (moral excellence), yi (morality), li (politeness), zhi (good character), and xin (integrity). Education was a key component of attaining these virtues and living a moral life, and the role of government, assumed to be monarchy, was to set an example for, and lead the people to, moral perfection.

For Confucius, the government mirrored the structure of the family, as outlined in the "five relationships." These were the relationships between ruler and subject, father and son, older and younger brother, husband and wife, and between friends. In each case except the last, the idea of one having power over another was key, and that power relationship carried an obligation to serve as a moral example. In Confucian terms, the conduct of ruler, father, elder brother, and husband was to be like the North Star—steady and centered, with all else revolving around it.

STANDARDS ADDRESSED IN THE CHAPTER

NCHS World History Content Standards, Grades 5–12:
- **Era 3—Standard 1A:** The student understands state-building, trade, and migrations that led to increasingly complex interrelations among peoples of the Mediterranean basin and Southwest Asia.
- **Era 3—Standard 2B:** The student understands the major cultural achievements of Greek civilization.
- **Era 3—Standard 3C:** The student understands how China became unified under the early imperial dynasties.

CCSS for Literacy in History/Social Studies, Grades 6–8 and 9–10:
- **6–8:** Cite specific textual evidence to support analysis of primary and secondary sources; Determine the central ideas or information of a primary or secondary source; Integrate visual information (e.g., in charts, graphs, photographs, videos, or maps) with other information in print and digital texts; Conduct short research projects to answer a question (including a self-generated question); Draw evidence from informational texts to support analysis, reflection, and research.
- **9–10:** Determine the central ideas or information of a primary or secondary source; Cite specific textual evidence to support analysis of primary and secondary sources, attending to such features as the date and origin of the information; Conduct short as well as more sustained research projects to answer a question (including a self-generated question) or solve a problem; Draw evidence from informational texts to support analysis, reflection, and research.

LESSON 1

ORGANIZING QUESTION

How did the teachings of Confucius reflect the values needed for a peaceful, orderly Chinese society?

STRATEGIES USED

Freewriting, Modeling, Modified Jigsaw

MATERIALS NEEDED

Handout 7.1: Excerpts From Confucius's *Analects* (ca. 500 BCE)

LESSON PLAN

Lesson Hook: *Freewriting*—Before class begins, display the following quote on the board:

> The Master said, "To rule a country of a thousand chariots, there must be reverent attention to business, and sincerity; economy in expenditure, and love for men; and the employment of the people at the proper seasons." (Confucius, ca. 500 BCE)

As class begins, have students spend 5 minutes writing their thoughts and opinions about the ideas expressed in the quote. They may agree or disagree on whether or not the advice is still relevant. Once students have written some of their thoughts on paper, let them discuss the main ideas in the quote and whether or not this advice is relevant for rulers and leaders in modern societies.

The Organizing Question: Tell students that the quote was written by Confucius in the *Analects*, a book of his teachings. Explain that they will read and analyze more of Confucius's teachings to help answer the organizing question: *How did the teachings of Confucius reflect the values needed for a peaceful, orderly Chinese society?*

Examine the Sources: Depending on when you choose to include this lesson in your unit, you may need to provide students with background about the warring states, Chinese dynasties, and Confucius's life as a government worker and teacher. Distribute Handout 7.1: Excerpts From Confucius's *Analects* (ca. 500 BCE).

Modeling—Explain to students that they will examine some excerpts from the *Analects* to determine the main ideas in Confucius's teachings and how they reflect the values needed for an orderly, stable Chinese society. Read the first three examples (1.2, 1.4, and 1.5) from Section 1 to students and ask them to determine the main idea from each piece of advice or story. Then, ask them what clues these might provide about Chinese values.

Modified Jigsaw—Once you have modeled Section 1 with the whole class, explain to students that they will use a jigsaw strategy to analyze the rest of the text.

- Expert Groups: Divide the class into four groups and assign each group a section of the text. Explain that students will become experts on their section. Their task is to read Confucius's teachings from their assigned section and discuss the main ideas with their group members. Remind them that each person will be responsible for teaching this section to others in the class in home groups. Encourage students to write notes and annotate main ideas in the margin of their handouts.
  - ☐ Group 1: Section 2
  - ☐ Group 2: Section 3
  - ☐ Group 3: Section 4
  - ☐ Group 4: Section 5

  After students complete their section discussion in expert groups, assign each student a letter (e.g., A–C or A–D, depending on the number of students in each group).
- Home Groups: For the second part of the modified jigsaw, students will go to "home" or letter groups. All of the "A" students, "B" students, and "C" students, for instance, should sit together. In that home group, there will be an expert on each section of the text. Students should take turns sharing their section, including the main ideas and what values they think are represented in those teachings. The other students in the group should write notes in the margins or annotate all of the sections of the text as they listen.

Make a Hypothesis: After all students in the home groups have shared their main ideas, have students write one or two hypotheses to answer the organizing question with multiple examples of evidence from the text. You may have students individually write their hypotheses and evidence as a formative assessment that you collect or have each group share the hypotheses and evidence in a class discussion. If time permits, return to the quote from the Lesson Hook section and have students discuss what other examples of effective leadership traits they found in the excerpts from *Analects*.

HANDOUT 7.1
EXCERPTS FROM CONFUCIUS'S *ANALECTS* (CA. 500 BCE)

Note: Line numbers indicate the book and chapter.
Characters:
- Master—Confucius
- Masters Yu, Tsang, and Tsze-hsia—followers of Confucius

SECTION 1

1.2 The philosopher Yu said, "They are few who, being filial and fraternal, are fond of offending against their superiors. There have been none, who, not liking to offend against their superiors, have been fond of stirring up confusion."

1.4 The philosopher Tsang said, "I daily examine myself on three points:—whether, in transacting business for others, I may have been not faithful;—whether, in intercourse with friends, I may have been not sincere;—whether I may have not mastered and practiced the instructions of my teacher."

1.5 The Master said, "To rule a country of a thousand chariots, there must be reverent attention to business, and sincerity; economy in expenditure, and love for men; and the employment of the people at the proper seasons."

SECTION 2

1.6 The Master said, "A youth, when at home, should be filial, and, abroad, respectful to his elders. He should be earnest and truthful. He should overflow in love to all, and cultivate the friendship of the good."

1.7 Tsze-hsia said, "If a man withdraws his mind from the love of beauty, and applies it as sincerely to the love of the virtuous; if, in serving his parents, he can exert his utmost strength; if, in serving his prince, he can devote his life; if, in his intercourse with his friends, his words are sincere:—although men say that he has not learned, I will certainly say that he has."

1.8 The Master said, "If the scholar be not grave, he will not call forth any veneration, and his learning will not be solid. Hold faithfulness and sincerity as first principles. Have no friends not equal to yourself. When you have faults, do not fear to abandon them."

1.9 The philosopher Tsang said, "Let there be a careful attention to perform the funeral rites to parents, and let them be followed when long gone with the ceremonies of sacrifice;—then the virtue of the people will resume its proper excellence."

SECTION 3

1.10 Tsze-ch'in asked Tsze-kung, saying, "When our master comes to any country, he does not fail to learn all about its government. Does he ask his information? or is it given to him?" Tsze-kung said, "Our master is benign, upright, courteous, temperate, and complaisant, and thus he gets his information. The master's mode of asking information!"

1.12 The philosopher Yu said, "In practising the rules of propriety, a natural ease is to be prized. In the ways prescribed by the ancient kings, this is the excellent quality, and in things

HANDOUT 7.1, CONTINUED

small and great we follow them. Yet it is not to be observed in all cases. If one, knowing how such ease should be prized, manifests it, without regulating it by the rules of propriety, this likewise is not to be done."

1.13 The philosopher Yu said, "When agreements are made according to what is right, what is spoken can be made good. When respect is shown according to what is proper, one keeps far from shame and disgrace. When the parties upon whom a man leans are proper persons to be intimate with, he can make them his guides and masters."

1.16 The Master said, "I will not be afflicted at men's not knowing me; I will be afflicted that I do not know men."

SECTION 4

2.1 The Master said, "He who exercises government by means of his virtue may be compared to the north polar star, which keeps its place and all the stars turn towards it."

2.3 The Master said, "If the people be led by laws, and uniformity sought to be given them by punishments, they will try to avoid the punishment, but have no sense of shame. If they be led by virtue, and uniformity sought to be given them by the rules of propriety, they will have the sense of shame, and moreover will become good."

4.14 The Master said, "A man should say, I am not concerned that I have no place, I am concerned how I may fit myself for one. I am not concerned that I am not known, I seek to be worthy to be known."

4.17 The Master said, "When we see men of worth, we should think of equaling them; when we see men of a contrary character, we should turn inwards and examine ourselves."

SECTION 5

4.18 The Master said, "In serving his parents, a son may remonstrate with them, but gently; when he sees that they do not incline to follow his advice, he shows an increased degree of reverence, but does not abandon his purpose; and should they punish him, he does not allow himself to murmur."

4.19 The Master said, "While his parents are alive, the son may not go abroad to a distance. If he does go abroad, he must have a fixed place to which he goes."

4.23 The Master said, "The cautious seldom err."

4.25 The Master said, "Virtue is not left to stand alone. He who practices it will have neighbors."

LESSON 2

ORGANIZING QUESTION

What does Hammurabi's Code of Laws reveal about daily life in Babylon?

STRATEGIES USED

Turn and Talk, Modeling, Sketching Through the Text

MATERIALS NEEDED

1. Handout 7.2: Excerpts From The Code of Hammurabi (ca. 1754 BCE)
2. Images of Hammurabi's Code of Laws (*Note*: These images are available on many websites, but the Louvre online collection includes images of the full monolith with background information for teachers and students in both written and video formats at https://www.louvre.fr/en/ oeuvre-notices/law-code-hammurabi-king-babylon.)
3. 2–3 pieces of chart paper, labeled "Sketching Through the Text— Hammurabi's Code of Laws" and divided into eight sections (numbered 1–8), posted on opposite sides of the room
4. Markers (one per group)

LESSON PLAN

Lesson Hook: *Turn and Talk*—Display pictures of Hammurabi's Law Code on cuneiform stones and the monolith. Display a picture of the top of the stone, which depicts King Hammurabi standing in front of Samash, the Babylonian god of the sun and justice. Ask students to discuss with a partner what this carving might represent and what message it might have conveyed to the Babylonian people. Give students a couple of minutes to discuss in pairs and then share their ideas with the whole class. (*Note*: The Louvre video mentioned in the Materials Needed section has information on the symbolism represented on the monolith.)

The Organizing Question: Explain to students that they will analyze some specific laws from Hammurabi's Code of Laws to look for clues to answer the organizing question: *What does Hammurabi's Code of Laws reveal about daily life in Babylon?*

Examine the Sources: First, depending on how much information the class has studied about Mesopotamian history and culture, you might need to provide students some background about the various kingdoms and people that occupied Mesopotamia, including information on King Hammurabi and his accomplishments in Babylon.

Modeling/Sketching Through the Text—Distribute Handout 7.2: Excerpts From the Code of Hammurabi (ca. 1754 BCE). Explain to students that they will read some laws and annotate main ideas from their assigned section. Next, they will choose two pictures that represent the main points of the laws they read. Before dividing the class into groups, read Section 1 to the class. During the reading, model annotating the laws for the main points, using context clues to understand challenging words, and analyzing what aspects of Babylonian daily life could be identified in Section 1. Next, ask students to help generate two visuals that would represent the main ideas of the laws from this section. Let student volunteers draw those visuals in Section 1 of the "Sketching Through the Text" poster.

Next, divide the class into seven groups and assign each group one section of the text (Sections 2–8). Explain that they are to read their assigned section, annotate the main ideas, and then decide on two visuals to draw on the "Sketching Through the Text" posters. Allow time for all groups to draw their pictures. Once all pictures are drawn, have each group summarize the laws in their section and explain their choice of drawings to the class. Encourage students to write the main ideas and make the drawings on their handouts. (*Note*: Handout 7.2 is divided into eight sections. For smaller classes, each group can analyze two sections of the text.)

Make a Hypothesis: After all groups have presented the main ideas and representative visuals, have students discuss, in their groups, the answer to the organizing question. Remind them to look back in the text to find multiple examples of references to Babylonian daily life. Depending on time available, you may have students discuss the organizing question as a class and require every group to contribute pieces of evidence that answer the question. You may also require students to individually write an answer to the question as an exit slip.

Optional Strategies/Extensions: Other strategies that work well with this lesson are a written position paper or class debate on whether or not Hammurabi's laws were (1) fair and consistent or (2) cruel and harsh. Students could be required to defend their position orally or in writing using examples from the laws themselves and their knowledge of the time period. You may also assess the lesson by having students compare and contrast Hammurabi's laws and punishments with those in the United States.

HANDOUT 7.2

EXCERPTS FROM THE CODE OF HAMMURABI (CA. 1754 BCE)

SECTION 1

3. If a man, in a case pending judgement, has uttered threats against the witnesses, or has not justified the word that he has spoken, if that case be a capital suit, that man shall be put to death.

5. If a judge has judged a judgement, decided a decision, granted a sealed sentence, and afterwards has altered his judgement, that judge, for the alteration of the judgement that he judged, one shall put him to account, and he shall pay twelvefold the penalty which was in the said judgement, and in the assembly one shall expel him from his judgement seat, and he shall not return, and with the judges at a judgement he shall not take his seat.

6. If a man has stolen the goods of temple or palace, that man shall be killed, and he who has received the stolen thing from his hand shall be put to death.

15. If a man has caused either a palace slave or palace maid, or a slave of a poor man or a poor man's maid, to go out of the gate, he shall be put to death.

16. If a man has harboured in his house a manservant or a maidservant, fugitive from the palace, or a poor man, and has not produced them at the demand of the commandant, the owner of that house shall be put to death.

SECTION 2

17. If a man has captured either a manservant or a maidservant, a fugitive, in the open country and has driven him back to his master, the owner of the slave shall pay him two shekels of silver.

22. If a man has carried on brigandage [i.e., piracy], and has been captured, that man shall be put to death.

27. If a ganger or a constable, who is diverted to the fortresses of the king, and after him one has given his field and his garden to another, and he has carried on his business, if he returns and regains his city, one shall return to him his field and his garden, and he shall carry on his business himself.

53. If a man has neglected to strengthen his bank of the canal, has not strengthened his bank, a breach has opened out itself in his bank, and the waters have carried away the meadow, the man in whose bank the breach has been opened shall render back the corn which he has caused to be lost.

HANDOUT 7.2, CONTINUED

SECTION 3

54. If he is not able to render back the corn, one shall give him and his goods for money, and the people of the meadow whose corn the water has carried away shall share it.

55. If a man has opened his runnel [i.e., a stream or channel for water] to water and has neglected it, and the field of his neighbour the waters have carried away, he shall pay corn like his neighbour.

108. If a wine merchant has not received corn as the price of drink, has received silver by the great stone, and has made the price of drink less than the price of corn, that wine merchant one shall put her to account and throw her into the water.

109. If a wine merchant has collected a riotous assembly in her house and has not seized those rioters and driven them to the palace, that wine merchant shall be put to death.

112. If a man stays away on a journey and has given silver, gold, precious stones, or treasures of his hand to a man, has caused him to take them for transport, and that man whatever was for transport, where he has transported has not given and has taken to himself, the owner of the transported object, that man, concerning whatever he had to transport and gave not, shall put him to account, and that man shall give to the owner of the transported object fivefold whatever was given him.

SECTION 4

127. If a man has caused the finger to be pointed against a votary [i.e., a holy person], or a man's wife, and has not justified himself, that man they shall throw down before the judge and brand his forehead.

195. If a man has struck his father, his hands one shall cut off.

196. If a man has caused the loss of a gentleman's eye, his eye one shall cause to be lost.

197. If he has shattered a gentleman's limb, one shall shatter his limb.

198. If he has caused a poor man to lose his eye or shattered a poor man's limb, he shall pay one mina of silver.

SECTION 5

199. If he has caused the loss of the eye of a gentleman's servant or has shattered the limb of a gentleman's servant, he shall pay half his price.

200. If a man has made the tooth of a man that is his equal to fall out, one shall make his tooth fall out.

201. If he has made the tooth of a poor man to fall out, he shall pay one-third of a mina of silver.

202. If a man has struck the strength of a man who is great above him, he shall be struck in the assembly with sixty strokes of a cow-hide whip.

205. If a gentleman's servant has struck the strength of a free-man, one shall cut off his ear.

HANDOUT 7.2, CONTINUED

SECTION 6

215. If a doctor has treated a gentleman for a severe wound with a bronze lancet and has cured the man, or has opened an abscess of the eye for a gentleman with the bronze lancet and has cured the eye of the gentleman, he shall take ten shekels of silver.

216. If he (the patient) be the son of a poor man, he shall take five shekels of silver.

217. If he be a gentleman's servant, the master of the servant shall give two shekels of silver to the doctor.

218. If the doctor has treated a gentleman for a severe wound with a lancet of bronze and has caused the gentleman to die, or has opened an abscess of the eye for a gentleman with the bronze lancet and has caused the loss of the gentleman's eye, one shall cut off his hands.

224. If a cow doctor or a sheep doctor has treated a cow or a sheep for a severe wound and cured it, the owner of the cow or sheep shall give one-sixth of a shekel of silver to the doctor as his fee.

SECTION 7

225. If he has treated a cow or a sheep for a severe wound and has caused it to die, he shall give a quarter of its price to the owner of the ox or sheep.

226. If a brander without consent of the owner of the slave has branded a slave with an indelible mark, one shall cut off the hands of that brander.

228. If a builder has built a house for a man and has completed it, he shall give him as his fee two shekels of silver *per sar* [i.e., a unit of measure roughly 36 square meters] of house.

229. If a builder has built a house for a man and has not made strong his work, and the house he built has fallen, and he has caused the death of the owner of the house, that builder shall be put to death.

234. If a boatman has navigated a ship of sixty *gur* [i.e., a unit of volume roughly equal to 18 cubic meters] for a man, he shall give him two shekels of silver for his fee.

SECTION 8

235. If a boatman has navigated a ship for a man and has not made his work trustworthy, and in that same year that he worked that ship it has suffered an injury, the boatman shall exchange that ship or shall make it strong at his own expense and shall give a strong ship to the owner of the ship.

236. If a man has given his ship to a boatman, on hire, and the boatman has been careless, has grounded the ship, or has caused it to be lost, the boatman shall render ship for ship to the owner.

257. If a man has hired a harvester, he shall give him eight *gur* of corn per year.

258. If a man has hired an ox-driver, he shall give him six *gur* of corn per year.

259. If a man has stolen a watering machine from the meadow, he shall give five shekels of silver to the owner of the watering machine.

LESSON 3

ORGANIZING QUESTION

How did theatre reflect the values and beliefs of the Greeks?

STRATEGIES USED

Picture Prediction, Student Research

MATERIALS NEEDED

1. Images:
    ✓ Painting: Cliff Spohn's *Greek Theater*, available at https://fineartam
    erica.com/featured/greek-theater-cliff-spohn.html
    ✓ Photograph: Mark Cartwright's *Theatre of Delphi*, available at
    https://www.ancient.eu/image/415
    ✓ Photograph: Mark Cartwright's *Terracotta Tragic Theatre Mask*,
    available at https://www.ancient.eu/image/3706
    ✓ Photograph: Mark Cartwright's *Greek Marble Comedy Mask*, avail-
    able at https://www.ancient.eu/image/3290

2. Computers or devices for student research on Greek theatre topics

LESSON PLAN

Lesson Hook: *Picture Prediction*—Display the *Greek Theater* painting for the class. Ask students to examine the painting and respond to these two questions in writing:

- What details do you notice in the painting?
- What might this visual predict about Greek theatre?

Prompt students to explain their predictions with details and evidence from the painting. Make a list of their predictions on the board.

Next, show the photographs *Theatre of Delphi*, *Terracotta Tragic Theatre Mask*, and *Greek Marble Comedy Mask*. Ask students what details they notice in these images and if or how they want to revise their list of predictions with the new clues.

The Organizing Question: Explain to students that they will work in groups and conduct research to determine whether or not their predictions were correct and to answer the organizing question: *How did theatre reflect the values and beliefs of the Greeks?*

Examine the Sources: *Student Research*—Divide the class into groups of 3–4 students, depending on the size of your class. Ask each group to choose a prediction from the list on the board. Once they know their topic, have groups develop a plan for researching the prediction statement and what sources they might use. Allow groups time to use textbooks, computers, or other resources to research answers to their chosen prediction statement. When students are finished discovering whether or not their prediction was correct, allow groups to share the facts they found. Ask students to write down the facts from all of the groups so that they have an overview of Greek theatre.

Make a Hypothesis: Once all groups are finished reporting their findings, have each group formulate a hypothesis that answers the organizing question. Challenge them to look for as many examples as possible from all groups' information and prepare to share textual evidence that proves their hypothesis. Allow them a few minutes to create their hypotheses with examples and have each group share with the class. At the end of the lesson, have students discuss whether or not their predictions about Greek theatre from the Lesson Hook section were correct or incorrect and the reasons why. If time permits, end the lesson by asking students which elements of Greek theatre are familiar in modern theatre.

Optional Extension: Have students read a scene or watch a video clip of a Greek comedy or tragedy and have them locate elements they learned from their research.

0-750

PART III

CLASSICAL ANTIQUITY

CHAPTER 8

RISE AND FALL OF EMPIRES

All things are subject to decay and change.

— *The General History of Polybius*

HISTORICAL CONTEXT:
WHAT DO I NEED TO KNOW?

Kings ruled Rome in its early days, from about 800–500 BCE, and Rome included a mix of Latin, Sabine, and Etruscan peoples. The king's power, called the *imperium*, spanned religious, military, and judicial affairs. The king was advised by a council of elders called the *fathers* (*patres* in Latin) or the *senate* (from the Latin word *senex*, meaning "old man"). In theory the senate was primarily an advisory body, but in practice it was quite powerful. Senators were often the heads of the most important families in Rome. The rest of the people, the bulk of Roman society who were free, were called *plebeians*. Most were ordinary people, although some were wealthy. Patricians monopolized the senate and priesthoods, and they did not intermarry with plebeians. Around 500 BCE, the city of Rome detached itself from the surrounding kingdom, while military pressure made it necessary to expand the body of loyal infantrymen, so native Romans decided to incorporate the immigrants into their community. Like the early Greeks, Romans moved toward citizenship based on military service, and within a few generations Rome went from a monarchy to a republic.

The turning point for Roman dominance came with the Punic Wars of 264–146 BCE. The conquest of Italy left Rome as one of two great powers in the central Mediterranean. Rome was a land power, however, while Rome's rival Carthage was an incredible sea power. The long and bloody war exhausted both sides. Rome emerged from the Punic Wars as the greatest power in the Mediterranean. It acquired new provinces in Sicily, Sardinia, Corsica, Spain, and North Africa, but governed its new provinces badly. Whether stealing bushels of wheat or bars of silver, greedy and corrupt governors milked the wealth of subject territories. Even without the corruption, the Roman Republic lacked the administrative structure to effectively govern such a far-flung empire. Most public functions, including basics such as tax collection, were auctioned off to the highest-bidding private companies. By 395 CE, internal and external divisions split the empire into the Eastern Roman Empire, with a capital in Constantinople, and the Western Roman Empire, with a capital in Rome.

Less is known about the early history of the Huns, who kept no written records of their own. Descriptions of their physical appearance, language, government, and culture all come from writers in the Roman Empire and Christians in Europe. As these writers considered the Huns to be either harbingers of the Antichrist or, at best, marauding bands of invaders, their perspective on the Hunnic peoples was clouded. The Goths, for example, described them in animalistic terms, while the Greeks saw them as barbarians. A migratory people from Central Asia, the Huns were less of a distinct ethnic group or empire than a loose confederation of warrior groups from Central Asia (possibly Mongols, Xiongnu, or others) who spoke a variety of languages inherited from conquered peoples. Their military tactics relied on horses, and they organized their armies along clan lines. Little is known about their religion other than that they probably worshipped a variety of gods and that shamans entered into trance states in order to communicate with deities.

They began to move west in the 300s CE, eventually attacking the eastern-most borders of the Eastern Roman Empire. More concerned with the Germanic tribes to their north and west in Europe, the Eastern Romans largely ignored the threat to the east, leaving the frontier lands there largely undefended. When Attila and his brother Bleda took control of the Huns, they negotiated a peace treaty with the Eastern Roman Empire in 435, and in exchange for annual tribute from Constantinople, the Huns and Romans together fought the Gauls to protect the western frontier of the Roman Empire. The Eastern Romans soon broke the treaty, leading Attila and the Huns to renew attacks upon the Eastern Roman Empire. The Huns maintained peace with the Western Empire until Honoria, the sister of the Western Emperor, asked Attila to save her from an arranged marriage. Attila claimed her as a bride, and spent the next 2 years making war, until he died in 453.

Far to the east, the Han Dynasty in China eventually grew from the culmination of the Qin attempts to unify the Warring States in 221 BCE. When that empire collapsed in 207 BCE, after a short period of civil war, the rebel leader Liu Bang became the emperor in 202 BCE. The Han Dynasty lasted until 202 CE. The word "Han" comes from a river in an area controlled by Liu Bang early in his career, and today most Chinese people are ethnic Han. Women in the Han Dynasty had more rights, generally, than earlier Chinese women and women in other world cultures at the time. They could own property and initiate court cases, and had some explicit rights under the law. The Han legal system followed Confucian principles. Torturous mutilation as punishment, common under the Qin, was abolished. Ancestor worship was common, as were animal sacrifices. Whether Confucian, Taoist, or Buddhist, most Chinese believed in two-part souls: one that passed into the afterlife and one that remained in the grave with the deceased body.

During the Han period, the Chinese developed more sophisticated metallurgy, including steel alloys. The development of seed drills in agriculture, the odometer for measuring distance, and waterwheels (for powering threshers, power hammers, and other mechanical devices) all came during the Han period. The Han also invented the idea of negative numbers in mathematics. The Han Dynasty period is considered a golden age of Chinese and world history.

STANDARDS ADDRESSED IN THE CHAPTER

NCHS World History Content Standards, Grades 5–12:
- **Era 3—Standard 3A:** The student understands the causes and consequences of the unification of the Mediterranean basin under Roman rule.
- **Era 4—Standard 1A:** The student understands the decline of the Roman and Han empires.

CCSS for Literacy in History/Social Studies, Grades 6–8 and 9–10:
- **6–8:** Cite specific textual evidence to support analysis of primary and secondary sources; Determine the central ideas or information of a primary or secondary source; Integrate visual information (e.g., in charts, graphs, photographs, videos, or maps) with other information in print and digital texts; Conduct short research projects to answer a question (including a self—generated question); Draw evidence from informational texts to support analysis, reflection, and research.
- **9–10:** Determine the central ideas or information of a primary or secondary source; Cite specific textual evidence to support analysis of

primary and secondary sources, attending to such features as the date and origin of the information; Conduct short as well as more sustained research projects to answer a question (including a self-generated question) or solve a problem; Draw evidence from informational texts to support analysis, reflection, and research.

LESSON 1

ORGANIZING QUESTION

How and where did the Roman Empire spread?

Note: This organizing question has been provided as a sample, but with the Question Formulation Technique (QFT; Rothstein & Santana, 2011), students will generate their own questions that will guide the lesson. Depending on the amount of time needed to research, this lesson may take two class periods. If the QFT strategy is new to you, visit the Right Question Institute's website (http://rightquestion.org) for more details, sample lessons, and resources.

STRATEGIES USED

Question Formulation Technique, Student Research

MATERIALS NEEDED

1. Handout 5.1: Question Formulation Technique (QFT)
2. A map of the growth of the Roman Empire (available at several websites)
3. World history textbooks or computers/devices for research

LESSON PLAN

Lesson Hook: *Question Formulation Technique*—Introduce students to the Question Focus (QFocus) for the QFT lesson (Rothstein & Santana, 2011). A QFocus is any type of prompt or stimulus used to encourage students to generate questions. For this lesson, the map of the growth of the Roman Empire is the QFocus. Distribute Handout 5.1 and remind students of the rules for producing questions. Display the Roman Empire map and give students 1–2 minutes to write down as many questions as possible in their notes.

The Organizing Question: Once students have generated questions for the map, explain that they are going to work together to categorize and prioritize their questions with groups, choose their best questions, and research answers about the Roman Empire.

Examine the Sources: Before students examine sources for information on the Roman Empire, have them complete the QFT process. Divide the class into groups of 3–4 students for the rest of the lesson.

- *Improving the questions*: Ask students to spend a few minutes sharing their own questions with others in their group. They should then label the questions as closed (C) or open (O), discuss the advantages and disadvantages of each type of question, and practice changing some questions from one type to another.
- *Prioritizing questions*: Ask students to come to a consensus in their groups on the three most important questions and write them on a sheet of paper in order to focus their research.
- *Next steps/student research*: Ask groups to develop a plan for how they will answer the questions and what sources they might use. Allow groups time to use textbooks, computers, or other resources to research answers to their own important questions. When students are finished finding text-based answers to their questions, allow groups to share their questions and the answers they found. Ask students to write down any questions and answers that were different from their group's so they learn more information about the Roman Empire's spread. Have students demonstrate locations on the map as they explain their questions and answers.

Make a Hypothesis: After all groups have shared their questions and answers, ask students to write a response to the organizing question for this lesson (or choose one of the student-generated questions). Ask them to cite evidence from their own research and the findings of other groups as well.

LESSON 2

ORGANIZING QUESTION

What were different ways that people viewed Attila and the Huns?

STRATEGIES USED

Close Reading, Annotation, Visual Representation of Text

MATERIALS NEEDED

1. Handout 8.1: Excerpts From *The Roman History of Ammianus Marcellinus* (ca. 380)
2. Handout 8.2: Priscus at the Court of Attila (ca. 448)
3. Painting: Eugene Delacroix's *Attila and His Hordes Overrun Italy and the Arts*, available at https://www.wikiart.org/en/eugene-delacroix/attila-and-his-hordes-overrun-italy-and-the-arts-1847
4. Map: William Shepherd's *Empire of Attila the Hun* (ca. 450), available at https://www.ancient.eu/image/3051
5. Highlighters and markers (one per student)
6. Blank paper (one sheet per pair of students)

LESSON PLAN

Lesson Hook: Display Eugene Delacroix's *Attila and His Hordes Overrun Italy and the Arts*. Explain to students that the figure in the center of the painting is Attila the Hun. Ask them to describe the details and what traits of Attila and the Huns that Delacroix might have been trying to portray.

The Organizing Question: Tell students that they are going to examine two primary sources about Attila the Hun to discover an answer to the organizing question: *What were different ways that people viewed Attila and the Huns?*

Examine the Sources: Begin this section of the lesson by showing students the map *Empire of Attila the Hun*. Ask them to describe what they noticed about the land Attila controlled. If needed, provide students with a brief background of the Huns and the Roman Empire.

Close Reading/Annotation—Next, divide the class into groups of four students. Explain to students that both of the sources they will read were written by someone who had visited the Huns in the fifth century. Give half of the groups Handout 8.1: Excerpts From *The Roman History of Ammianus Marcellinus* (ca. 380) and the other half Handout 8.2: Priscus at the Court of Attila (ca. 448). Explain to students that they will work with their groups to carefully read their assigned text and annotate any facts in the text that provide clues about Attila and/or the Huns. Once students have read their text, annotated the clues, and shared their annotations with their group, ask them to write on the bottom of the handout what their author's opinions were about Attila and the Huns. Students should be able to support their writing with evidence from their annotations.

Visual Representation of Text—Next have students find a partner who read a different text. With their new partner, have them summarize the source they read, share their annotations, and discuss the author's opinion of Attila and the Huns. While students are sharing their texts, distribute a blank sheet of paper to every pair. When they finish, they should create a visual of Attila and the Huns using two descriptions from both of the texts. Give students a few minutes to create a drawing, and then have students share their work with the class and explain what their drawing means. Prompt them to support their visual with examples from both texts.

Make a Hypothesis: When all partners have shared their drawings, ask students to respond to the organizing question either as an individual exit slip or as a whole-class discussion. Students might find it helpful to have the visuals displayed in the room to help prompt their thinking. Remind them to use evidence from both texts. If time permits, show Delacroix's painting again and have students add to their ideas from the Lesson Hook section.

HANDOUT 8.1

EXCERPTS FROM *THE ROMAN HISTORY OF AMMIANUS MARCELLINUS* (CA. 380)

Note: The Roman historian Ammianus Marcellinus was a fourth-century Roman historian who described the Huns as the most barbaric of Rome's enemies.

The people of the Huns, but little known from ancient records, dwelling beyond the Maeotic Sea near the ice-bound ocean, exceed every degree of savagery. . . . They all have compact, strong limbs and thick necks, and are so monstrously ugly and misshapen, that one might take them for two-legged beasts or for the stumps, rough-hewn into images, that are used in putting sides to bridges. But although they have the form of men, however ugly, they are so hardy in their mode of life that they have no need of fire nor of savory food, but eat the roots of wild plants and the half-raw flesh of any kind of animal whatever. . . .

They are never protected by any buildings, but they avoid these like tombs, which are set apart from everyday use. For not even a hut thatched with reed can be found among them. But roaming at large amid the mountains and woods, they learn from the cradle to endure cold, hunger, and thirst. When away from their homes they never enter a house unless compelled by extreme necessity; for they think they are not safe when staying under a roof.

They dress in linen cloth or in the skins of field-mice sewn together, and they wear the same clothing indoors and out. But when they have once put their necks into a faded tunic, it is not taken off or changed until by long wear and tear it has been reduced to rags and fallen from them bit by bit. They cover their heads with round caps and protect their hairy legs with goat-skins; their shoes are formed upon no lasts, and so prevent their walking with free step. For this reason they are not at all adapted to battles on foot, but they are almost glued to their horses, which are hardy, it is true, but ugly, and sometimes they sit on them woman-fashion and thus perform their ordinary tasks. From their horses by night or day every one of that nation buys and sells, eats and drinks, and bowed over the narrow neck of the animal relaxes into a sleep so deep as to be accompanied by many dreams.

And when deliberation is called for about weighty matters, they all consult as a common body in that fashion. They are subject to no royal restraint, but they are content with the disorderly government of their important men, and led by them they force their way through every obstacle.

They also sometimes fight when provoked, and then they enter the battle drawn up in wedge-shaped masses, while their medley of voices makes a savage noise. And as they are lightly equipped for swift motion, and unexpected in action, they purposely divide suddenly into scattered bands and attack, rushing about in disorder here and there, dealing terrific slaughter; and because of their extraordinary rapidity of movement they are never seen to attack a rampart or pillage an enemy's camp.

And on this account you would not hesitate to call them the most terrible of all warriors, because they fight from a distance with missiles having sharp bone, instead of their usual points, joined to the shafts with wonderful skill; then they gallop over the intervening spaces and fight hand to hand with swords, regardless of their own lives; and while the enemy are guarding against wounds from the sabre-thrusts, they throw strips of cloth plaited into nooses over their opponents and so entangle them that they fetter their limbs and take from them the power of riding or walking. . . .

Like unreasoning beasts, they are utterly ignorant of the difference between right and wrong; they are deceitful and ambiguous in speech, never bound by any reverence for religion or for superstition. They burn with an infinite thirst for gold, and they are so fickle and prone to anger, that they often quarrel with their allies without provocation, more than once on the same day, and make friends with them again without a mediator.

HANDOUT 8.2

PRISCUS AT THE COURT OF ATTILA (CA. 448)

Note: Priscus was a Greek writer who visited Attila in 448 and described his impressions.

Attila's residence, which was situated here, was said to be more splendid than his houses in other places. It was made of polished boards, and surrounded with wooden enclosures, designed not so much for protection as for appearance' sake. . . . Not far from the inclosure was a large bath. . . . The stones for this bath had been brought from Pannonia, for the barbarians in this district had no stones or trees, but used imported material. . . .

The next day I entered the enclosure of Attila's palace, bearing gifts to his wife, whose name was Kreka. . . . Within the inclosures were numerous buildings, some of carved boards beautifully fitted together, others of straight planed beams, without carving, fastened on round wooden blocks which rose to a moderate height from the ground. Attila's wife lived here; and, having been admitted by the barbarians at the door, I found her reclining on a soft couch. The floor of the room was covered with woolen mats for walking on. A number of servants stood round her, and maids sitting on the floor in front of her embroidered with colors linen cloths intended to be placed over the Scythian dress for ornament. Having approached, saluted her, and presented the gifts, I went out and walked to the other houses. . . .

I saw a number of people advancing, and a great commotion and noise, Attila's egress being expected. And he came forth from the house with a dignified strut, looking round on this side and on that. He was accompanied by Onegesius, and stood in front of the house; and many persons who had lawsuits with one another came up and received his judgment. . . .

[We were invited to a banquet with Attila at three o'clock] When the hour arrived we went to the palace, along with the embassy from the western Romans, and stood on the threshold of the hall in the presence of Attila. The cupbearers gave us a cup, according to the national custom, that we might pray before we sat down. Having tasted the cup, we proceeded to take our seats, all the chairs being ranged along the walls of the room on either side. Attila sat in the middle on a couch; a second couch was set behind him, and from it steps led up to his bed, which was covered with linen sheets and wrought coverlets for ornament, such as Greeks and Romans used to deck bridal beds. The places on the right of Attila were held chief in honor—those on the left, where we sat, were only second. . . .

Tables, large enough for three or four, or even more, to sit at, were placed next the table of Attila, so that each could take of the food on the dishes without leaving his seat. The attendant of Attila first entered with a dish of meat, and behind him came the other attendants with bread and viands, which they laid on the tables. A luxurious meal, served on silver plate, had been made ready for us and the barbarian guests, but Attila ate nothing but meat on a wooden trencher. In everything else, too, he showed himself temperate—his cup was of wood, while to the guests were given goblets of gold and silver. His dress, too, was quite simple, affecting only to be clean. The sword he carried at his side, the ratchets of his Scythian shoes, the bridle of his horse were not adorned, like those of the other Scythians, with gold or gems or anything costly.

When the viands of the first course had been consumed, we all stood up, and did not resume our seats until each one, in the order before observed, drank to the health of Attila in the goblet of wine presented to him. We then sat down, and a second dish was placed on each table with eatables of another kind. After this course the same ceremony was observed as after the first, When evening fell torches were lit, and two barbarians coming forward in front of Attila sang songs they had composed, celebrating his victories and deeds of valor in war.

CHAPTER 9

CHRISTIANITY

The triumph of Christianity is actually a very remarkable historical phenomenon . . . . We begin with a small group from the backwaters of the Roman Empire and after two, three centuries go by, lo and behold that same group and its descendants have somehow taken over the Roman Empire and have become the official religion, in fact the only tolerated religion, of the Roman Empire by the end of the 4th century.

—Shaye I. D. Cohen, Professor of Religious Studies, Brown University

HISTORICAL CONTEXT: WHAT DO I NEED TO KNOW?

By the first century BCE, the Roman Republic was on stable footing religiously. Early Roman religion in general was animistic, meaning that people believed that there were spirits in objects—trees, clouds, rocks, doors, crops, and so forth. Under the influence of expansion and colonization, the Romans adopted Greek gods to their own culture in a process called *syncretization*, and also anthropomorphized them and gave them human characteristics. The spirit of the hearth (the central fire in the house) used for cooking and warmth became Vesta, goddess of the home, of the family, and of the hearth. The Romans also gave the Greek gods Romanized names, so Dionysus became Bacchus, Zeus became Jupiter, Poseidon became Neptune, and so on. As Rome expanded, it tended to incorporate foreign religions. Roman polytheism was tolerant of all forms of religious expression and allowed for the addition of new gods—which required approval by the Roman Senate—that Romans encountered through trade or conquest. Romans who worshipped particular gods could do so as long as it did not threaten the power of the state and as long as they continued to acknowledge the cult of the Emperor, especially in the Republic period. Romans were also generally suspicious of religions practiced in secret or those that required secret oaths.

By the first century BCE, the Jews had lived successively under the Babylonians, the Egyptians, the Persians, the Greeks, and then the Romans, working to maintain a unique cultural and religious identity. In the first century BCE, two schools of Jewish thought emerged with different views regarding written and oral tradition, and with different outlooks on the law and how to worship. Sadducees, who generally came from the elite of Jewish society, recognized the written Torah and resisted new ideas that threatened traditions. They also tended to support the balance of power that had been established between Jews and Romans in Judea. The Pharisees focused on the spiritual needs of ordinary folk, believed that law was central to Judaism but argued that it could be interpreted flexibly, believed in the superiority of spiritual to political matters, emphasized charity toward the poor, spoke in parables to make their teaching accessible, and, unlike many Jews, accepted the idea of an afterlife and of the resurrection of the body. Pharisees also accepted the concept of a Messiah, who would bring a reign of divine justice to Earth.

Christianity has its roots in the Pharisaic tradition, and early followers of Jesus saw themselves as Jews for whom Jesus's life served as a model. To these early followers, Jesus was the Messianic fulfillment of Hebrew scripture. That simple doctrine changed with Paul, a Pharisee and a native speaker of Aramaic, who knew Hebrew and Greek. The key to Paul's faith was not Jesus's life, although that was a model for Christian ethics, but Jesus's death and resurrection. He also began to convert Gentiles to Christianity.

Early Christianity frightened conservative Romans because Christians met in small groups, had secret rituals, and refused to make patriotic sacrifices to the emperor cults. Still, although Romans persecuted Christians from time to time, the general attitude was one of tacit toleration as long as Christians kept their religion private and did not proselytize in public places, put up inscriptions or monuments, or build churches. That changed with the Emperor Constantine, who legalized Christianity and other religious cults with the Edict of Milan in 313 CE, after seeing what he believed was a vision commanding him to make a sign of Christ on his soldiers' shields before a crucial battle. The Council of Nicaea in 325 brought Christians of different beliefs together to standardize an understanding of Jesus's divine nature.

Although Constantine was responsible for the acceptance of Christianity in the Roman Empire, Charlemagne created the idea of a Christian kingdom in

Europe. Most of what is known about Charlemagne comes from his biographer, Einhard, a German-speaking member of Charlemagne's court who may have been married to Charlemagne's daughter. It was not until Charlemagne, who was sometimes called the "Father of Europe" for having brought together most of the kingdoms in the West, that Europe would find itself united under a single emperor whose power included domain over the churches within his realm. In the West, the idea of the "divine right of rule"—the belief that the power of the monarch derived from God, and the king or queen was answerable only to God (as opposed to the people in a democracy or to a parliament in some modern monarchical systems)—had its origins in the story of Saul and David in I Samuel, as well as in the deity-kings of ancient Mesopotamia. The concept developed in Europe from the time of Charlemagne through the Middle Ages. By the Renaissance, royalists argued that Charles I represented the heir of Adam, the first king.

STANDARDS ADDRESSED IN THE CHAPTER

NCHS World History Content Standards, Grades 5–12:
- **Era 3—Standard 3B:** The student understands the emergence of Christianity in the context of the Roman Empire.
- **Era 4—Standard 1B:** The student understands the expansion of Christianity and Buddhism beyond the lands of their origin.
- **Era 4—Standard 4A:** The student understands the foundations of a new civilization in Western Christendom in the 500 years following the breakup of the western Roman Empire.

CCSS for Literacy in History/Social Studies, Grades 6–8 and 9–10:
- **6–8:** Cite specific textual evidence to support analysis of primary and secondary sources; Determine the central ideas or information of a primary or secondary source; Integrate visual information (e.g., in charts, graphs, photographs, videos, or maps) with other information in print and digital texts; Conduct short research projects to answer a question (including a self-generated question); Draw evidence from informational texts to support analysis, reflection, and research.
- **9–10:** Determine the central ideas or information of a primary or secondary source; Cite specific textual evidence to support analysis of primary and secondary sources, attending to such features as the date and origin of the information; Conduct short as well as more sustained research projects to answer a question (including a self-generated question) or solve a problem; Draw evidence from informational texts to support analysis, reflection, and research.

LESSON 1

ORGANIZING QUESTION

How did the basic beliefs of Christianity conflict with Roman religious beliefs?

STRATEGIES USED

Analyzing Art, Very Important Points, Give One/Get One

MATERIALS NEEDED

1. Handout 9.1: Excerpts From the New Testament of the Bible
2. Painting: Cosimo Roselli's *Sermon on the Mount* (ca. 1481–1482), available at https://commons.wikimedia.org/wiki/File:Cosimo_Rosselli_Sermone_della_Montagna.jpg
3. The Library of Congress's "Teacher's Guide: Analyzing Photographs and Prints," available at https://loc.gov/teachers/usingprimarysources/guides.html
4. Timer

LESSON PLAN

Note: This lesson works best after students have studied the Roman Empire, including Roman customs and religious beliefs.

Lesson Hook: *Analyzing Art*—Display an image of Cosimo Roselli's fresco *Sermon on the Mount*. Display and review the Library of Congress's "Teacher's Guide: Analyzing Photographs and Prints." Ask students to work with a partner to write down notes in response to the Observe-Reflect-Question sections on the template. Allow them to share responses and questions.

The Organizing Question: Explain to students that the *Sermon on the Mount* fresco is a Renaissance artist's depiction of a scene from the New Testament of the Bible. Explain to students that they will read and discuss excerpts from Jesus's teachings to answer the following organizing question: *How did the basic beliefs of Christianity conflict with Roman religious beliefs?*

Examine the Sources: Depending on previous lessons, students might need some background about Roman religious beliefs, Jesus, and early Christianity. Distribute Handout 9.1: Excerpts From the New Testament of the Bible. Continuing to work with the same partner, students should read the text, annotating main ideas as they read.

Very Important Points (VIPs)—Give students time to read the excerpts and complete their annotations with their partner. Then explain to students that they will choose five VIPs that they feel reflect the most important beliefs of Christianity. Ask them to discuss these with their partner and place stars in the text by their five VIPs.

Give One/Get One—Next have students stand up and find a new partner. They should "give" one of their VIPs and explain why they chose it. They should then "get" a VIP and a rationale from their new partner. Encourage students to write down any new VIPs that they get from other students. Continue Give One/Get One until students have had a chance to share their ideas with multiple partners. A timer set for 1–2 minutes can keep this exercise moving efficiently.

Make a Hypothesis: Once students have discussed their VIPs with several others, have them return to their original partner. Either keep students working in the same pairs or combine pairs to make groups of four. Ask students to create a hypothesis that answers the organizing question. You may need to let them use their text or previous notes to review Roman religious beliefs. Give groups time to discuss and then allow all groups to share their hypotheses with specific examples of evidence. If time permits, this would also be a good writing task to use as a formative assessment for the lesson.

HANDOUT 9.1
EXCERPTS FROM THE NEW TESTAMENT OF THE BIBLE

MATTHEW 5: 1–7, AMERICAN STANDARD VERSION

When Jesus saw the crowds, He went up on the mountain; and after He sat down, His disciples came to Him. He opened His mouth and began to teach them, saying,

"Blessed are the poor in spirit, for theirs is the kingdom of heaven.

"Blessed are those who mourn, for they shall be comforted.

"Blessed are the gentle, for they shall inherit the earth.

"Blessed are those who hunger and thirst for righteousness, for they shall be satisfied.

"Blessed are the merciful, for they shall receive mercy.

"Blessed are the pure in heart, for they shall see God.

"Blessed are the peacemakers, for they shall be called sons of God.

"Blessed are those who have been persecuted for the sake of righteousness, for theirs is the kingdom of heaven.

"Blessed are you when people insult you and persecute you, and falsely say all kinds of evil against you because of Me. Rejoice and be glad, for your reward in heaven is great; for in the same way they persecuted the prophets who were before you."

MATTHEW 5: 14–16

"You are the light of the world. A city set on a hill cannot be hidden; nor does anyone light a lamp and put it under a basket, but on the lampstand, and it gives light to all who are in the house. Let your light shine before men in such a way that they may see your good works, and glorify your Father who is in heaven."

MATTHEW 5: 38–40

"You have heard that it was said, 'An eye for an eye, and a tooth for a tooth.' But I say to you, do not resist an evil person; but whoever slaps you on your right cheek, turn the other to him also. If anyone wants to sue you and take your shirt, let him have your coat also. Whoever forces you to go one mile, go with him two. Give to him who asks of you, and do not turn away from him who wants to borrow from you."

MATTHEW 22: 36–40

"Teacher, which is the great commandment in the Law?" And He said to him, "'You shall love the Lord your God with all your heart, and with all your soul, and with all your mind.' This is the great and foremost commandment. The second is like it, 'You shall love your neighbor as yourself.' On these two commandments depend the whole Law and the Prophets."

LESSON 2

ORGANIZING QUESTION

How and why did Christianity spread throughout the Roman Empire?

STRATEGIES USED

I Notice/I Wonder, Pair Reading, Student Research

MATERIALS NEEDED

1. Student access to Francis S. Betten's "The Milan Decree of A.D. 313: Translation and Comment," available at https://www.jstor.org/stable/25011854?seq=2#metadata_info_tab_contents
2. Map showing the spread of Christianity from 300–600
3. World history textbooks or computers/devices for research

LESSON PLAN

Lesson Hook: *I Notice/I Wonder*—Display a map of the spread of Christianity. Ask students to draw a column down the middle of a sheet of paper. Have them title the left column "I Notice" and the right column "I Wonder." Give them a few minutes to write down anything they notice, as well as any questions, about the map. Then, allow them to share their thoughts and questions. The lesson can be facilitated by writing common questions on the board to help guide the rest of the lesson.

The Organizing Question: Explain to students that they will read and analyze a primary source and do some research to answer their "I Wonder" questions, as well as the following organizing question: *How and why did Christianity spread throughout the Roman Empire?*

Examine the Sources: If you have not talked about Christianity in the context of the Roman Empire, start this part of the lesson with background about the Roman Empire, Constantine, and the beginnings of Christianity.

Pair Reading—Explain to students that they will work with a partner to read the Edict of Milan and determine the main ideas. In partner reading, students take turns reading and discussing a paragraph together. The first partner reads out loud, and the second partner summarizes the paragraph and begins a discussion of the main points. Readers switch roles for the next paragraph. Because this text has long paragraphs, it can help to have students read only 2–3 sentences at a time, and then stop to discuss them. If needed, model a few sentences together to show students how to read and understand complex texts. Encourage them to locate difficult words and use context clues or dictionaries to determine their meanings. Once students have read and discussed the text, ask them to share the main ideas of the Edict of Milan and consider how it might help them understand the spread of Christianity.

Student Research—Ask each group to choose one question from their "I Wonder" list (from the Lesson Hook section) to use for this mini-research task. Allow groups time to use textbooks, computers, or other resources to research answers to their question and see if they can find more clues to answer the lesson's organizing question. When students are finished finding text-based answers to their questions, allow groups to share their questions and the answers they found. Ask students to write down any questions and answers that were different from theirs so they learn more information about the spread of Christianity. Have students demonstrate locations on the map as they explain their questions and answers.

Make a Hypothesis: After all groups have shared questions and answers, ask students to write a response to the organizing question for this lesson. They should cite evidence in their answer from their own research and the findings of other groups as well. End the lesson by having them discuss how important they think the Edict of Milan was to the spread of Christianity.

LESSON 3

ORGANIZING QUESTION

How effective was Charlemagne as Holy Roman Emperor?

STRATEGIES USED

Brainstorming, Very Important Points (VIPs), Modified Jigsaw

MATERIALS NEEDED

1. Handout 9.2: Excerpts From Einhard's *Life of Charlemagne* (ca. 830)
2. Video: History Channel's "Charlemagne," available at https://www.his tory.com/topics/charlemagne/videos/charlemagne
3. Map: Charlemagne's empire, available online

LESSON PLAN

Lesson Hook: *Brainstorming*—Ask students to think of their favorite hero, real or fictional. Have them write down three amazing facts about this person that justify him or her being classified a hero. Allow them to discuss these facts with a partner. Next, ask students: *If you were going to write a biography about this person, how would you make this biography interesting to the public?* Remind students that their goal is not only to praise the hero, but also to sell books. Give partners a chance to brainstorm this together and discuss these ideas with the class.

The Organizing Question: Explain to students that in this lesson they will read and analyze excerpts from a biography about Charlemagne and use the information to answer the organizing question: *How effective was Charlemagne as Holy Roman Emperor?*

Examine the Sources: *Very Important Points (VIPs)*—Begin this section of the lesson by playing History Channel's "Charlemagne" video. As students watch the video, have them write down five VIPs about Charlemagne. After the video, ask students to turn and talk to a partner and share their VIPs. Next, have them write down two questions they are wondering about Charlemagne. Show them the map of Charlemagne's empire as an introduction to the primary source they will read.

Modified Jigsaw—Distribute Handout 9.2: Excerpts From Einhard's *Life of Charlemagne* (ca. 830). Explain that students will read an excerpt of the biography and annotate the text for clues about Charlemagne's reign. Read the first section (Chapter XV) to the class and practice highlighting important facts that might help answer the organizing question. Once you have modeled the process of annotating, explain to students that they will use a jigsaw strategy to analyze the rest of the text.

- Expert Groups: Divide the class into eight numbered groups and assign each group a chapter excerpt. Explain that they will become experts on their section. Their task is to read Einhard's description of Charlemagne and discuss the main ideas with their group members. Remind them that each person will be responsible for teaching the assigned section to others in the class in home groups. Encourage students to write notes and annotate main ideas in the margin of their handouts.
  - Group 1: Chapter XVI
  - Group 2: Chapter XVII
  - Group 3: Chapter XXII
  - Group 4: Chapter XXIV
  - Group 5: Chapter XXV
  - Group 6: Chapter XXVI
  - Group 7: Chapter XXVIII
  - Group 8: Chapter XXIX

    After students complete their section discussion in expert groups, assign each student a letter in alphabetical order (e.g., A–C or A–D, depending on the number of students in each group).
- Home Groups: For the second part of the modified jigsaw, students will go to "home" or letter groups. All of the "A" students, "B" students, and "C" students, for instance, should sit together. In that home group, they will have an expert on each section of the text. Students should take turns sharing their section, including main ideas and what clues about Charlemagne's reign are found in that section. The other students in the group should annotate all of the sections of the text as they listen.

Make a Hypothesis: After all students in the home groups have shared their main ideas, have students write a hypothesis statement that answers the organizing question with multiple examples of evidence from the biography. You may have students individually write their hypothesis and evidence as a formative assessment or choose to have each group share the hypothesis and evidence in a class discussion. If time permits, return to the ideas about a biography that you discussed in the Lesson Hook section and have students evaluate whether they think Einhard might have exaggerated in the biography. You could also have them compare the accomplishments mentioned in the biography with a textbook or online encyclopedia source about Charlemagne's accomplishments.

HANDOUT 9.2
EXCERPTS FROM EINHARD'S
LIFE OF CHARLEMAGNE (CA. 830)

XV.

Such are the wars, most skillfully planned and successfully fought, which this most powerful king waged during the forty seven years of his reign. He so largely increased the Frank kingdom, which was already great and strong when he received it at his father's hands, that more than double its former territory was added to it. . . . In fine, he vanquished and made tributary all the wild and barbarous tribes dwelling in Germany between the Rhine and the Vistula, the Ocean and the Danube, all of which speak very much the same language, but differ widely from one another in customs and dress.

XVI.

He added to the glory of his reign by gaining the goodwill of several kings and nations; so close, indeed, was the alliance that he contracted with Alphonso, King of Galicia and Asturias, that the latter, when sending letters or ambassadors to Charles, invariably styled himself his man. His munificence won the kings of the Scots also to pay such deference to his wishes that they never gave him any other title than lord, or themselves than subjects and slaves: there are letters from them extant in which these feelings in his regard are expressed. . . . His relations with Aaron, King of the Persians, who ruled over almost the whole of the East, India excepted, were so friendly that this prince preferred his favour to that of all the kings and potentates of the earth, and considered that to him alone marks of honour and munificence were due. Accordingly, when the ambassadors sent by Charles to visit the most holy sepulchre and place of resurrection of our Lord and Saviour presented themselves before him with gifts, and made known their master's wishes, he not only granted what was asked, but gave possession of that holy and blessed spot. . . . In fact, the power of the Franks was always viewed by the Greeks and Romans with a jealous eye, whence the Greek proverb "Have the Frank for your friend, but not for your neighbour."

XVII.

This King, who showed himself so great in extending his empire and subduing foreign nations, and was constantly occupied with plans to that end, under took also very many works calculated to adorn and benefit his kingdom, and brought several of them to completion. Among these, the most deserving of mention are the basilica of the Holy Mother of God at Aixla-Chapelle, built in the most admirable manner, and a bridge over the Rhine at Mayence, half a mile long, the breadth of the river at this point. This bridge gia was destroyed by fire the year before Charles died, but, owing to his death so soon after, could not be repaired, although he had intended to rebuild it in stone. He began two palaces of beautiful workmanship. He also fitted out a fleet for the war with the Northmen; the vessels required for this purpose were built on the rivers that flow from Gaul and Germany into the Northern Ocean. Moreover, since the Northmen continually overran and laid waste the Gallic and German coasts, he caused watch

HANDOUT 9.2, CONTINUED

and ward to be kept in all the harbours, and at the mouths of rivers large enough to admit the entrance of vessels, to prevent the enemy from disembarking. . . .

XXII.

Charles was large and strong, and of lofty stature, though not disproportionately tall (his height is well known to have been seven times the length of his foot); the upper part of his head was round, his eyes very large and animated, nose a little long, hair fair, and face laughing and merry. Thus his appearance was always stately and dignified, whether he was standing or sitting; although his neck was thick and somewhat short, and his belly rather prominent; but the symmetry of the rest of his body concealed these defects. His gait was firm, his whole carriage manly, and his voice clear, but not so strong as his size led one to expect. His health was excellent, except during the four years preceding his death, when he was subject to frequent fevers; at the last he even limped a little with one foot. Even in those years he consulted rather his own inclinations than the advice of physicians, who were almost hateful to him, because they wanted him to give up roasts, to which he was accustomed, and to eat boiled meat instead. In accordance with the national custom, he took frequent exercise on horseback and in the chase, accomplishments in which scarcely any people in the world can equal the Franks. He enjoyed the exhalations from natural warm springs, and often practised swimming, in which he was such an adept that none could surpass him; and hence it was that he built his palace at Aix-la-Chapelle, and lived there constantly during his latter years until his death.

XXIV.

Charles was temperate in eating, and particularly so in drinking, for he abominated drunkenness in anybody, much more in himself and those of his household; but he could not easily abstain from food, and often complained that fasts injured his health. He very rarely gave entertainment, only on great feast-days, and then to large numbers of people. His meals ordinarily consisted of four courses, not counting the roast, which his huntsmen used to bring in on the spit; he was more fond of this than of any other dish. While at table, he listened to reading or music. The subjects of the readings were the stories and deeds of olden time: he was fond, too, of St. Augustine's books, and especially of the one entitled "The City of God." He was so moderate in the use of wine and all sorts of drink that he rarely allowed himself more than three cups in the course of a meal. In summer, after the midday meal, he would eat some fruit, drain a single cup, put off his clothes and shoes, just as he did for the night, and rest for two or three hours. He was in the habit of awaking and rising from bed four or five times during the night. While he was dressing and putting on his shoes, he not only gave audience to his friends, but if the Count of the Palace told him of any suit in which his judgment was necessary, he had the parties brought be ore him forthwith, took cognizance of the case, and gave his decision, just as if he were sitting on the judgment-seat. This was not the only business that he transacted at this time, but he performed any duty of the day whatever, whether he had to attend to the matter himself, or to give commands concerning it to his officers.

HANDOUT 9.2, CONTINUED

XXV.

Charles had the gift of ready and fluent speech, and could express whatever he had to say with the utmost clearness. He was not satisfied with command of his native language merely, but gave attention to the study of foreign ones, and in particular was such a master of Latin that he could speak it as well as his native tongue; but he could understand Greek better than he could speak it. He was so eloquent, in deed, that he might have passed for a teacher of eloquence. He most zealously cultivated the liberal arts, held those who taught them in great esteem, and conferred great honours upon them. The King spent much time and labour with him studying rhetoric, dialectics, and especially astronomy; he learned to reckon, and used to investigate the motions of the heavenly bodies most curiously, with an intelligent scrutiny. He also tried to write, and used to keep tablets and blanks in bed under his pillow, that at leisure hours he might accustom his hand to form the letters; however, as he did not begin his efforts in due season, but late in life, they met with ill success.

XXVI.

He cherished with the greatest fervour and devotion the principles of the Christian religion, which had been instilled into him from infancy. . . . He was a constant worshipper at this church as long as his health permitted, going morning and evening, even after nightfall, besides attending mass; and he took care that all the services there conducted should be administered with the utmost possible propriety.

XXVIII.

When he made his last journey thither, he had also other ends in view. The Romans had inflicted many injuries upon the Pontiff Leo, tearing out his eyes and cutting out his tongue, so that he had been compelled to call upon the King for help. Charles accordingly went to Rome, to set in order the affairs of the Church, which were in great confusion, and passed the whole winter there. It was then that he received the titles of Emperor and Augustus, to which he at first had such an aversion that he declared that he would not have set foot in the Church the day that they were conferred, although it was a great feast-day, if he could have foreseen the design of the Pope. He bore very patiently with the jealousy which the Roman emperors showed upon his assuming these titles, for they took this step very ill; and by dint of frequent embassies and letters, in which he addressed, them as brothers, he made their haughtiness yield to his magnanimity, a quality in which he was unquestionably much their superior.

HANDOUT 9.2, CONTINUED

XXIX.

It was after he had received the imperial name that, finding the laws of his people very defective (the Franks have two sets of laws, very different in many particulars), he determined to add what was wanting, to reconcile the discrepancies, and to correct what was vicious and wrongly cited in them. However, he went no further in this matter than to supplement the laws by a few capitularies, and those imperfect ones; but he caused the unwritten laws of all the tribes that came under his rule to be compiled and reduced to writing. He also had the old rude songs that celebrate the deeds and wars of the ancient kings written out for transmission to posterity. He began a grammar of his native language. He gave the months names in his own tongue, in place of the Latin and barbarous names by which they were formerly known among the Franks.

CHAPTER 10

ISLAM

In Islam, it is not just your right, but your responsibility to get education.
—Malala Yousafzai

HISTORICAL CONTEXT:
WHAT DO I NEED TO KNOW?

In the seventh century, the Arab world encompassed a great deal of territory, and politics were turbulent. The area had long been dominated by the Roman and Persian empires. People lived in close-knit clans and formed tribes through various associations. Like the Germanic tribes, Arab tribes were complex groupings of relatives, allies, and political or economic clients. Arabs tended to be pagan, although there were also Jews and Christians. Economically, Bedouins (nomadic traders) herded sheep and goats, engaged in small-scale trading, and raided one another's camps and caravans. There was some small-scale farming, although in many areas the soil was poor and the rain irregular. Cities supported trade routes and traders who brought luxury goods, such as spices, incense, and perfumes, from the Indian Ocean and eastern Mediterranean. Traders formed the economic elite and led the tribes. A solution to the intertribal competition and warfare was the institution of the haram, or sanctuary where parties could settle their differences peacefully. Mecca was one of the chief harams in Arabia, and its founding was attributed to the Jewish patriarch Abraham.

Muhammad was born in 750 and raised by his grandparents. By the age of 20 he became a financial advisor to a wealthy widow named Khadija, who became his wife in 595. They remained married until she died. Always a very spiritual man, Muhammad received his first of many revelations in 610, commanding him to teach people a new faith that had an unquestioning belief in one god, Allah, and a commitment to social justice for all believers. He began teaching in Mecca, but won few converts outside of his own family—his wife was his first convert. Some Meccans didn't like his new teachings, fearing that they would upset the established religious, social, and political order. By 619, a group of citizens from Medina asked him to establish a haram in that city. In 622, he made his way to Medina, joining a group of his followers already there. That journey, the hijra (heezh-ra), marks the beginning of the Islamic calendar. Muhammad gained political control of Medina, but Mecca remained the center of his attention. In 630, he returned to Mecca in triumph and then set off to convert the Bedouins of the desert. By his death in 632, he had converted most of Arabia.

The tenets of the faith include surrender to Allah—people were asked to make al-Islam, or "the surrender." Those who surrendered became Muslims and joined the umma muslima—a community in which membership depended only on the belief in Allah and acceptance of Muhammad as Allah's prophet. Those in the umma had a personal and communal responsibility to all other members. The Five Pillars formed the core of the new religion: (1) the profession of faith, "There is no God but Allah, and Muhammad is his prophet," (2) individual prayer five times daily (plus group prayers at noon on Friday in a Mosque), (3) a sunup-to-sundown fast for one month each year during Ramadan, (4) the donation of alms to the poor, and (5) a pilgrimage to Mecca at least once in a lifetime.

In the early decades of Islam, the Five Pillars built up a sense of community. After Muhammad's death, his closest followers organized his recitations into 114 suras, or chapters, and gathered them in the Koran, which contains legal wisdom and moral teachings, as well as regulations on diet and personal conduct, much like the Christian and Jewish Bibles. Initially the Koran was interpreted rather freely, mostly because there was no clergy to impose an interpretation. After Muhammad's death, some felt the need for an authoritative set of teachings, much in the same way that Christians had done. The result was the sunna—literally "good practice"—which was a set of guidelines on how to practice the faith.

After Muhammad's death in 632, the Meccan elite chose Abu Bakr as caliph, or "successor to the prophet." He maintained a united Arabia while his successor, Umar, another Meccan, initiated conquests of the Roman and Persian empires. Umar also started a policy of giving the best positions in the expanding caliphate—the Arab empire—to the older converts and ranking the members of the caliphate in importance according to the order in which they converted. Some of these men became emirs, or governors, of the various provinces. Others became administrators. His successor, Uthman, was a great administrator, regulating the finances of the provinces, preparing a definitive text of the Koran, and choosing emirs based on their skills. In 656, Uthman was succeeded by Ali, son-in-law of Muhammad. Subsequently, followers of Ali formed a "Party of Ali," called the *Shi'a*.

Ali's successor was a governor of Syria and belonged to the Umayyad family, which ruled from 661–750. The Umayyads completed the centralization process of the growing empire by introducing a unified system of coinage, Arabizing the administration, taking tight control of the provincial governments, and moving the capital to Damascus, which was more centrally located as well as the center of Ali's power. The Umayyads also presided over the final territorial expansion of the caliphate. In the west, the caliph's forces took North Africa and Spain, and conducted raids deep into Gaul. In the east, although unable to take Constantinople, the frontier nevertheless expanded against the Roman empire, which was contracting. Although it took Rome 350 years to reach the height of its expansion, the Islamic caliphate reached the height of its power after only 100 years.

STANDARDS ADDRESSED IN THE CHAPTER

NCHS World History Content Standards, Grades 5–12:

- **Era 4—Standard 2A:** The student understands the emergence of Islam and how it spread in Southwest Asia, North Africa, and Europe.
- **Era 4—Standard 2B:** The student understands the significance of the Abbasid Caliphate as a center of cultural innovation and hub of interregional trade in the 8th–10th centuries.

CCSS for Literacy in History/Social Studies, Grades 6–8 and 9–10:

- **6–8:** Cite specific textual evidence to support analysis of primary and secondary sources; Determine the central ideas or information of a primary or secondary source; Integrate visual information (e.g., in charts, graphs, photographs, videos, or maps) with the other information in print and digital texts.
- **9–10:** Cite specific textual evidence to support analysis of primary and secondary sources; Determine the central ideas or information of a primary or secondary source.

LESSON 1

ORGANIZING QUESTION

What are the basic beliefs and practices of Islam?

STRATEGIES USED

I Notice/I Wonder, Gallery Walk, Student Research

MATERIALS NEEDED

1. Images of the following paintings:
    ✓ *Journey of the Prophet Muhammad in the Majmac al-tawarikh* (ca. 1425), available at https://en.wikipedia.org/wiki/Depictions_of_Muhammad#/media/File:Muhammad-Majmac-al-tawarikh-2.jpg
    ✓ *Miniature of Muhammad Rededicating the Black Stone at the Kaaba* (ca. 1315), available at https://en.wikipedia.org/wiki/Depictions_of_Muhammad#/media/File:Mohammed_kaaba_1315.jpg

2. The following images placed around the room for a gallery walk:
    ✓ Painting: Theodor Hosemann's *Die Berufung Mohammeds durch den Engel Gabriel* (1847), available at https://en.wikipedia.org/wiki/Depictions_of_Muhammad#/media/File:Mohammeds_Berufung,_Hosemann_1847.jpg
    ✓ Photograph: Steve Allen's *Qur'an*, available at https://www.thoughtco.com/quran-2004556
    ✓ Photograph: Al Jazeera's *The Kaaba and the Sacred Mosque During Hajj*, available at https://en.wikipedia.org/wiki/Kaaba#/media/File:Al-Haram_mosque_-_Flickr_-_Al_Jazeera_English.jpg
    ✓ Photograph: One of the photos from Christina Lee's article "The Significance of Islamic Prayer Mats," available at https://classroom.synonym.com/the-significance-of-islamic-prayer-mats-12085591.html
    ✓ Graphic: *The Five Pillars of Islam*, available at https://www.religionworld.in/five-pillars-islam
    ✓ Map: *The Spread of Islam, 630–1700*, available at https://ilmfeed.com/wp-content/uploads/2014/02/islamspread.jpg

3. Chart paper placed beside each image in the gallery walk and divided into two columns: "I Notice" and "I Wonder"

4. Markers (1–2 per group)
5. World history textbooks or computers/devices for research

LESSON PLAN

Lesson Hook: *I Notice/I Wonder*—Display a picture of *Journey of the Prophet Muhammad in the Majmac al-tawarikh*. Ask students to draw a line down the middle of a sheet of paper and make an "I Notice" and an "I Wonder" column. Give students 2 minutes to write down any details they notice in the painting and what questions they have about it. Discuss the painting and their questions. Next show them *Miniature of Muhammad Rededicating the Black Stone at the Kaaba* and have them write down things they notice and questions. Ask them to share their ideas and discuss if they see any similarities between the two paintings. Write some of the common questions on the board to use later in the lesson. End this section by asking students if these two paintings give them any clues about Islam.

The Organizing Question: Explain to students that they will examine other images for information to help them answer the organizing question: *What are the basic beliefs and practices of Islam?*

Examine the Sources: *Gallery Walk*—Tell students that they will examine a variety of images to make some predictions about the beliefs and practices of Islam. Divide the class into groups of 3–4 students, give each group a marker, and then assign them to a station to begin the gallery walk. Their task is to examine the image first, and then write on the chart paper what details they notice ("I Notice" column) and what questions they have ("I Wonder" column). Have students rotate clockwise, adding their comments and responding to others' written ideas. When they have returned to the image where they started, have them read all of the responses and report to the class some of the best ideas and questions. Write some of the best student questions on the board and use them for the rest of the lesson.

Student Research—Have each group pick one of the questions as a research focus. Remind them that they are looking for answers to their question as well as learning about the basic beliefs and practices of Islam. Allow students to use textbooks and online sources to find answers to their questions. Based on time needed, this part of the lesson may carry over into a second day. Once students have researched their topics, allow each group to share its findings. Encourage students to write down information from all of the groups to use in the hypothesis section of the lesson.

Make a Hypothesis: Once all groups have shared answers to their research questions, have students work with their group to make a hypothesis that answers the organizing question. They should use evidence from the paintings, the gallery walk images, and any group's research information. End the lesson with a whole-group discussion asking students to find examples of how the images and research sources corroborated information and whether or not their responses during the gallery walk were supported by their research. The organizing question could also be used as an individual, written formative assessment.

LESSON 2

ORGANIZING QUESTION

What insights about Muslim beliefs can be found in excerpts from the Koran?

STRATEGIES USED

Inside/Outside Circle, Modified Jigsaw

MATERIALS NEEDED

1. Handout 10.1: Excerpts From the Koran
2. Index cards (one per student)
3. Timer

LESSON PLAN

Note: It may be helpful to teach the basic beliefs of Islam before using this lesson, or you might use the lesson as the introduction, making predictions or inferences about Muslim beliefs from the text. This would also be a good follow-up lesson to the gallery walk in Lesson 1 of this chapter. See the Optional Extension at the end of this lesson.

Lesson Hook: *Inside/Outside Circle*—Distribute index cards and ask students to spend 5 minutes jotting down their thoughts on the following questions, one on each side of the card:

- What does it mean to live a good life?
- How does a person learn his or her code of behavior (i.e., how to be "good")?

Next, have students stand and create two concentric circles, with the students in the inner circle facing the students in the outer circle. Each student should be facing a partner. Explain that they will have 2 minutes to share their thoughts about the first question with this partner. A timer can help keep this moving quickly. (*Note*: You can adjust the time if needed. You can also do this activity with two lines instead of circles if there are space constraints.) Once the timer goes off, only the outside circle of students should move one position clockwise. The students should then have a discussion of the first question again with their new partners. Continue 3–4 times per question, based on the interest level of the students, and allow them to discuss both questions with multiple partners.

The Organizing Question: Explain to students that the types of challenging questions they discussed are the basis of many religions and religious texts. Review previous religions and texts that students have studied, such as Buddhism, Hinduism, Judaism, and Christianity. Explain to students that they will read and analyze excerpts from the Islamic sacred text to find answers to the organizing question: *What insights about Muslim beliefs can be found in excerpts from the Koran?*

Examine the Sources: Depending on students' background knowledge or previous lessons taught in the unit, it can help to begin by showing Mecca and Medina on a map and explaining background about Muhammad, important dates, and information about the origins of Islam.

Modified Jigsaw—Distribute Handout 10.1: Excerpts From the Koran. Explain to students that they will examine excerpts from the Koran to infer some basic beliefs of Islam. If students need help analyzing the complex text, model a few lines from the opening section together. Ask students to determine the main idea from every few lines and what clues these might provide about Muslim beliefs. Encourage students to write their annotations or notes in the margins of the text.

- Expert Groups: Divide the class into four numbered groups and assign each group a section of the text. Explain that they will become experts on their section. Their task is to read excerpts from their assigned section and discuss the main ideas with their group members. Remind them that each person will be responsible for teaching this section to others in the class in home groups. Encourage students to write notes and annotate main ideas in the margin of their handouts.
  - ☐ Group 1: Section 1
  - ☐ Group 2: Section 2
  - ☐ Group 3: Section 3
  - ☐ Group 4: Section 4

  After students complete their section discussion in expert groups, assign each student a letter in alphabetical order (e.g., A–C or A–D, depending on the number of students in each group).
- Home Groups: For the second part of the modified jigsaw, students will go to "home" or letter groups. All of the "A" students, "B" students, and "C" students, for instance, should sit together. In that home group, they will have an expert on each section of the text. Students should take turns sharing their section, including main ideas and what Muslim

beliefs they think are represented in those teachings. The other students in the group should write notes in the margins or annotate all of the sections of the text as they listen.

Make a Hypothesis: After all students in the home groups have shared their main ideas, have students write one or two hypotheses to answer the organizing question with multiple examples of evidence from the text. You may have each student individually write hypotheses and evidence as a formative assessment or share the hypotheses and evidence in a class discussion. If time permits, return to the questions from the Lesson Hook section and have students discuss whether or not they found any advice that would add insight to their thinking from their Inside/Outside Circle discussion.

Optional Extension: You may have students review their textbook or notes if you have previously taught beliefs of Islam. If this is new information for students, simply assign them a secondary source (a textbook section, video, or an online article) about Islam. While they read or watch a secondary source on the topic, they should look or listen for any similar ideas from the Koran excerpts.

HANDOUT 10.1
EXCERPTS FROM THE KORAN

SECTION 1

The Opening:

In the name of Allah, the Beneficent, the Merciful. [1.1] All praise is due to Allah, the Lord of the Worlds.

[1.2] The Beneficent, the Merciful.

[1.3] Master of the Day of Judgment.

[1.4] Thee do we serve and Thee do we beseech for help.

[1.5] Keep us on the right path.

[1.6] The path of those upon whom Thou hast bestowed favors. Not (the path) of those upon whom Thy wrath is brought down, nor of those who go astray.

SECTION 2

The Women:

[4.17] Repentance with Allah is only for those who do evil in ignorance, then turn (to Allah) soon, so these it is to whom Allah turns (mercifully), and Allah is ever Knowing, Wise.

[4.18] And repentance is not for those who go on doing evil deeds, until when death comes to one of them, he says: Surely now I repent; nor (for) those who die while they are unbelievers. These are they for whom We have prepared a painful chastisement.

[4.36] And serve Allah and do not associate any thing with Him and be good to the parents and to the near of kin and the orphans and the needy and the neighbor of (your) kin and the alien neighbor, and the companion in a journey and the wayfarer and those whom your right hands possess; surely Allah does not love him who is proud, boastful;

[4.106] And ask forgiveness of Allah; surely Allah is Forgiving, Merciful.

[4.107] And do not plead on behalf of those who act unfaithfully to their souls; surely Allah does not love him who is treacherous, sinful.

SECTION 3

[4.134] Whoever desires the reward of this world, then with Allah is the reward of this world and the hereafter; and Allah is Hearing, Seeing.

[4.135] O you who believe! be maintainers of justice, bearers of witness of Allah's sake, though it may be against your own selves or (your) parents or near relatives; if he be rich or poor, Allah is nearer to them both in compassion; therefore do not follow (your) low desires, lest you deviate; and if you swerve or turn aside, then surely Allah is aware of what you do.

[4.136] O you who believe! believe in Allah and His Apostle and the Book which He has revealed to His Apostle and the Book which He revealed before; and whoever disbelieves in Allah and His angels and His apostles and the last day, he indeed strays off into a remote error.

HANDOUT 10.1, CONTINUED

The Pilgrimage:

[22.27] And proclaim among men the Pilgrimage: they will come to you on foot and on every lean camel, coming from every remote path,

[22.28] That they may witness advantages for them and mention the name of Allah during stated days over what He has given them of the cattle quadrupeds, then eat of them and feed the distressed one, the needy.

[22.29] Then let them accomplish their needful acts of shaving and cleansing, and let them fulfil their vows and let them go round the Ancient House.

[22.30] That (shall be so); and whoever respects the sacred ordinances of Allah, it is better for him with his Lord; and the cattle are made lawful for you, except that which is recited to you, therefore avoid the uncleanness of the idols and avoid false words.

SECTION 4

[22.69] Allah will judge between you on the day of resurrection respecting that in which you differ.

[22.75] Allah chooses messengers from among the angels and from among the men; surely Allah is Hearing, Seeing.

[22.77] O you who believe! bow down and prostrate yourselves and serve your Lord, and do good that you may succeed.

[22.78] And strive hard in (the way of) Allah, (such) a striving a is due to Him; He has chosen you and has not laid upon you an hardship in religion; the faith of your father Ibrahim; He named you Muslims before and in this, that the Apostle may be a bearer of witness to you, and you may be bearers of witness to the people; therefore keep up prayer and pay the poor-rate and hold fast by Allah; He is your Guardian; how excellent the Guardian and how excellent the Helper!

LESSON 3

ORGANIZING QUESTION

What were the achievements of the Golden Age of Islam?

STRATEGIES USED

Clue Stations, Student Research

MATERIALS NEEDED

1. Video: NowThis World's "The Rise and Fall of Islam's Golden Age," available https://www.youtube.com/watch?v=FFfXDZvvmrg
2. Images of any of the following illustrations from the Islamic Golden Age, available at https://en.wikipedia.org/wiki/Islamic_Golden_Age
   - ✓ Painting: *Scholars at an Abbasid Library*
   - ✓ Map: *Expansion of the Caliphates, 622–750 CE*
   - ✓ Picture: *A Manuscript Written on Paper During the Abbasid Era*
   - ✓ Picture: *An Arabic Manuscript From the 13th Century Depicting Socrates*
   - ✓ Picture: *Geometric Patterns*
   - ✓ Picture: *A Triangle Labelled With the Components of the Law of Sines*
   - ✓ Picture: *The Eye, According to Hunain ibn Ishaq*
   - ✓ Drawing: *Entrance to the Qawaloon Complex*

3. Illustration: Any of the doctor/patient illustrations from "How Early Islamic Science Advanced Medicine," available at https://www.nationalgeographic.com/archaeology-and-history/magazine/2016/11-12/muslim-medicine-scientific-discovery-islam
4. World history textbooks or computers/devices for research (*Note*: Several websites outline the achievements of the Islamic Golden Age and should be easy for students to find.)

LESSON PLAN

Lesson Hook: Before class, write the words "Golden Age" on the board. Ask students what they think this phrase means and why historians would label something a golden age. Once they have brainstormed some reasons, show the video "The Rise and Fall of Islam's Golden Age." Have students write down Islamic achievements that are mentioned in the video.

The Organizing Question: Explain to students that they are going to examine some pictures of artifacts from the Islamic Golden Age as clues to help them answer the organizing question: *What were the achievements of the Golden Age of Islam?*

Examine the Sources: *Clue Stations*—Before class begins, display images of the Golden Age around the room in clue stations. Divide the class into groups and assign each group a clue station. Their task is to carefully examine the clue at their assigned station for what it tells them about Islamic achievements. Encourage them to add some notes about their clue to the list of achievements from the Lesson Hook section.

Student Research—Once students have carefully examined their clue, have them use a textbook or computer to research the achievements of the Islamic Golden Age and try to understand how their clue illustrates one of the achievements. Once all of the groups have found some answers, have them share their clues and give background about how each clue illustrates one of the accomplishments of the Golden Age. Encourage students to write down the examples as groups report.

Make a Hypothesis: After all groups have shared the research information, have them answer the organizing question using multiple examples of achievements from a variety of clues and student research findings. Ask students to respond to whether or not they think the title "Golden Age" was accurate based on the content they learned. This section could either be a whole-class discussion or a written formative assessment task.

CHAPTER 11
ECONOMY AND TRADE

I did not write half of what I saw, for I knew I would not be believed.

—Marco Polo

HISTORICAL CONTEXT: WHAT DO I NEED TO KNOW?

For as long as humans have been leaving traces in history, they have engaged in trade. Formalized, regular, long-distance trade routes appear in the earliest human records at the beginning of the Bronze Age. Long-distance trade allowed an empire to supplement meager natural resources or import luxury goods. The early "incense route" (600s BCE–200s CE) brought, among other things, frankincense and myrrh from Arabia and Africa into Roman-held Jerusalem. One of the most legendary trade routes is the Silk Road, which linked China to the Mediterranean Sea. The term *Silk Road* was coined in the 1800s CE and might bring to mind a single road connecting two endpoints; however, the Silk Road was a network of overland and overseas routes that connected China, Java in the south, India, Persia, Central Asia, the eastern coast of Africa, Egypt, and Europe. Moreover, silk was only one of very many commodities that moved along the routes. In that sense, the Silk Road was always more of a concept than an exact path.

In the period of its existence, from 130 BCE to 1353 CE, the Silk Road helped connect eastern, central, and western Asia into a vast trade network, with goods flowing in multiple directions and with starting and stopping points all along the routes. Goods moving to China included the very large horses favored by the Dayuan in Central Asia, glassware, gold and silver, exotic animals, weapons, and slaves. Goods moving out of China included silk, tea, dyes, ivory, rice, paper, and porcelain. Archaeologists working along the routes have found Roman coins in China, as well as the graves of people from Afghanistan, India, and the Mediterranean. They have even discovered evidence of a postal route, as well as a trade in marijuana and opium. Most goods that moved over long distances were portable, valuable, and intended for the wealthiest in each area. Cotton and raw silk were moved to the Mediterranean, where they were made into cloth in Egypt and Byzantium. Paper and pottery were moved around the Muslim world. Asian spices and perfumes were sought everywhere. The Byzantines traded in silk cloth, fine ivories, and delicate products of the goldsmiths' and silversmiths' art, slaves, and naval stores. Trade in the West included some high-value luxury goods but mainly ordinary items, such as plain pottery, raw wool, wool cloth, millstones, weapons, and slaves.

As with any trade network, the most important commodity was ideas. Along the Silk Road, people learned more about each other's languages, culture, and political systems. Of long-lasting importance was the transmission of Buddhism, Christianity, Islam, Judaism, and Hinduism along the route. A significant effect of a trade in ideas along the Silk Road was the appearance in Islamic art of heretofore forbidden human figures in the 1200s CE, transforming techniques, styles, and even the media on which art was made, as silk became an important canvas for painting in the Islamic world. In the same century, the knowledge of how to make gunpowder moved from China to Europe, radically influencing the use of armor and the construction of castles, and, on a larger scale, allowing European expansion into Africa and the Americas.

Beginning in the 1450s with the invention of the moveable-type printing press in Europe, information became more accessible than ever. The printing press made it possible to print thousands of copies of a work, and travel narratives about exotic lands became wildly popular among the European elite. The most important of these was Marco Polo's *Travels*, an account of one Venetian merchant's travels to China in the 1200s. *Travels* circulated widely among European elites and led many people to believe that they could trade directly with China in ocean-going vessels.

The Silk Road connection to Africa was one small part of the trade between Africa and Europe, and within Africa itself. With the Sahara Desert separating the northern, Mediterranean-oriented African lands from the southern African kingdoms, trade inside of Africa required pack animals that could endure the fierce heat, as well as supplies to keep both animals and humans alive during the trek. For humans, aside from water, salt was the next most crucial commodity—sometimes more valuable than gold. Taking in extra salt helps the body retain water, and in a time when medical knowledge was more primitive, extra salt could mean the difference between life and death. The spread of Islam into central and southern Africa brought camels from Asia via the Silk Road. These became the desert animal of choice, known as "the ships of the desert" because their fatty humps could store enough water for them to go days without drinking.

Even so, a low population density, and therefore a lack of large cities or even towns, in the interior of Africa meant that most African trade was coastal. In particular, gold, salt, and cloth were especially prized, and African cloth-making was considered by both Europeans and Africans to be vastly superior to European products. Although Africa is often conceived of as one large, uni-form "place," coastal Africa had a dozen or more kingdoms with dozens, if not hundreds, of languages by the end of the first millennium. Some of these king-doms, such as that of the Akan people, were pushed west from the east coast by Christian Ethiopia. The origins of dozens of others are shrouded in mystery due to lack of written records or agreed-upon oral tradition.

Ghana, along with Mali, is an example of an early large trading empire for which the Sahara was an ocean navigated by the "ships of the desert." Unlike most kingdoms along the coasts, Ghana sat at the edge of the Sahara with no access to either the Mediterranean or the Atlantic. The Kingdom of Ghana con-trolled trade in salt and gold by taxing both commodities as they moved from one side of Africa to the other. Some generalizations about the cultures out-side of the Islamic-influenced kingdoms can be made. In West Africa all social relations were centered on kinship and kinship lines, stretching backward to include the dead. These kinship lines were vitally important to the individual in locating himself or herself in the local society. These cultures also shared certain religious principles and ritual patterns. Widespread among the societies on the west coast of Africa was the belief in a Supreme Creator of the cosmos and a pantheon of lesser gods who were associated with forces in nature, such as rain, animals, and the fertility of the earth. These gods were believed to have the power to intervene in the affairs of humankind. In the West African belief system, ancestors also had the power to affect the welfare of village life, for they mediated between the living and the lesser gods. It was therefore important to ensure the entrance of deceased family members into the spiritual world with elaborate funeral rites that honored them properly for the role they would play after death. Finally, West Africans believed in spirit possession, in which the gods spoke to men and women through priests and other religious "experts."

STANDARDS ADDRESSED IN THE CHAPTER

NCHS World History Content Standards, Grades 5–12:

- **Era 4—Standard 2B:** The student understands the significance of the Abbasid Caliphate as a center of cultural innovation and hub of interregional trade in the 8th–10th centuries.
- **Era 4—Standard 5A:** The student understands state-building in Northeast and West Africa and the southward migrations of Bantu-speaking peoples.
- **Era 5—Standard 1D:** The student understands how interregional communication and trade led to intensified cultural exchanges among diverse peoples of Eurasia and Africa.

CCSS for Literacy in History/Social Studies, Grades 6–8 and 9–10:

- **6–8:** Cite specific textual evidence to support analysis of primary and secondary sources; Determine the central ideas or information of a primary or secondary source; Integrate visual information (e.g., in charts, graphs, photographs, videos, or maps) with other information in print and digital texts; Conduct short research projects to answer a question (including a self-generated question); Draw evidence from informational texts to support analysis, reflection, and research.
- **9–10:** Determine the central ideas or information of a primary or secondary source; Cite specific textual evidence to support analysis of primary and secondary sources, attending to such features as the date and origin of the information; Conduct short as well as more sustained research projects to answer a question (including a self-generated question) or solve a problem; Draw evidence from informational texts to support analysis, reflection, and research.

LESSON 1

ORGANIZING QUESTION

How did the Silk Road link the East and the West?

STRATEGIES USED

Map Analysis, Role-Play, Annotating Text

MATERIALS NEEDED

1. Handout 11.1: Silk Road Role-Play Cards (cut out in advance; one card per student)
2. Handout 11.2: Goods Traded Along the Silk Road
3. Handout 11.3: Excerpts From *The Travels of Marco Polo* (ca. 1290s)
4. Map: *The Silk Road*, available at https://en.wikipedia.org/wiki/Silk_Road#/media/File:SeidenstrasseGMT.JPG
5. Highlighters (one per group)

LESSON PLAN

Lesson Hook: *Map Analysis*—Display *The Silk Road* map. Ask students to take 2 minutes to write down as many details as possible that they notice from the map. These could be trade routes, mountains, rivers, or any other detail. Then, have students share their ideas with the class. Ask them why travel on the Silk Road might have been difficult and what country might benefit the most from the Silk Road.

Organizing Question: Next, explain to students that they are going to role-play a scenario and then examine excerpts from the writings of Marco Polo, a Silk Road traveler, to answer the organizing question: *How did the Silk Road link the East and the West?*

Examine the Sources: Keep the map of the Silk Road displayed during this portion of the lesson. Before explaining the roles, introduce students to the countries that are considered "East" and "West" on the map, as well as countries and continents that can't be seen on this particular map.

Role-Play—Distribute one Silk Road role-play card to each student (see Handout 11.1). Tell students that there are eight different roles for this activity, including Eastern and Western merchants, kings/queens, wealthy nobles, and soldiers. Ask students to form groups with other classmates who share their role (creating eight groups). Then, distribute Handout 11.2: Goods Traded Along the Silk Road. Ask students to work with their groups to choose the top four products that they want from the "other side." Remind them to think like their particular role would as they choose these products. They should also be able to explain their reasons for choosing the products they did. As they are working, circulate and prompt discussion about why they might want certain products and what the products might be used for. Ask each group to make a list to present to the rest of the class. Have each group share choices and reasons.

Annotating Text—Next give a brief introduction to Marco Polo, his journeys, and his writing. Distribute Handout 11.3: Excerpts From *The Travels of Marco Polo* (ca. 1290s) to each student. Explain to students that they are going to read excerpts from Marco Polo's book about his travel experiences. Their task is to circle or highlight any clues about trade and specific products that Marco Polo encountered. Model this process by reading the Chapter III excerpt to students, and then asking them to circle clues and discuss their annotations.

Divide the class into 12 groups and assign each group a chapter excerpt to read and annotate. Once students have circled or annotated their clues, have them return to the list of goods (Handout 11.2) and highlight any products from the list mentioned in Marco Polo's writing. Ask groups to share with the class what products they found in their excerpt and have the class highlight all products mentioned.

Make a Hypothesis: Once all groups have reported their products, have students work with their groups to create an answer to the organizing question that uses examples from the map, the role-play, the product list, and Marco Polo's book. This could also be an individual writing prompt used as a formative assessment for the lesson.

HANDOUT 11.1

SILK ROAD ROLE-PLAY CARDS

Teacher directions: Cut out the cards below and distribute to students. Each student should receive one card.

EASTERN MERCHANT	**WESTERN MERCHANT**
EASTERN KING/QUEEN	**WESTERN KING/QUEEN**
EASTERN WEALTHY NOBLE	**WESTERN WEALTHY NOBLE**
EASTERN SOLDIER	**WESTERN SOLDIER**

HANDOUT 11.2
GOODS TRADED ALONG THE SILK ROAD

Directions: Considering your role on the Silk Road, circle which four products you would like to receive from the "other side." You should be able to support your choices with reasoning.

From West to East	From East to West
Gold	Lacquer
Silver	Porcelain
Ivory	Jade
Gems	Bronze (Ornaments, Mirrors)
Glass	Fur
Pomegranates	Silk
Carrots	Iron
Salt	Umbrellas
Copper	Varnish
Tin	Medicines
Dates	Perfumes
Saffron Powder	Tea
Frankincense	Rice
Myrrh	Skins
Pistachios	Corals
Sandalwood	Ivory
Grapes	Cinnamon
Horses	Ginger
String Beans	Turtle Shells
Onions	
Figs	
Cotton Fabric	
Carpets	
Blankets	
Camels	
Military Equipment	
Skins	
Wool	
Gold Embroidery	
Melons	
Peaches	
Sheep	
Hunting Dogs	
Leopards	
Lions	

HANDOUT 11.3
EXCERPTS FROM *THE TRAVELS OF MARCO POLO*
(CA. 1290s)

CHAPTER III: OF THE PROVINCE CALLED TURKOMANIA WHERE ARE THE CITIES OF KOGNI, KAISARIAH, AND SEVASTA, AND OF ITS COMMERCE

The other classes are Greeks and Armenians, who reside in the cities and fortified places, and gain their living by commerce and manufacture. The best and handsomest carpets in the world are wrought here, and also silks of crimson and other rich colours.

CHAPTER VI: OF THE PROVINCE OF MOSUL AND ITS DIFFERENT INHABITANTS OF THE PEOPLE NAMED KURDS AND OF THE TRADE OF THIS COUNTRY

All those cloths of gold and of silk which we call muslins are of the manufacture of Mosul, and all the great merchants termed Mossulini, who convey spices and drugs, in large quantities, from one country to another, are from this province. In the mountainous parts there is a race of people named Kurds. . . . They are all an unprincipled people, whose occupation it is to rob the merchants. In the vicinity of this province there are places named Mus and Maredin, where cotton is produced in great abundance, of which they prepare the cloths called boccasini, and many other fabrics. The inhabitants are manufacturers and traders. . . .

CHAPTER IX: OF THE NOBLE CITY OF TAURIS, IN IRAK, AND OF ITS COMMERCIAL AND OTHER INHABITANTS

Tauris is a large and very noble city belonging to the province of Irak, which contains many other cities and fortified places, but this is the most eminent and most populous. The inhabitants support themselves principally by commerce and manufactures, which latter consist of various kinds of silk, some of them interwoven with gold, and of high price. It is so advantageously situated for trade, that merchants from India, from Baldach, Mosul, Cremessor, as well as from different parts of Europe, resort thither to purchase and to sell a number of articles. Precious stones and pearls in abundance may be procured at this place. The merchants concerned in foreign commerce acquire considerable wealth, but the inhabitants in general are poor.

CHAPTER XII: OF THE NAMES OF THE EIGHT KINGDOMS THAT CONSTITUTE THE PROVINCES OF PERSIA, AND OF THE BREED OF HORSES AND OF ASSES FOUND THEREIN

The country is distinguished for its excellent breed of horses, many of which are carried for sale to India, and bring high prices. . . . It produces also the largest and handsomest breed of asses in the world, which sell (on the spot) at higher prices than the horses, because they are more easily fed, are capable of carrying heavier burthens, and travel further in the day than either horses or mules, which cannot support an equal degree of fatigue. The merchants, there-

HANDOUT 11.3, CONTINUED

fore, who in travelling from one province to another are obliged to pass extensive deserts and tracts of sand, where no kind of herbage is to be met with, and where, on account of the distance between the wells or other watering places, it is necessary to make long journeys in the course of the day, are desirous of providing themselves with asses in preference, as they get sooner over the ground and require a smaller allowance of food. Camels also are employed here, and these in like manner carry great weights and are maintained at little cost, but they are not so swift as the asses.

CHAPTER XII: OF THE CITY OF YASDI AND ITS MANUFACTURES, AND OF THE ANIMALS FOUND IN THE COUNTRY BETWEEN THAT PLACE AND KIERMAN

Yasdi is a considerable city on the confines of Persia, where there is much traffic. A species of cloth of silk and gold manufactured there is known by the appellation of Yasdi, and is carried from thence by the merchants to all parts of the world. Its inhabitants are of the Mahometan religion. Those who travel from that city, employ eight days in passing over a plain, in the course of which they meet with only three places that afford accommodation. The road lies through extensive groves of the date-bearing palm, in which there is abundance of game, as well beasts as partridges and quails; and those travellers who are fond of the amusements of the chase, may here enjoy excellent sport.

CHAPTER XXIII: OF A FERTILE PLAIN OF SIX DAYS JOURNEY, SUCCEEDED BY A DESERT OF EIGHT, TO BE PASSED IN THE WAY TO THE CITY OF SAPURGAN OF THE EXCELLENT MELONS PRODUCED THERE AND OF THE CITY OF BALACH

At the end of the sixth day's journey, he arrives at a town named Sapurgan, which is plentifully supplied with every kind of provision, and is particularly celebrated for producing the best melons in the world. These are preserved in the following manner. They are cut spirally, in thin slices, as the pumpkin with us, and after they have been dried in the sun, are sent, in large quantities, for sale, to the neighbouring countries; where they are eagerly sought for, being sweet as honey.

CHAPTER XXVI: OF THE PROVINCE OF BALASHAN OF THE PRECIOUS STONES FOUND THERE AND WHICH BECOME THE PROPERTY OF THE KING OF THE HORSES AND THE FALCONS OF THE COUNTRY OF THE SALUBRIOUS AIR OF THE MOUNTAINS AND OF THE DRESS WITH WHICH THE WOMEN ADORN THEIR PERSONS

In this country are found the precious stones called balass rubies, of fine quality and great value, so called from the name of the province. They are imbedded in the high mountains, but are searched for only in one, named Sikinan. In this the king causes mines to be worked, in the same manner as for gold or silver; and through this channel alone they are obtained. . . . Some he sends as complimentary gifts to other kings and princes; some he delivers as tribute (to his superior lord); and some also he exchanges for gold and silver. These he allows to be exported. There are mountains likewise in which are found veins of lapis lazuli, the stone which yields the azure colour (ultramarine), here the finest in the world. The mines of silver, copper, and lead, are likewise very productive.

CHAPTER XXXIII: OF THE CITY OF KOTAN, WHICH IS ABUNDANTLY SUPPLIED WITH ALL THE NECESSARIES OF LIFE

Following a course between north-east and east, you next come to the province of Kotan, the extent of which is eight days journey. It is under the dominion of the grand khan, and the people are Mahometans. It contains many cities and fortified places, but the principal city, and which gives its name to the province, is Kotan. Everything necessary for human life is here in the greatest plenty. It yields likewise cotton, flax, hemp, grain, wine, and other articles. The inhabitants cultivate farms and vineyards, and have numerous gardens. They support themselves also by trade and manufactures, but they are not good soldiers.

CHAPTER XVII: OF THE MULTITUDE OF PERSONS WHO CONTINUALLY RESORT TO AND DEPART FROM THE CITY OF KANBALU AND OF THE COMMERCE OF THE PLACE

To this city everything that is most rare and valuable in all parts of the world finds its way; and more especially does this apply to India, which furnishes precious stones, pearls, and various drugs and spices. From the provinces of Cathay itself, as well as from the other provinces of the empire, whatever there is of value is carried thither, to supply the demands of those multitudes who are induced to establish their residence in the vicinity of the court. The quantity of merchandise sold there exceeds also the traffic of any other place; for no fewer than a thousand carriages and pack-horses, loaded with raw silk, make their daily entry; and gold tissues and silks of various kinds are manufactured to an immense extent.

CHAPTER XXIII: OF THE KIND OF WINE MADE IN THE PROVINCE OF CATHAY AND OF THE STONES USED THERE FOR BURNING IN THE MANNER OF CHARCOAL

The greater part of the inhabitants of the province of Cathay drink a sort of wine made from rice mixed with a variety of spices and drugs. This beverage, or wine as it may be termed is so good and well flavoured that they do not wish for better. It is clear, bright, and pleasant to the taste, and being (made) very hot, has the quality of inebriating sooner than any other. Throughout this province there is found a sort of black stone, which they dig out of the mountains, where it runs in veins. When lighted, it burns like charcoal, and retains the fire much better than wood; insomuch that it may be preserved during the night, and in the morning be found still burning. These stones do not flame, excepting a little when first lighted, but during their ignition give out a considerable heat. It is true there is no scarcity of wood in the country, but the multitude of inhabitants is so immense, and their stoves and baths, which they are continually heating, so numerous, that the quantity could not supply the demand; for there is no person who does not frequent the warm bath at least three times in the week, and during the winter daily, if it is in their power. Every man of rank or wealth has one in his house for his own use; and the stock of wood must soon prove inadequate to such consumption; whereas these stories may be had in the greatest abundance, and at a cheap rate.

CHAPTER XXXIII: OF THE CITY OF KA-CHAN-FU

Having crossed this river and travelled three days journey, you arrive at a city named Ka-chan-fu whose inhabitants are idolaters. They carry on a considerable traffic, and work at a variety of manufactures. The country produces in great abundance, silk, ginger, galangal, spikenard, and many drugs that are nearly unknown in our part of the world. Here they weave gold tissues, as well as every other kind of silken cloth.

CHAPTER XXXIV: OF THE CITY OF KEN-ZAN-FU

Departing from Ka-chan-fu, and proceeding eight days' journey in a westerly direction, you continually meet with cities and commercial towns, and pass many gardens and cultivated grounds, with abundance of the mulberry or tree that contributes to the production of silk. . . . It is a country of great commerce, and eminent for its manufactures. Raw silk is produced in large quantities, and tissues of gold and every other kind of silk are woven there. At this place likewise they prepare every article necessary for the equipment of an army. All species of provisions are in abundance, and to be procured at a moderate price.

CHAPTER XXXIX: OF THE GREAT PROVINCE OF KARAIAN, AND OF YACHI ITS PRINCIPAL CITY

In this country there are salt-springs, from which they manufacture salt by boiling it in small pans. When the water has boiled for an hour, it becomes a kind of paste, which is formed into cakes of the value of twopence each. These, which are flat on the lower, and convex on the upper side, are placed upon hot tiles, near a fire, in order to dry and harden. On this latter species of money the stamp of the grand khan is impressed, and it cannot be prepared by any other than his own officers. Eighty of the cakes are made to pass for a saggio of gold.

But when these are carried by the traders amongst the inhabitants of the mountains and other parts little frequented, they obtain a saggio of gold for sixty, fifty, or even forty of the salt cakes, in proportion as they find the natives less civilized, further removed from the towns, and more accustomed to remain on the same spot; inasmuch as people so circumstanced cannot always have a market for their gold, musk, and other commodities. And yet even at this rate it answers well to them who collect the gold-dust from the beds of the rivers, as has been men-

HANDOUT 11.3, CONTINUED

tioned. The same merchants travel in like manner through the mountainous and other parts of the province of Thebeth, last spoken of, where the money of salt has equal currency. Their profits are considerable, because these country people consume the salt with their food, and regard it as an indispensable necessary; whereas the inhabitants of the cities use for the same purpose only the broken fragments of the cakes, putting the whole cakes into circulation as money. . . .

This province likewise produces cloves. The tree is small; the branches and leaves resemble those of the laurel, but are somewhat longer and narrower. Its flowers are white and small, as are the cloves themselves, but as they ripen they become dark-coloured. Ginger grows there and also cassia in abundance, besides many other drugs, of which no quantity is ever brought to Europe.

LESSON 2

ORGANIZING QUESTION

How were salt, gold, and camels important to West African kingdoms?

STRATEGIES USED

Brainstorming, Picture Prediction, Student Research

MATERIALS NEEDED

1. Images:
   - ✓ Two or three desert scenes
   - ✓ Clue 1—Map: *Timbuktu: A Center for Trade*, available at https://malitradevseuropeantrade.weebly.com/uploads/1/5/2/2/15224772/709840085_orig.jpg
   - ✓ Clue 2—Photograph: Vladimir Wrangel's *Camel Caravan in the Sahara, Morocco*, available at https://www.britannica.com/topic/caravan-desert-transport/media/94606/112204
   - ✓ Clue 3—Photograph: Picture of gold, available at https://industrialminingmagazine.com/gold-fields-to-explore-new-mining-methods-at-south-deep-mine-in-south-africa
   - ✓ Clue 4—Photograph: Image cover for "$50m Salt Project for Maknoadze," available at https://www.modernghana.com/news/338596/50m-salt-project-for-mankoadze.html
   - ✓ Clue 5—Map: Jeff Israel's *Pre-colonial African Kingdoms*, available at https://en.wikipedia.org/wiki/African_empires#/media/File:African-civilizations-map-pre-colonial.svg

2. World history textbooks or computers/devices for research

LESSON PLAN

Lesson Hook: *Brainstorming*—Show students pictures of life in a desert. Have students brainstorm ideas to this question: *What is it like to live in a desert?* Give them a couple of minutes to write and share responses.

The Organizing Question: Explain that in this lesson students will do some research to determine answers to the organizing question: *How were salt, gold, and camels important to West African kingdoms?*

Examine the Sources: *Picture Prediction*—Tell students that they will examine five pictures (clues; see Materials Needed) to help them make predictions about the organizing question. Display Clue 1 and have students write down what they notice about the map (e.g., trade routes, Sahara Desert, Atlantic Ocean). Next, ask them to write down ideas about how the map might help them answer the organizing question. Show Clues 2–5 and have students repeat the process. Review the pictures and have students write down a question they are wondering about from the pictures.

Student Research—Divide the class into groups of 3–4 students. Assign each group one of the West African trading kingdoms to research: Axum, Ghana, Mali, and Songhai. Explain that their task is to discover the following facts about their kingdom:

- its location,
- the time period in which it existed,
- the goods traded there, and
- important rulers or facts about the kingdom.

Give students a few minutes to use textbooks, computers, or other resources to research information on their kingdom. Then reorganize groups of students so that each new group contains a student who researched each kingdom. Ask students to share their research facts about their kingdom with the other students. Encourage students to make a chart in their notes of information about all four kingdoms. Also have them discuss any answers to their own written questions they might have found.

Make a Hypothesis: Once all students have presented, keep the groups together and have them create a hypothesis statement that answers the organizing question. They should use examples from all four kingdoms as evidence to support their hypothesis. This could be a whole-class discussion in which each group shares the hypothesis and evidence, or it could be an individual exit slip used as a formative assessment.

750-1500

PART IV

THE WORLD IN TRANSITION

CHAPTER 12

KINGDOMS OF ASIA AND AFRICA

Whenever I can find the time, I read history books and the classics so as to avoid idle living. I constantly remind myself that the world is so vast and state affairs so important that I cannot succumb to laziness and complacency for even a moment. Once one has succumbed to laziness and complacency, everything will become stagnant.

—Yongle Emperor (1360–1424)

HISTORICAL CONTEXT: WHAT DO I NEED TO KNOW?

In 1324, Emperor Mansa Musa of Mali made the pilgrimage to Mecca that is expected of all good Muslims. His caravan left from the east coast and crossed 3,500 miles of Central Africa. Emperor Musa's pilgrimage created quite a stir because of its remarkable size and wealth, and he is still listed as the wealthiest person in history. Not much is known about Musa's life, other than that he succeeded to the throne after his father took a fleet of ships to try to discover the edge of the world and never returned. Musa's journey to Mecca, though, had a massive effect on the economies in Africa and Arabia. He brought some 60,000 people on his journey, including a reported 12,000 slaves who each carried several pounds of gold. Some five dozen camels carried massive bags of gold dust. Musa distributed so much gold to the poor along the way that he single-handedly disrupted the economies of those regions.

The empire that Musa ruled was one of the largest West Africa has ever seen. As in the Babylonian and Roman Empires, the Malian government was decentralized, relying on local villages and districts to collect taxes and supply men for the army. Mali's wealth was established through a combination of gold mining and tribute collected from Musa's large empire, as well as connections to Middle Eastern and African trade networks, including trade in slaves. The majority of the wealth in the kingdom came from its position as a center of trade, and from taxing the cross-Sahara trade that ended at Timbuktu. Likewise, gold was common in Mali—so much so that gold dust was a standard currency. Salt also served as currency.

Emperor Musa's effect on Europe was just as profound as his pilgrimage was to Africa. Stories about African riches spread throughout the Mediterranean, and pictures in maps and atlases illustrate their impact. One map, called the Catalan Atlas of 1375, left most of Africa undefined but gave the Mali Empire a prominent position, showing Emperor Musa himself seated on an ornate throne, holding a scepter in one hand and a huge gold nugget in the other. By the 14th century, European merchants' manuals often included more information about Africa than about Europe.

In China, the Ming Dynasty succeeded the Yuan Dynasty in 1368. Under the Ming Dynasty, China saw, if not a golden age, then certainly a series of cultural achievements that have lasted well into the modern era. Born out of what might be considered an ethnic rebellion, the Han-dominated Ming overthrew the Mongol Yuan in 1368 and immediately consolidated rule by securing borders and towns, as well as through a purging of non-Han ethnic peoples in the government. The reorganization outlasted the Ming Empire itself as the administration of 13 provinces with prefectures, subprefectures, and counties became much more stable and efficient. This became the model for modern-day Chinese governmental organization.

The Ming Dynasty saw a number of long-lasting contributions to Chinese and world history, including a resurgence of art that remains culturally significant to this day. Artists known as the "Four Masters of the Ming Dynasty" created works of varied styles, from unadorned landscapes, to landscapes coupled with lyrical poetry, to calligraphy, to images of gardens, flowers, and religious figures. Art during the Ming period was considered so culturally relevant that artists could earn a living through patronage or by selling their pieces at very high prices. The greatest extent of the Great Wall of China, with more than 5,000 miles and around 25,000 watchtowers, was built between 1368 and 1644. The Yongle Emperor (1402–1424) also established Beijing as the capital of China, and constructed China's famous Forbidden City, which served as the imperial palace from 1420–1912. The Yongle Emperor sent the admiral Zheng

He and a fleet of ships on a series of voyages around the Indian Ocean, the coast of Africa, and the coasts of Thailand, Java, and Arabia.

In 1578, Li Zhizhen finished work on *Bencao Gangmu*, or the *Compendium of Materia Medica*. Considered the most complete and authoritative book on traditional Chinese medicine, the *Compendium* describes almost anything found in nature that could have medicinal properties. It also contains instructions, with colorized illustrations, for mixing and administering herbal cures. The greater value of the tome, which is still in use, is as a resource for insight into Ming-era understandings of the natural world. Color illustrations were made possible by important advances in Chinese woodblock printing techniques during this period. The scholar Hua Sui developed China's first metal movable type printing in 1490, seemingly independent of a similar Korean invention in the 1200s, and the European invention in 1450. Metal type greatly facilitated the spread of literature throughout the dynasty. In 1408, some 2,000 scholars completed the more than 11,000-page volume *Yongle Encyclopedia*, the largest print encyclopedia in the world. Unlike the *Compendium*, the encyclopedia was handwritten, and not widely distributed, and only a small portion survives.

Japan had been undergoing a similar transformation. The year 1185 saw the beginning of what is known as the Kamakura Period of Japanese history. Although important for the development of a more complex and diverse form of Buddhism, known as "New Buddhism," the Kamakura period is more well-known for the Kamakura Shogunate, a time when the government was characterized by a feudal system headed by a shogun, or military dictator who replaced the emperor and local administrators. Under the shogunate, a single military ruler, or shogun, used de facto military occupation to enforce the law. The emperor remained but had little more than symbolic authority. The shogun usually delegated regional authority—including taxation, law enforcement, judicial affairs, and defense—to local lords called *daimyō* in return for loyalty and service. The shogun class, a military class made up of local nobility trained as officers in the local armies, sat underneath the shogun and the daimyō in this hierarchy.

There had been a samurai class since the 700s, and as their numbers grew, they formed into larger groups, and eventually began to elect a head of their group. The Kamakura Shogunate saw the consolidation of power for samurai and shoguns, and the political and cultural dominance of the samurai. Under the influence of Zen Buddhism and Shinto, the samurai developed a code of conduct and system of beliefs that focused on warrior ideals, ritual, and bravery. Above all, the warrior was to be completely devoted to, and to be willing to sacrifice his life for, his master. Although the Kamakura period would come to an end in 1333, the feudal shogun system would endure until 1868, when it was replaced with a government ruled by the Emperor and deliberative assemblies as well as an expansion of the empire.

STANDARDS ADDRESSED IN THE CHAPTER

NCHS World History Content Standards, Grades 5–12:

- **Era 4—Standard 3B:** The student understands developments in Japan, Korea, and Southeast Asia in an era of Chinese ascendancy.
- **Era 5—Standard 1A:** The student understands China's extensive urbanization and commercial expansion between the 10th and 13th centuries.
- **Era 5—Standard 1B:** The student understands developments in Japanese and Southeast Asian civilization.
- **Era 5—Standard 1D:** The student understands how interregional communication and trade led to intensified cultural exchanges among diverse peoples of Eurasia and Africa.
- **Era 5—Standard 4A:** The student understands the growth of imperial states in West Africa and Ethiopia.

CCSS for Literacy in History/Social Studies, Grades 6–8 and 9–10:

- **6–8:** Cite specific textual evidence to support analysis of primary and secondary sources; Determine the central ideas or information of a primary or secondary source; Integrate visual information (e.g., in charts, graphs, photographs, videos, or maps) with other information in print and digital texts; Conduct short research projects to answer a question (including a self-generated question); Draw evidence from informational texts to support analysis, reflection, and research.
- **9–10:** Determine the central ideas or information of a primary or secondary source; Cite specific textual evidence to support analysis of primary and secondary sources, attending to such features as the date and origin of the information; Conduct short as well as more sustained research projects to answer a question (including a self-generated question) or solve a problem; Draw evidence from informational texts to support analysis, reflection, and research.

LESSON 1

ORGANIZING QUESTION

How did Mansa Musa build a powerful kingdom in Mali during the 14th century?

STRATEGIES USED

Brainstorming, Clue Stations

MATERIALS NEEDED

1. Handout 12.1: Clue Stations
2. The following clues placed around the room in clue stations (*Note*: Depending on the number of students in your class, you may set up two of each station to allow easier access and keep students on task):
   ✓ Station 1—Atlas: Two versions of Abraham Cresques's *Catalan Atlas*: the entire atlas picture (available at https://upload.wikimedia.org/wikipedia/commons/3/35/1375_Atlas_Catalan_Abraham_Cresques.jpg) and a close image of West Africa and Mansa Musa (available at https://commons.wikimedia.org/wiki/File:Catalan_Atlas_BNF_Sheet_6_Mansa_Musa.jpg)
   ✓ Station 2—Travel account: Arab historian Chihab Al-Umari's account of Mansa Musa's visit to Cairo, available at http://www.digitalhistory.uh.edu/active_learning/explorations/1492/mansa_musa_visit.cfm
   ✓ Station 3—Map: *Timbuktu: A Center for Trade*, available at https://malitradevseuropeantrade.weebly.com/uploads/1/5/2/2/15224772/709840085_orig.jpg
   ✓ Station 4—Photographs: The Djinguereber Mosque in Timbuktu and the University of Sankore, available from several websites
   ✓ Station 5—Textbooks, encyclopedias, or computers for student research on Mali and Mansa Musa

LESSON PLAN

Lesson Hook: *Brainstorming*—Ask students to image that they are a king in the 14th century and want to build a powerful kingdom that is respected by other countries. Give them 2 minutes to brainstorm any strategies they can think of for creating this empire. You may need to prompt them to think about government, economics, a military, or other important elements. Ask them to share their ideas and look for patterns or themes that may emerge. Write these ideas on the board to use at the end of the lesson.

The Organizing Question: Explain to students that they are going to look at a variety of primary and secondary sources (clues) around the room to learn about Mansa Musa, a 14th-century African king, to determine answers to the organizing question: *How did Mansa Musa build a powerful kingdom in Mali during the 14th century?*

Examine the Sources: *Clue Stations*—Divide the class into groups of 3–4 students and distribute Handout 12.1: Clue Stations. If students are not used to independently analyzing sources, model one with them so they see how to collect evidence on the clue sheet. Assign groups to specific stations to begin looking at clues and completing the handout. Have them rotate around the room in a clockwise manner until all clues have been analyzed.

Make a Hypothesis: When groups have finished at all clue stations, have them return to their seats and sit with their groups. Their next task is to develop hypotheses about the organizing question using evidence from several clues they examined. Give them time to work with their group to develop one or two hypotheses about how Mansa Musa built his kingdom. Encourage them to write down the hypotheses at the bottom of the clue sheet along with what specific evidence supports the hypotheses. Ask each group to present one of their hypotheses with supporting evidence. If time permits, end the lesson by looking at students' list of ideas on the board from the Lesson Hook section and compare/contrast those with Mansa Musa's strategies and accomplishments.

HANDOUT 12.1
CLUE STATIONS

Directions: Examine the evidence or clues posted around the room. Write down what details you notice and what each clue might tell you about the organizing question. Your group will use this information to make hypotheses that answer this organizing question.

ORGANIZING QUESTION: How did Mansa Musa build a powerful kingdom in Mali during the 14th century?

	What details can you learn from this clue?	**What does this clue tell you about the organizing question?**
Clue #1 _____		
Clue #2 _____		
Clue #3 _____		
Clue #4 _____		
Clue #5 _____		
Clue #6 _____		

Based on the clues/evidence you examined, what are your hypotheses about the organizing question?

LESSON 2

ORGANIZING QUESTION

What were the major accomplishments of the Ming Dynasty in China?

Note: This organizing question has been provided as a sample, but with the Question Formulation Technique (QFT; Rothstein & Santana, 2011), students will generate their own questions that will guide the lesson. Depending on the amount of time needed to research, this lesson may take two class periods. If the QFT strategy is new to you, visit the Right Question Institute's website (http://rightquestion.org) for more details, sample lessons, and resources.

STRATEGIES USED

Question Formulation Technique, Student Research

MATERIALS NEEDED

1. Handout 5.1: Question Formulation Technique (QFT)
2. Images of the Great Wall of China and the Forbidden City
3. World history textbooks or computers/devices for research

LESSON PLAN

Lesson Hook: *Question Formulation Technique*—Introduce students to the Question Focus (QFocus) for this QFT lesson (Rothstein & Santana, 2011). A QFocus is any type of prompt or stimulus used to encourage students to generate questions. For this lesson, pictures of the Great Wall and the Forbidden City are the QFocus visuals. Distribute Handout 5.1: Question Formulation Technique (QFT) and remind students of the rules for producing questions. Display the two pictures and give students 1–2 minutes to write down as many questions as possible in their notes.

The Organizing Question: Once students have generated questions about the photographs, explain that they are going to work together to categorize and prioritize their questions with groups, choose their best questions, and research answers about the accomplishments of the Ming Dynasty.

Examine the Sources: Before students examine sources for information about the Ming Dynasty, they should have completed the QFT process. Divide the class into groups of 3–4 students for the rest of the lesson.

- *Improving the questions*: Ask students to spend a few minutes sharing their own questions with others in their group. They should then label the questions as closed (C) or open (O), discuss the advantages and disadvantages of each type of question, and practice changing some questions from one type to another.

- *Prioritizing questions*: Ask students to come to a consensus in their groups on the three most important questions and write them on a sheet of paper in order to focus the research.

- *Next steps/student research*: Ask groups to develop a plan for how they will answer the questions and what sources they might use. Allow groups time to use textbooks, computers, or other resources to research answers to their own important questions. When students are finished finding text-based answers to their questions, allow groups to share their questions and the answers they found. Ask students to write down any questions and answers that were different from their group's so that they learn more information about accomplishments of the Ming Dynasty.

Make a Hypothesis: After all groups have shared their questions and answers, ask students to write a response to the organizing question for this lesson (or one of the student-generated questions). Ask them to cite evidence in their answer from their own research and the findings of other groups. You may choose to end this lesson with a discussion that references the photographs instead of having students write their responses to the organizing question.

LESSON 3

ORGANIZING QUESTION

What virtues were practiced by samurai warriors in feudal Japan?

STRATEGIES USED

Picture Prediction, Modified Jigsaw

MATERIALS NEEDED

1. Handout 12.2: Excerpts From Inazo Nitobe's *Bushido: The Soul of Japan* (1908)
2. Images:
   ✓ Painting: *Samurai on Horseback* (ca. 1868), available at https://upload.wikimedia.org/wikipedia/commons/a/a6/Samurai_on_horseback0.jpg
   ✓ Armor: Ian Armstrong's photo of Samurai o-yoroi armor from Kamakura period, available at https://en.wikipedia.org/wiki/Samurai#/media/File:Samurai_o-yoroi.jpg
   ✓ Painting: *Samurai and Defensive Wall at Hakata* (ca. 1293), available at https://en.wikipedia.org/wiki/Samurai#/media/File:Takezaki_suenaga_ekotoba_bourui.jpg

LESSON PLAN

Note: This lesson could be used as an introduction to the role of samurai in the structure of feudal Japan, including the development of the shogunate and role of the daimyo in maintaining order.

Lesson Hook: *Picture Prediction*—Tell students that they will look at images depicting Japanese samurai warriors. As they look at each image, have them write down in their notes some predictions they can make about samurai from these clues. Display *Samurai on Horseback* (ca. 1868) and give students a few minutes to write down their ideas. Continue this process with the armor photograph and the painting *Samurai and Defensive Wall at Hakata* (ca. 1293). Allow students to share their samurai predictions and write some on the board to use later in the lesson.

The Organizing Question: Explain to students that they will be reading and analyzing excerpts from *Bushido: The Soul of Japan* to answer the organizing question: *What virtues were practiced by samurai warriors in feudal Japan?*

Examine the Sources: *Modeling*—Distribute Handout 12.2: Excerpts From Inazo Nitobe's *Bushido: The Soul of Japan* (1908). Explain to students that this book is a secondary source about feudal Japan, but that it is considered one of the earliest sources to describe the code of bushido practiced by Japanese samurai. With students following along, read the first section of the text out loud. Ask students to determine the main ideas about samurai and bushido from this section. Encourage students to write their annotations or notes in the margins of the text.

Modified Jigsaw—Once you have modeled the first section with the whole class, explain to students that they will do a modified jigsaw strategy to analyze the rest of the text.

- Expert Groups: Divide the class into five numbered groups and assign each group a section of the text. Explain that they will become experts on their section. Their task is to read their assigned section and discuss the main ideas with their group members. Remind them that each person will be responsible for teaching this section to others in the class in home groups. Encourage students to write notes and annotate main ideas in the margin of their handouts.
  - Group 1: Section 2
  - Group 2: Section 3
  - Group 3: Section 4
  - Group 4: Section 5
  - Group 5: Section 6

  After students complete their section discussion in expert groups, assign each student a letter in alphabetical order (e.g., A–C or A–D, depending on the number of students in each group).
- Home Groups: For the second part of the modified jigsaw, students will go to "home" or letter groups. All of the "A" students, "B" students, and "C" students, for instance, should sit together. In that home group, they will have an expert on each section of the text. Students should take turns sharing their section, including main ideas and what samurai virtues they found. The other students in the group should write notes in the margins or annotate all of the sections of the text as they listen.

Making a Hypothesis: With their home groups, ask students to make a hypothesis that answers the organizing question. They should be prepared to give evidence from multiple sections of the text to support their hypothesis. Allow groups to share their hypotheses when finished. Then, review their predictions from the Lesson Hook section and evaluate how accurate they were. You may also want to discuss similarities between the role of samurai/bushido in Japan and knights/chivalry in medieval Europe.

HANDOUT 12.2
EXCERPTS FROM INAZO NITOBE'S *BUSHIDO: THE SOUL OF JAPAN* (1908)

Note: Sections have been added by authors for the purposes of this lesson.

SECTION 1

Bu-shi-do means literally Military-Knight-Ways—the ways which fighting nobles should observe in their daily life as well as in their vocation; in a word, the "Precepts of Knighthood," the *noblesse oblige* of the warrior class. . . . Bushido, then, is the code. . . . The Japanese word which I have roughly rendered Chivalry, is, in the original, more expressive than Horsemanship. *Bu-shi-do* means literally Military-Knight-Ways—the ways of moral principles which the knights were required or instructed to observe. It is not a written code; at best it consists of a few maxims handed down from mouth to mouth or coming from the pen of some well-known warrior or savant. More frequently it is a code unuttered and unwritten, possessing all the more the powerful sanction of veritable deed, and of a law written on the fleshly tablets of the heart. It was founded not on the creation of one brain, however able, or on the life of a single personage, however renowned. It was an organic growth of decades and centuries of military career. . . .

In Japan as in Europe, when feudalism was formally inaugurated, the professional class of warriors naturally came into prominence. These were known as *samurai*, meaning literally, like the old English *cniht* (knecht, knight), guards or attendants. . . . They were a privileged class, and must originally have been a rough breed who made fighting their vocation. This class was naturally recruited, in a long period of constant warfare, from the manliest and the most adventurous, and all the while the process of elimination went on, the timid and the feeble being sorted out, and only "a rude race, all masculine, with brutish strength," to borrow Emerson's phrase, surviving to form families and the ranks of the *samurai*. Coming to profess great honor and great privileges, and correspondingly great responsibilities, they soon felt the need of a common standard of behavior.

SECTION 2

RECTITUDE OR JUSTICE, the most cogent precept in the code of the samurai. Nothing is more loathsome to him than underhand dealings and crooked undertakings. The conception of Rectitude may be erroneous—it may be narrow. A well-known bushi defines it as a power of resolution;—"Rectitude is the power of deciding upon a certain course of conduct in accordance with reason, without wavering;—to die when it is right to die, to strike when to strike is right. . . ."

COURAGE, THE SPIRIT OF DARING AND BEARING, to the consideration of which we shall now return. Courage was scarcely deemed worthy to be counted among virtues, unless it was exercised in the cause of Righteousness. . . . Valor, Fortitude, Bravery, Fearlessness, Courage, being the qualities of soul which appeal most easily to juvenile minds, and which can be trained by exercise and example, were, so to speak, the most popular virtues, early emulated among the youth. Stories of military exploits were repeated almost before boys left their mother's breast. . . . The spiritual aspect of valor is evidenced by composure—calm presence of mind. Tranquillity is

HANDOUT 12.2, CONTINUED

courage in repose. It is a statical manifestation of valor, as daring deeds are a dynamical. A truly brave man is ever serene; he is never taken by surprise; nothing ruffles the equanimity of his spirit. In the heat of battle he remains cool; in the midst of catastrophes he keeps level his mind. Earthquakes do not shake him, he laughs at storms. We admire him as truly great, who, in the menacing presence of danger or death, retains his self-possession.

SECTION 3

BENEVOLENCE, THE FEELING OF DISTRESS, love, magnanimity, affection for others, sympathy and pity, which were ever recognized to be supreme virtues, the highest of all the attributes of the human soul. Benevolence was deemed a princely virtue in a twofold sense;—princely among the manifold attributes of a noble spirit; princely as particularly befitting a princely profession. . . .

The cultivation of tender feelings breeds considerate regard for the sufferings of others. Modesty and complaisance, actuated by respect for others' feelings, are at the root of POLITENESS, that courtesy and urbanity of manners which has been noticed by every foreign tourist as a marked Japanese trait. Politeness is a poor virtue, if it is actuated only by a fear of offending good taste, whereas it should be the outward manifestation of a sympathetic regard for the feelings of others. It also implies a due regard for the fitness of things, therefore due respect to social positions.

SECTION 4

VERACITY OR TRUTHFULNESS, without which Politeness is a farce and a show. . . . The bushi held that his high social position demanded a loftier standard of veracity than that of the tradesman and peasant. . . . His word carried such weight with it that promises were generally made and fulfilled without a written pledge, which would have been deemed quite beneath his dignity. . . . HONOR . . . The sense of honor, implying a vivid consciousness of personal dignity and worth, could not fail to characterize the samurai, born and bred to value the duties and privileges of their profession. . . .

Life itself was thought cheap if honor and fame could be attained therewith: hence, whenever a cause presented itself which was considered dearer than life, with utmost serenity and celerity was life laid down.

SECTION 5

Of the causes in comparison with which no life was too dear to sacrifice, was THE DUTY OF LOYALTY, which was the key-stone making feudal virtues a symmetrical arch. Other virtues feudal morality shares in common with other systems of ethics, with other classes of people, but this virtue—homage and fealty to a superior—is its distinctive feature. . . .

SELF-CONTROL, which was universally required of samurai. . . . It was considered unmanly for a samurai to betray his emotions on his face. . . . Calmness of behavior, composure of mind, should not be disturbed by passion of any kind.

HANDOUT 12.2, CONTINUED

SECTION 6

It is easy to infer that the sword played an important part in social discipline and life. The saying passed as an axiom which called THE SWORD THE SOUL OF THE SAMURAI, and made it the emblem of power and prowess. . . . Very early the samurai boy learned to wield it. It was a momentous occasion for him when at the age of five he was apparelled in the paraphernalia of samurai costume . . . and initiated into the rights of the military profession by having thrust into his girdle a real sword, instead of the toy dirk with which he had been playing. After this first ceremony of *adoptio per arma*, he was no more to be seen outside his father's gates without this badge of his status, even if it was usually substituted for every-day wear by a gilded wooden dirk. Not many years pass before he wears constantly the genuine steel, though blunt, and then the sham arms are thrown aside and with enjoyment keener than his newly acquired blades, he marches out to try their edge on wood and stone. When he reaches man's estate at the age of fifteen, being given independence of action, he can now pride himself upon the possession of arms sharp enough for any work. The very possession of the dangerous instrument imparts to him a feeling and an air of self-respect and responsibility.

CHAPTER 13

KINGDOMS OF EUROPE

A King's raw material and instruments of rule are a well-peopled land, and he must have men of prayer, men of war, and men of work.

—Alfred the Great

HISTORICAL CONTEXT: WHAT DO I NEED TO KNOW?

The Crusades occurred from 1099–1270 and were the result of many different factors, although three are very important. First, Spain had been conquered by Muslim Arabs, called Moors, from North Africa after year 711, and although Charlemagne (768–814) had established a small Christian outpost in the county of Barcelona, Spain had remained Arab ever since. With its capital in Cordoba, the Muslim government had strong ties to the main Muslim capital of Baghdad, but also complete political independence. The Moorish civilization remained politically stable until about 1031, when internal dissensions led to the breakdown of the caliphate into about a dozen rival principalities.

In the year 1000, the Christian King Sancho I of Navarre launched an offensive against the Muslims in a process that became known as the Reconquest. The papacy became involved and encouraged volunteers from the rest of Europe to join the Christian forces in Spain in a crusade against the Muslims. This call was heeded particularly by second sons of noble families seeking their fortune in war.

The second major influence was a change in the social character of the Christian Kingdoms, beginning in the 11th century. The Frankish king Charlemagne had connected personal loyalty (vassalage) with public office and material reward (the fief). This brought about the rise of Feudalism as well as the concept of chivalry. At the same time, the character of the family had changed. Noble families began to practice primogeniture, which meant that there were very few paths to power for those who were not first-born noblemen. Second and third sons had to either find glory on the battlefield or else join a monastery and gain honor through service to the church.

The final impetus for the Crusades came from a major defeat for the Byzantines in Asia Minor at the hands of a new invading group from Central Asia, the Seljuk Turks. An Asian tribe that adopted Islam and moved into the Islamic Empire proper, they began their reign by a process of expansion similar to the earlier stages of Islamic kingdoms, capturing most of Asia Minor. In the late 11th century, the Byzantine emperor Alexius I (1081–1118) decided to recapture territory lost to the Turks. Because he did not have enough men of his own to accomplish his task, he turned to the papacy for some assistance. He used the plea that Christian pilgrims were being harassed on their way to the Holy Land. Pope Urban II heard this plea and felt that he could use this cause to build his power and bring about a reunification between the Latin and Greek churches. Therefore, at the Council of Clermont in 1095, Urban II preached a call for Crusade.

The response was overwhelming, with frenzied crowds of nobles and clergy at Clermont responding with cries of "Deus volt, Deus volt" (God wills it). Eventually around 130,000 men, women, and children from France, Italy, and Southern and Western Germany took up arms and headed off for the First Crusade. However popular this Crusade was, it did not appeal to all—many Western Europeans did not respond at all to the pope's call.

The members of the First Crusade arrived in Jerusalem in early June 1099, and because Jerusalem was too large to be surrounded, they laid siege to the city. For a month the Christian armies maneuvered around the city, creeping closer, filling in the defensive ditches, and listening to Christian sermons preached in the areas outside the walls. On July 15, a pair of knights breached some defenses in the city wall, followed by a few more knights. Soon thousands of Christians poured into the city, capturing it. They celebrated by plundering the city and slaughtering Muslim and Jewish inhabitants. The only people left alive in the city were 500 elites who were able to pay a ransom.

Charlemagne's first major achievement was a new ruling ideology in the Latin West. In 789, Charlemagne required all men to swear an oath of allegiance to him, and he compared himself to a biblical king in his responsibility to his people. No distinctions were to be made among Franks or Saxons—everyone was to be equal in allegiance to the king. To Charlemagne, no boundary existed between church and state. Religion and state were complementary attributes of a political body whose end was salvation, not victory in war, domestic security, or personal fulfillment. In personal governance, Charlemagne had connected personal loyalty (vassalage) with public office and material reward (the fief). In the 10th and 11th centuries, versions of this arrangement spread all over Europe. The result is sometimes called *the feudal system*. A specific code of conduct, chivalry, belonged to the warrior aristocracy.

Despite the consolidation of power and major advancements, by 1300 Europe was on the edge of disaster. Changes brought on by wars, plagues, and religious controversy affected the structure and dynamics of families, the organization of work, and the culture in many parts of Europe. After nearly three centuries of dramatic growth, European society was overpopulated and threatened by drastic economic and social problems. Estimates of Europe's population in 1300 have ranged from about 80 million to as high as 100 million. Despite farming improvements, it became increasingly difficult for the towns and countryside to feed and support the growing population, and millions died around Europe during the Great Famine of 1315–1322.

On top of this, in 1348 bubonic plague returned to Western Europe for the first time in 600 years. Genoese traders contracted the plague in Caffa on the Black Sea coast, and infected sailors carried the disease south into Egypt and west to Sicily. From there it followed established trade routes and spread throughout Europe. The bacillus that caused "the great mortality," as contemporaries called it, was *Yersinia pestis*.

In its bubonic form, the plague attacks the lymphatic system, bringing painful, discolored swelling under the armpits and in the groin or lower abdomen. Those who survived the first days of high fever and internal hemorrhaging recovered from the bubonic plague. No one, however, survived the rarer pneumonic or septicemic forms of the plague, which attacked the lungs and circulatory system. In the initial infestation of 1348–1351, up to 60% of the population of some areas died. After the initial outbreak, the plague returned again in 1363, and then returned every 25 years or so for three more centuries. Less is known about the spread of the plague in Asia and the Middle East, although mortality rates would likely have been about the same.

Yet it was the young, the elderly, and the poor—those least likely to pay taxes, own shops, or produce new children—who were the most common victims. Even in towns with the highest mortality rates, economic recovery was rapid. Government offices were closed at most for only a few weeks. Markets reopened as soon as the death rate began to decline. Within 2 years tax receipts were back at pre-plague levels, but the shape of society had changed.

STANDARDS ADDRESSED IN THE CHAPTER

NCHS World History Content Standards, Grades 5–12:

- **Era 5—Standard 2B:** The student understands the expansion of Christian Europe after 1000.
- **Era 5—Standard 2C:** The student understands the patterns of social change and cultural achievement in Europe's emerging civilizations.
- **Era 5—Standard 5A:** The student understands the consequences of Black Death and recurring plague pandemic in the 14th century.

CCSS for Literacy in History/Social Studies, Grades 6–8 and 9–10:

- **6–8:** Cite specific textual evidence to support analysis of primary and secondary sources; Determine the central ideas or information of a primary or secondary source; Analyze the relationship between a primary and secondary source on the same topic.
- **9–10:** Cite specific textual evidence to support analysis of primary and secondary sources, attending to such features as the date and origin of the information; Determine the central ideas or information of a primary or secondary source; Compare and contrast treatments of the same topic in several primary and secondary sources.

LESSON 1

ORGANIZING QUESTION

How did both sides experience the attack on Jerusalem during the Crusades?

STRATEGIES USED

5W Review (Who? What? When? Where? Why?), Partner Read/Annotating Text

MATERIALS NEEDED

1. Handout 13.1: Excerpts From Raymond d'Aguilers's *A History of the Franks, Who Have Taken Jerusalem* (ca. 1100)
2. Handout 13.2: Excerpts From Ibn Al-Athir's "The Seizure of Jerusalem" (ca. 1200)
3. Book: Jon Scieszka's *The True Story of the Three Little Pigs* (teacher copy)

LESSON PLAN

Note: This lesson works best after students have studied the Catholic Church in the Middle Ages and background about the Crusades.

Lesson Hook: Have students write down the "facts" from the traditional story of the three little pigs. Ask them to list the characters, any details about the setting they remember, and describe the sequence of events that happened. Allow several students to share their version of the story. Read *The True Story of the Three Little Pigs* to the class and have students consider how well it matches their story. Have students listen for similarities and differences between their story and the book's version. Ask them to think about why the stories might be so different and lead them, if needed, to the concept of multiple perspectives. Have them share examples of multiple perspectives on historical events they have already learned in class.

The Organizing Question: Explain that students will examine two different primary source accounts to help answer the organizing question: *How did both sides experience the attack on Jerusalem during the Crusades?*

Examine the Sources: *5W Review (Who? What? When? Where? Why?)*—Have students write the 5W questions in their notes. Have them review the Crusades with a partner by writing down answers to the 5W questions:

- Who was involved?
- What was it?
- When did it happen?
- Where did it take place?
- Why was it important?

Partner Read/Annotating Text—Explain to students they will examine two accounts of the seizure of Jerusalem from Christian and Muslim writers. Divide the class in half and give one half Raymond d'Aguilers's text (Handout 13.1) and the other half Ibn Al-Athir's text (Handout 13.2). Allow students to partner with someone who has the same text. As they are reading, have them annotate main ideas and look for answers to the organizing question. As they find clues to the question, have them mark or highlight those clues in the text. Encourage them to read one paragraph at a time, stop and discuss it, and then write main ideas in the margins beside that section.

As partner groups finish reading and analyzing their text, have them find two people who read the other text and form a group of four. Their task is to explain their sources and to share the main ideas and clues they located.

Make a Hypothesis: After students share both texts, have them work as a group to create a hypothesis that answers the organizing question. Require them to use both accounts as evidence to support their hypothesis. Allow groups to share hypotheses with the class and evaluate how well other groups use evidence as support.

HANDOUT 13.1

EXCERPTS FROM RAYMOND D'AGUILERS'S
A HISTORY OF THE FRANKS, WHO HAVE TAKEN JERUSALEM (CA. 1100)

The appointed day arrived and the attack began. However, I want to say this first, that, according to our estimate and that of many others, there were sixty thousand fighting men within the city, not counting the women and those unable to bear arms, and there were not many of these. At the most we did not have more than twelve thousand able to bear arms, for there were many poor people and many sick. . . . I say this that you may realize that nothing, whether great or small, which is undertaken in the name of the Lord can fail, as the following pages show.

Our men began to undermine the towers and walls. From every side stones were hurled . . . and so many arrows that they fell like hail. . . . The battle showed no indication of victory, but when the machines were drawn nearer to the walls, they hurled not only stones and arrows, but also burning wood and straw. The wood was dipped in pitch, wax, and sulphur; then straw and tow were fastened on by an iron band, and, when lighted, these firebrands were shot from the machines. (They were) all bound together by an iron band, I say, so that wherever they fell, the whole mass held together and continued to burn. . . . Thus the fight continued from the rising to the setting sun in such splendid fashion that it is difficult to believe anything more glorious was ever done. Then we called on Almighty God, our Leader and Guide, confident in His mercy. Night brought fear to both sides. . . . We gladly labored to capture the city for the glory of God, they less willingly strove to resist our efforts for the sake of the laws of Mohammed. . . .

. . . our men began to take heart, and some began to batter down the wall, while others began to ascend by means of scaling ladders and ropes. Our archers shot burning firebrands. . . . Then the Count quickly released the long drawbridge which had protected the side of the wooden tower next to the wall, and it swung down from the top, being fastened to the middle of the tower, making a bridge over which the men began to enter Jerusalem bravely and fearlessly.

But now that our men had possession of the walls and towers, wonderful sights were to be seen. Some of our men (and this was more merciful) cut off the heads of their enemies; others shot them with arrows, so that they fell from the towers; others tortured them longer by casting them into the flames. Piles of heads, hands, and feet were to be seen in the streets of the city. It was necessary to pick one's way over the bodies of men and horses . . . men rode in blood up to their knees and bridle reins. Indeed, it was a just and splendid judgment of God that this place should be filled with the blood of the unbelievers, since it had suffered so long from their blasphemies. The city was filled with corpses and blood. . . .

Now that the city was taken, it was well worth all our previous labors and hardships to see the devotion of the pilgrims at the Holy Sepulchre. How they rejoiced and exulted and sang a new song to the Lord! For their hearts offered prayers of praise to God, victorious and triumphant, which cannot be told in words.

HANDOUT 13.2

EXCERPTS FROM IBN AL-ATHIR'S "THE SEIZURE OF JERUSALEM" (CA. 1200)

After their vain attempt to take Acre by siege, the Franks moved onto Jerusalem and besieged it for more than six weeks. They built two towers, one of which, near Sion, the Muslims burnt down, killing everyone inside it. It had scarcely ceased to burn before a messenger arrived to ask for help and to bring the news that the other side of the city had fallen. In fact Jerusalem was taken from the north on the morning of Friday 22, sha'ban 492. The population was put to the sword by the Franks, who pillaged the area for a week. A band of Muslims barricaded themselves into the Oratory of David and fought on for several days. They were granted their lives in return for surrendering. The Franks honored their word, and the group left by night for Ascalon.

In the Masjid alAqsa the Franks slaughtered more than 70,000 people, among them a large number of Imams and Muslim scholars, devout and ascetic men who had left their homelands to live lives of pious seclusion in the Holy Place. The Franks stripped the Dome of the Rock of more than forty silver candelabra, each of them weighing 3,600 drams, and a great silver lamp weighing forty four Syrian pounds, as well as a hundred and fifty smaller silver candelabra and more than twenty gold ones, and a great deal more booty.

Refugees from Syria reached Baghdad in Ramadan, among them the qadi Abu Sa'd al Harawi. They told the Caliph's ministers a story that wrung their hearts and brought tears to their eyes. On Friday they went to the Cathedral Mosque and begged for help, weeping so that their hearers wept with them as they described the sufferings of the Muslims in that Holy City: the men killed, the women and children taken prisoner, the homes pillaged. Because of the terrible hardships they had suffered, they were allowed to break the fast.

It was the discord between the Muslim princes . . . that enabled the Franks to overrun the country.

LESSON 2

ORGANIZING QUESTION

How did the Magna Carta limit the power of the English king and impact future political systems?

STRATEGIES USED

Inside/Outside Circle, Modeling, Annotating Text

MATERIALS NEEDED

1. Handout 13.3: Excerpts From the Magna Carta (1215)
2. Highlighters or colored pencils (two different colors per student)
3. Timer

Note: Visit the British Library's Magna Carta website (https://www.bl.uk/treasures/magnacarta/index.html) for background information and frequently asked questions about the Magna Carta.

LESSON PLAN

Lesson Hook: *Inside/Outside Circle*—Before class, post the following questions on the board:

- What is a right?
- What rights do you have?
- How do you have those rights?
- What is the most important right you have?

Give student 5 minutes to jot down their ideas about the questions. Next, have students stand and create two concentric circles, with the students in the inner circle facing the students in the outer circle. Each student should be facing a partner. Explain that they will have 2 minutes to share their thoughts about the first question with this partner. A timer can help keep this moving quickly. (*Note*: You can adjust the time if needed. You can also do this activity with two lines instead of circles if there are space constraints.) Once the timer goes off, only the outside circle of students should move one position clockwise. The students should then have a discussion of the first question again with their new partners. Continue 3–4 times per question, based on the interest level of the students, and allow them to discuss each question with multiple partners.

The Organizing Question: Explain to students that they will examine a primary source from the medieval era—The Great Charter, or Magna Carta—to look for clues to the following organizing question: *How did the Magna Carta limit the power of the English king and impact future political systems?*

Examine the Sources: Depending on where you are in your unit, students might need some background about medieval England, King John, and the historical context of the Magna Carta. Distribute Handout 13.3: Excerpts From the Magna Carta (1215).

Modeling—Explain to students that they will examine some excerpts from the Magna Carta to explore two aspects of the document: (1) how it limits the power of the English king (examples are listed in the text) and (2) how it impacts other political systems (this will require students to make inferences and connections to other governments). Read the first section of the document to students to help them understand the context for the rest of the points they will read in groups. As you are reading, ask students to consider what clues these points might provide in each area of the organizing question. Explain to students that they will code or mark the text in different colors—one color for limits to the king's power and the second color for influences on other governments.

Annotating Text—Once you have modeled Section 1 with the whole class and color-coded the text as appropriate, explain to students that they will work in small groups to analyze the rest of the text. Divide the class into groups of 3–4 students, depending on your class size. Each group should read Sections 2, 3, and 4 of the text, highlighting in two colors any clues they find. Encourage them to use the sections dividers as stopping points to read and discuss their highlights with their group. (*Note*: Alternatively, you can assign each group one particular section to be responsible for and allow each group to share its annotations with the whole class.)

Make a Hypothesis: After students have read and discussed the text, have them work with their group to make a hypothesis to answer both parts of the organizing question with multiple examples of evidence from the text. You may have each student individually write his or her hypothesis and evidence as a formative assessment that you collect, or you may choose to have each group share the hypotheses and evidence in a class discussion. If time permits, revisit students' ideas about rights from the Lesson Hook section and have them discuss any of those they might have seen mentioned in the Magna Carta.

HANDOUT 13.3
EXCERPTS FROM THE MAGNA CARTA (1215)

SECTION 1

JOHN, by the grace of God King of England, Lord of Ireland, Duke of Normandy and Aquitaine, and Count of Anjou, to his archbishops, bishops, abbots, earls, barons, justices, foresters, sheriffs, stewards, servants, and to all his officials and loyal subjects, Greeting.

KNOW THAT BEFORE GOD, for the health of our soul and those of our ancestors and heirs, to the honour of God, the exaltation of the holy Church, and the better ordering of our kingdom. . . .

(1) FIRST, THAT WE HAVE GRANTED TO GOD, and by this present charter have confirmed for us and our heirs in perpetuity, that the English Church shall be free, and shall have its rights undiminished, and its liberties unimpaired. That we wish this so to be observed, appears from the fact that of our own free will, before the outbreak of the present dispute between us and our barons, we granted and confirmed by charter the freedom of the Church's elections—a right reckoned to be of the greatest necessity and importance to it—and caused this to be confirmed by Pope Innocent III. This freedom we shall observe ourselves, and desire to be observed in good faith by our heirs in perpetuity.

TO ALL FREE MEN OF OUR KINGDOM we have also granted, for us and our heirs for ever, all the liberties written out below, to have and to keep for them and their heirs, of us and our heirs.

SECTION 2

(12) No 'scutage' or 'aid' may be levied in our kingdom without its general consent, unless it is for the ransom of our person, to make our eldest son a knight, and (once) to marry our eldest daughter. For these purposes only a reasonable 'aid' may be levied. 'Aids' from the city of London are to be treated similarly.

(13) The city of London shall enjoy all its ancient liberties and free customs, both by land and by water. We also will and grant that all other cities, boroughs, towns, and ports shall enjoy all their liberties and free customs. . . .

(18) We ourselves, or in our absence abroad our chief justice, will send two justices to each county four times a year, and these justices, with four knights of the county elected by the county itself, shall hold the assizes in the county court, on the day and in the place where the court meets. . . .

(20) For a trivial offence, a free man shall be fined only in proportion to the degree of his offence, and for a serious offence correspondingly, but not so heavily as to deprive him of his livelihood. In the same way, a merchant shall be spared his merchandise, and a villein the implements of his husbandry, if they fall upon the mercy of a royal court. None of these fines shall be imposed except by the assessment on oath of reputable men of the neighbourhood.

(21) Earls and barons shall be fined only by their equals, and in proportion to the gravity of their offence. . . .

(28) No constable or other royal official shall take corn or other movable goods from any man without immediate payment, unless the seller voluntarily offers postponement of this.

HANDOUT 13.3, CONTINUED

SECTION 3

(30) No sheriff, royal official, or other person shall take horses or carts for transport from any free man, without his consent.

(31) Neither we nor any royal official will take wood for our castle, or for any other purpose, without the consent of the owner. . . .

(35) There shall be standard measures of wine, ale, and corn (the London quarter), throughout the kingdom. There shall also be a standard width of dyed cloth, russet, and haberject, namely two ells within the selvedges. Weights are to be standardised similarly. . . .

(38) In future no official shall place a man on trial upon his own unsupported statement, without producing credible witnesses to the truth of it.

(39) No free man shall be seized or imprisoned, or stripped of his rights or possessions, or outlawed or exiled, or deprived of his standing in any other way, nor will we proceed with force against him, or send others to do so, except by the lawful judgement of his equals or by the law of the land.

(40) To no one will we sell, to no one deny or delay right or justice.

SECTION 4

(45) We will appoint as justices, constables, sheriffs, or other officials, only men that know the law of the realm and are minded to keep it well. . . .

(52) To any man whom we have deprived or dispossessed of lands, castles, liberties, or rights, without the lawful judgement of his equals, we will at once restore these. In cases of dispute the matter shall be resolved by the judgement of the twenty-five barons referred to below in the clause for securing the peace. . . .

(55) All fines that have been given to us unjustly and against the law of the land, and all fines that we have exacted unjustly, shall be entirely remitted or the matter decided by a majority judgement of the twenty-five barons referred to below in the clause for securing the peace together with Stephen, archbishop of Canterbury, if he can be present, and such others as he wishes to bring with him. . . .

(61) SINCE WE HAVE GRANTED ALL THESE THINGS for God, for the better ordering of our kingdom, and to allay the discord that has arisen between us and our barons, and since we desire that they shall be enjoyed in their entirety, with lasting strength, for ever, we give and grant to the barons the following security: The barons shall elect twenty-five of their number to keep, and cause to be observed with all their might, the peace and liberties granted and confirmed to them by this charter. If we, our chief justice, our officials, or any of our servants offend in any respect against any man, or transgress any of the articles of the peace or of this security, and the offence is made known to four of the said twenty-five barons, they shall come to us—or in our absence from the kingdom to the chief justice—to declare it and claim immediate redress. . . .

(63) IT IS ACCORDINGLY OUR WISH AND COMMAND that the English Church shall be free, and that men in our kingdom shall have and keep all these liberties, rights, and conces-

sions, well and peaceably in their fullness and entirety for them and their heirs, of us and our heirs, in all things and all places for ever.

Both we and the barons have sworn that all this shall be observed in good faith and without deceit. Witness the above-mentioned people and many others. Given by our hand in the meadow that is called Runnymede, between Windsor and Staines, on the fifteenth day of June in the seventeenth year of our reign[1].

---

1   Year 1215; the new regnal year began on 28 May.

LESSON 3

ORGANIZING QUESTION

In what ways did the Black Death affect the city of Florence?

STRATEGIES USED

Give One/Get One, Reciprocal Reading

MATERIALS NEEDED

1. Handout 13.4: Excerpts From Giovanni Boccaccio's *Decameron* (ca. 1353)
2. Painting: Josse Lieferinxe's *St. Sebastian Interceding for the Plague Stricken* (ca. 1497–1499), available at http://art.thewalters.org/detail/6193/saint-sebastian-interceding-for-the-plague-stricken
3. Timer
4. Highlighters (one per student)

LESSON PLAN

Lesson Hook: *Give One/Get One*—Display the painting *St. Sebastian Interceding for the Plague Stricken*. Ask students to individually write down as many details as they can about what they notice, as well as some questions they have about the painting. After a couple of minutes, allow students to find a partner. Set a timer for one minute and instruct students to "give" one idea from their list and "get" one idea from their partner. Allow students to switch partners 3–4 times. Have students share their responses and chart their questions on the board.

The Organizing Question: Explain to students that they will look for answers to their questions by reading and analyzing excerpts from Boccaccio's *Decameron* describing the Bubonic Plague, or Black Death, that struck Florence, Italy, in 1348. As they are reading the text, they should look for clues to answer the organizing question: *In what ways did the Black Death affect the city of Florence?*

Examine the Sources: *Reciprocal Reading*—Explain to students that they are going to use a reciprocal reading strategy to analyze and discuss the text. Distribute Handout 13.4: Excerpts From Giovanni Boccaccio's *Decameron* (ca. 1353).

Take a few minutes to clarify the following four reciprocal reading roles used in this lesson:

- Reader: Reads the passage out loud, stopping after every 2–3 sentences.
- Main Idea Master: For each 2–3-sentence passage, helps the group determine the main idea from that section.
- Vocabulary Locator: Locates difficult vocabulary words and tries to use context clues to help determine their meaning.
- Clarifier/Clue Finder: At the end of each passage, helps the group clarify the meaning of the sentences and decide if that section provides any clues to answer the organizing question or the class-generated questions on the board.

Read the first section of the text to the class and help students annotate it. For this modeling section, you can assign certain areas of the room one of the roles. Stop at the end of the first section and have students discuss it as their role (main idea master, vocabulary locator, or clarifier/clue finder) as practice for working in small groups.

Next divide the class into groups of four and have students choose roles. (*Note*: You can choose to use only three of these roles and have groups of three if that works better for your class size.) Direct them to read Section 2, annotating key ideas and clues. At the end of the section, they should stop and discuss it from the focus area of their assigned role. After the discussion of Section 2, each student should switch to a new role for Section 3. Continue the same process for Section 4. Make sure to circulate around the room helping students decipher this challenging text and engage in effective discussions.

Make a Hypothesis: Once groups are finished discussing all sections of the text, have them formulate a hypothesis that answers the organizing question. Challenge them to look for as many examples as possible and prepare to share textual evidence that proves their hypotheses. Allow them a few minutes to create their hypotheses with examples and have each group share with the class. At the end of the lesson, have students discuss what answers they found to their list of student-generated questions from the Lesson Hook section. Next, have them discuss what questions still remain and how or where they could locate information to answer them.

HANDOUT 13.4

EXCERPTS FROM GIOVANNI BOCCACCIO'S
DECAMERON (CA. 1353)

SECTION 1

I say, then, that the years of the beatific incarnation of the Son of God had reached the tale of one thousand three hundred and forty-eight when in the illustrious city of Florence, the fairest of all the cities of Italy, there made its appearance that deadly pestilence, which, whether disseminated by the influence of the celestial bodies, or sent upon us mortals by God in His just wrath by way of retribution for our iniquities, had had its origin some years before in the East, whence, after destroying an innumerable multitude of living beings, it had propagated itself without respite from place to place, and so, calamitously, had spread into the West.

In Florence, despite all that human wisdom and forethought could devise to avert it, as the cleansing of the city from many impurities by officials appointed for the purpose, the refusal of entrance to all sick folk, and the adoption of many precautions for the preservation of health; despite also humble supplications addressed to God, and often repeated both in public procession and otherwise, by the devout; towards the beginning of the spring of the said year the doleful effects of the pestilence began to be horribly apparent by symptoms that shewed as if miraculous.

SECTION 2

Not such were they [effects of the plague] as in the East, where an issue of blood from the nose was a manifest sign of inevitable death; but in men and women alike it first betrayed itself by the emergence of certain tumours in the groin or the armpits, some of which grew as large as a common apple, others as an egg, some more, some less, which the common folk called gavoccioli. From the two said parts of the body this deadly gavocciolo soon began to propagate and spread itself in all directions indifferently; after which the form of the malady began to change, black spots or livid making their appearance in many cases on the arm or the thigh or elsewhere, now few and large, now minute and numerous. . . .

Not merely were those that recovered few, but almost all within three days from the appearance of the said symptoms, sooner or later, died, and in most cases without any fever or other attendant malady. . . . for not merely by speech or association with the sick was the malady communicated to the healthy with consequent peril of common death; but any that touched the cloth of the sick or aught else that had been touched or used by them, seemed thereby to contract the disease.

So marvellous sounds that which I have now to relate, that, had not many, and I among them, observed it with their own eyes, I had hardly dared to credit it, much less to set it down in writing, though I had had it from the lips of a credible witness.

I say, then, that such was the energy of the contagion of the said pestilence, that it was not merely propagated from man to man but, what is much more startling, it was frequently observed, that things which had belonged to one sick or dead of the disease, if touched by some other living creature, not of the human species, were the occasion, not merely of sickening, but of an almost instantaneous death. Whereof my own eyes (as I said a little before) had cogni-

HANDOUT 13.4, CONTINUED

sance, one day among others, by the following experience. The rags of a poor man who had died of the disease being strewn about the open street, two hogs came thither, and after, as is their wont, no little trifling with their snouts, took the rags between their teeth and tossed them to and fro about their chaps; whereupon, almost immediately, they gave a few turns, and fell down dead, as if by poison, upon the rags which in an evil hour they had disturbed.

SECTION 3

In which circumstances, not to speak of many others of a similar or even graver complexion, divers apprehensions and imaginations were engendered in the minds of such as were left alive, inclining almost all of them to the same harsh resolution, to wit, to shun and abhor all contact with the sick and all that belonged to them, thinking thereby to make each his own health secure. Among whom there were those who thought that to live temperately and avoid all excess would count for much as a preservative against seizures of this kind. Wherefore they banded together, and, dissociating themselves from all others, formed communities in houses where there were no sick, and lived a separate and secluded life, which they regulated with the utmost care, avoiding every kind of luxury, but eating and drinking very moderately of the most delicate viands and the finest wines, holding converse with none but one another, lest tidings of sickness or death should reach them, and diverting their minds with music and such other delights as they could devise.

Others, the bias of whose minds was in the opposite direction, maintained, that to drink freely, frequent places of public resort, and take their pleasure with song and revel, sparing to satisfy no appetite, and to laugh and mock at no event, was the sovereign remedy for so great an evil: and that which they affirmed they also put in practice, so far as they were able, resorting day and night, now to this tavern, now to that, drinking with an entire disregard of rule or measure, and by preference making the houses of others, as it were, their inns....

Not a few there were who belonged to neither of the two said parties, but kept a middle course between them, neither laying the same restraint upon their diet as the former, nor allowing themselves the same license in drinking and other dissipations as the latter, but living with a degree of freedom sufficient to satisfy their appetites, and not as recluses. They therefore walked abroad, carrying in their hands flowers or fragrant herbs or divers sorts of spices, which they frequently raised to their noses, deeming it an excellent thing thus to comfort the brain with such perfumes, because the air seemed to be everywhere laden and reeking with the stench emitted by the dead and the dying and the odours of drugs.

Some again, the most sound, perhaps, in judgment, as they were also the most harsh in temper, of all, affirmed that there was no medicine for the disease superior or equal in efficacy to flight; following which prescription a multitude of men and women, negligent of all but themselves, deserted their city, their houses, their estate, their kinsfolk, their goods, and went into voluntary exile, or migrated to the country parts.

HANDOUT 13.4, CONTINUED

SECTION 4

Tedious were it to recount, how citizen avoided citizen, how among neighbours was scarce found any that shewed fellow-feeling for another, how kinsfolk held aloof, and never met, or but rarely; enough that this sore affliction entered so deep into the minds of men and women, that in the horror thereof brother was forsaken by brother, nephew by uncle, brother by sister, and oftentimes husband by wife; nay, what is more, and scarcely to be believed, fathers and mothers were found to abandon their own children, untended, unvisited, to their fate, as if they had been strangers. Wherefore the sick of both sexes, whose number could not be estimated, were left without resource but in the charity of friends (and few such there were), or the interest of servants. . . .

Few also there were whose bodies were attended to the church by more than ten or twelve of their neighbours, and those not the honourable and respected citizens; but a sort of corpse-carriers drawn from the baser ranks who called themselves becchini (1) and performed such offices for hire, would shoulder the bier, and with hurried steps carry it, not to the church of the dead man's choice, but to that which was nearest at hand. . . .

Many died daily or nightly in the public streets; of many others, who died at home, the departure was hardly observed by their neighbours, until the stench of their putrefying bodies carried the tidings; and what with their corpses and the corpses of others who died on every hand the whole place was a sepulchre.

CHAPTER 14

CIVILIZATIONS IN THE AMERICAS

> We did not know there were other people besides the Indian until about one hundred winters ago, when some men with white faces came to our country.
>
> —Chief Joseph

HISTORICAL CONTEXT: WHAT DO I NEED TO KNOW?

Up until its conquest by Spain in 1533, the Inca Empire, at the time of European encounters, was the latest and largest in a long line of complex civilizations in that area of the Americas. Prior to the early 1400s, a people known as the Tiwanaku dominated the region around Lake Titicaca, while the Wari people controlled the area that included what would become the Inca capital of Cuzco. The decline of those two empires set the stage for the rise of the Inca. Called *Tawantinsuyu*, which means "four provinces" in Quechua, the Inca empire was a union of four regions in the Andes. The ruler of the Tawantinsuyu was known as the *Sapa Inca*, the "son of the sun," and it was from this term that Spaniards named the empire. Although not a phrase used at the time by the Inca, this "divine right of rule" fit with many kingdoms' understanding of monarchy at the time.

In the early 16th century, the Sapa Inca Atahualpa presided over a far-flung civilization of perhaps 2 million people and a governing structure spread over mountainous, difficult terrain. The area lacked animals such as oxen, so the Inca never developed wheeled vehicles. Unlike other cultures around the world, they did not develop ironworking or, most unusually, a writing system, instead relying on a complex system of knotted strings called *quipu*. Despite these differences, the Inca had a sophisticated system of mathematics, built monumental architecture, including Machu Picchu, and united their empire through a sophisticated system of taxation that included mandatory public service and a "distributive economy" in which goods flowed from the peripheries to the center, and then back out again to the peripheries. The Inca calendar was built on the movements of the stars, with the time of day measured by the movement of the sun or the length of different tasks.

To the north, a diverse array of peoples and cultures utilizing hundreds of distinct languages lived in pre-Columbian Mesoamerica. The Aztec culture, the largest and most powerful by the 15th century, grew out of the arrival of the Mexica people in the central valley of Mexico in the mid-13th century. After initial clashes with other local city-states—including an incident in which a Mexica priest supposedly sacrificed the daughter of a nearby king and wore her skin to a festival in her honor—the Mexica eventually settled on the western shores of lake Texcoco, where they built the city of Tenochtitlan out into the lake through the use of floating gardens called *chinampas*. Over time the Mexica absorbed the surrounding city-states, either through tribute, political alliance, or outright conquest. Like the Inca and Egyptians, the Aztec engaged in monumental architecture, building large pyramids similar to those of the Sumerians and Babylonians and probably meant to house their gods. In contrast to the Inca, the Aztec empire engaged in a tributary economy by sending goods to local markets as well as to Tenochtitlan as tribute to the Aztec ruler Moctezuma. By 1519, when the Spaniard Hernán Cortés arrived, the population of Tenochtitlan, the Aztec capital, had reached more than 200,000, with a total population of perhaps 2–5 million in the empire. Within a few decades of Spanish conquest that number dropped by more than half.

Farther north still, North America was home to numerous smaller tribes, kingdoms, and city-states, and a diverse array of cultures, economies, and political systems. Although none reached the size and scope of the Inca or Aztec, some groups controlled large territories, and some, such as the Mississippian Woodlands people, built large structures, including the mounds at present-day Cahokia. That site was likely home to as many as 20,000 people at its height. There were some generalities among the people. In societies that relied on hunting large animals for food, that task usually went to men, while women gathered food and produced clothing. That kind of sexual division of labor was universal among hunting peoples regardless of location. Agricultural societies varied in how they divided the labor. Descendants of the Anasazi, called the

Pueblo, defined agriculture as men's work. Most of the tribes in the east, on the other hand, saw agriculture as women's work, although men cleared the land. In native societies that practiced agriculture, many families were defined matrilineally, or through a female line of descent. By contrast, the nomadic bands of the Great Plains were linked patrilineally, or through the male line. In almost every Native American culture, political power was divided between civil and military leaders who had authority only as long as they had the support of their people. In some Native societies, women held power. Autocratic power of the kind in Inca or Aztec societies was unusual. For Native Americans in North America, there was no concept of land ownership in the sense that Europeans understood it. For Native Americans, land could be used, and people could gain the rights to take the produce of the land—hunting, fishing, farming, even extraction of metals—but nobody had long-term ownership. Land treaties for Indians, therefore, only meant usage, not ownership, and even then, the usage was not intended to be exclusive.

STANDARDS ADDRESSED IN THE CHAPTER

NCHS World History Content Standards, Grades 5–12:
- **Era 5—Standard 6A:** The student understands the development of complex societies and states in North America and Mesoamerica.
- **Era 5—Standard 6B:** The student understands the development of the Inca empire in Andean South America.

CCSS for Literacy in History/Social Studies, Grades 6–8 and 9–10:
- **6–8:** Cite specific textual evidence to support analysis of primary and secondary sources; Determine the central ideas or information of a primary or secondary source; Integrate visual information (e.g., in charts, graphs, photographs, videos, or maps) with the other information in print and digital texts.
- **9–10:** Cite specific textual evidence to support analysis of primary and secondary sources; Determine the central ideas or information of a primary or secondary source; Compare and contrast treatments of the same topic in several primary and secondary sources.

LESSON 1

ORGANIZING QUESTION

What was life like in the Inca empire in the 16th century?

STRATEGIES USED

Cooperative Learning, Gallery Walk

MATERIALS NEEDED

1. Handout 14.1: Clue Sheet: Life in the 16th-Century Inca Empire
2. Image of an archaeology dig
3. Chart paper and markers (per group of 3–4 students)
4. The following images displayed around the room for a gallery walk:
   ✓ Drawing: Felipe Guaman Poma de Ayala's *Incan Quipu* (ca. 1600), available at https://www.granger.com/results.asp?image=0027226
   ✓ Drawing: Felipe Guaman Poma de Ayala's *Inca Man Holding a Quipu* (ca. 1600), available at https://www.granger.com/results.asp?image= 0272578
   ✓ Woodcut: *Inca Harvest Festival* (1633), available at https://www. granger.com/results.asp?image=0044220
   ✓ Woodcut: Felipe Guaman Poma de Ayala's *Incan King* (1583), available at https://www.granger.com/results.asp?image=0038003
   ✓ Drawing: Felipe Guaman Poma de Ayala's *Inca Farmers* (1583), available at https://www.granger.com/results.asp?image=0007493
   ✓ Photograph: Any image of the Machu Picchu ruins in Peru
   ✓ Map: Manco Capac's *Inca Road System*, available at https://com mons.wikimedia.org/wiki/Atlas_of_the_Inca_Empire#/media/ File:Inca_road_system_map-en.svg

LESSON PLAN

Note: This lesson works well as an introduction to the Incas. Display students' posters in your classroom and prove or disprove their hypotheses as they learn more about the Incas.

Lesson Hook: Display a picture of an archaeology dig on the screen. Ask students to brainstorm what they know about the job of an archaeologist from movies, television, or books. Discuss their responses and clarify if needed.

The Organizing Question: Explain the following task to students:

Your help is needed with a very important historical project! You have been hired as an archaeology team to help determine what the Incan culture was like in the 16th century. Your task is to analyze the clues around the room in order to answer the organizing question: *What was life like in the Inca empire in the 16th century?*

Examine the Sources: *Cooperative Learning*—Divide the class into groups of 3–4 students, assigning each group member a role of Recorder, Reporter, Sketch Artist, and/or Project Manager. Discuss the duties of each role:
- Recorder: Writes the group's ideas on the clue sheet.
- Reporter: Shares the group's hypothesis and evidence with the class.
- Sketch Artist: Designs the group's visual depiction on chart paper.
- Project Manager: Keeps the group focused on the task of examining clues and makes sure everyone participates in creating hypotheses and visuals.

Modify these roles and responsibilities as needed for the size of your groups and student needs.

Gallery Walk—Distribute Handout 14.1: Clue Sheet: Life in the 16th-Century Inca Empire. Model analyzing one of the images at the stations with students so that they can see how to collect the evidence on the clue sheet. Give students time to view the images and artifacts, to take notes on their clue sheets, and to discuss the findings with their team.

Make a Hypothesis: Explain to the archaeology teams that they will make a hypothesis about the Inca culture and use chart paper and markers to provide a visual depiction of their hypothesis. Teams should be prepared to explain their hypothesis and visual depiction using evidence from the clues around the room. After students have been given adequate time, have groups present their posters to the class. As students learn more about the Incas, they can prove or disprove their hypotheses.

HANDOUT 14.1

CLUE SHEET: LIFE IN THE 16TH-CENTURY INCA EMPIRE

Directions: Using the clues around the room, collect evidence and take notes on the things you notice about life in the Inca Empire in the 16th century. Then, organize your notes using the categories. You may not have something in every box. Use the evidence to form a hypothesis answering the question: *What was life like in the Inca Empire in the 16th century?*

NOTES/IDEAS/QUESTIONS
GOVERNMENT
ROLES OF MEN OR WOMEN
GEOGRAPHY OF THE AREA
ACHIEVEMENTS OF THE INCAS

HANDOUT 14.1, CONTINUED

TRADE
WARFARE
FOOD
RELIGIOUS BELIEFS

1. Our hypothesis is:

2. The evidence to support this hypothesis is:

3. Questions we still have about the Incas:

LESSON 2

ORGANIZING QUESTION

What was the Aztec civilization in Mesoamerica like in the 16th century?

STRATEGIES USED

Think Aloud, Analyzing Maps

MATERIALS NEEDED

1. A modern map of the United States, your state, or city
2. Laptop or tablet (per group of three students)
3. Map: *Tenochtitlan, 1521*, available at https://www.wdl.org/en/item/503
4. Map: *Tenochtitlan*, from Hernán Cortés's Second Letter to Charles V (1524), available at https://www.wdl.org/en/item/19994
5. The Library of Congress's "Teacher's Guide: Analyzing Maps" template, available at https://www.loc.gov/teachers/usingprimarysources/guides.html
6. Computers/devices for student research (one per group)
7. White paper (one sheet per student)

LESSON PLAN

Lesson Hook: Give students a sheet of white paper as they enter the class-room. Begin by asking students to describe how they get directions or find where they need to go on a trip. Most will say Google Maps or another map app on their phones. Ask students if they know what a cartographer is. Explain the following task to students and give them 10 minutes to complete it:

Today you will be a cartographer. Your assignment is to draw a detailed map of the classroom using a blank piece of paper. Use the entire space on the paper and put in objects located throughout the classroom. As you draw your desk, place a star over it.

Once students finish the task, have them trade maps with a partner and briefly determine if they can understand their partner's map to the starred desk. Then, ask them these questions:

- What was difficult about this task?
- Does your map accurately represent the objects in the classroom?
- Where do you see spatial errors in your map?

The Organizing Question: Explain that in this lesson students will analyze two maps of the city of Tenochtitlan for clues to help answer the organizing question: *What was the Aztec civilization in Mesoamerica like in the 16th century?*

Examine the Sources: *Think Aloud*—Display and review the Library of Congress's "Teacher's Guide: Analyzing Maps." Then, display any modern map of the United States, your state, or your city. With the class, practice analyzing the map using the Analyzing Maps template. Do a "think aloud" with students and describe what details you notice in the map. Let students help answer some of the questions from the Observe, Reflect, and Question sections of the template. End your map analysis by asking students what clues they learned about the specific place from the map details. Explain that they will look at some 16th century maps for information about the Aztecs.

Analyzing Maps—Before beginning this section, show students where the Aztecs were located and give them some background on the time period. Then divide students into groups of 2–3 with a computer or device for each group. Assign them one of the two Tenochtitlan maps. Ask students to use the questions in the Observe, Reflect, and Question sections of the Analyzing Maps template to prompt their analysis of the map. Have students zoom in on the maps if possible and try to decipher the smaller images. Encourage them to read the text on the websites for more background information.

Make a Hypothesis: Next, ask students to partner with a group that looked at a different map. Give them a few minutes to share clues from their map and discuss similarities and differences in the maps. End the lesson by having students work with their newly formed group to develop a hypothesis for the organizing question that can be answered with details from both maps. This could be used as an exit slip for the lesson or could be shared in a whole-group discussion. If students are required to share their hypotheses, write them on the board to use for the next lesson.

Optional Extension: Have students review the hypotheses about the Aztec civilization that they created from the maps. Have them look for more information to prove or disprove their hypotheses from either secondary sources or excerpts from a primary source, such as Hernán Cortés's letters to Charles V.

LESSON 3

ORGANIZING QUESTION

What was life like in a 16th-century Powhatan village in the Eastern Woodlands of North America?

STRATEGIES USED

Cooperative Learning, Gallery Walk

MATERIALS NEEDED

1. Handout 14.2: Clue Sheet: Life in the 16th-Century Powhatan Culture in North America
2. Web image of an archaeology dig
3. Chart paper and markers (per group of 3–5 students)
4. The following sources displayed in stations around the room:
   ✓ Handout 14.3: Excerpts From Gabriel Archer's "A Brief Description of the People" (1607)
   ✓ Engravings by Theodor de Bry (available at http://historyisfun.org/pdf/In-the-Words-of- Pocahontas/PIndians_Images.pdf):
     » *The Town of Pomeiooc*
     » *Their Manner of Feeding*
     » *The Town of Secota*
     » *Their Manner of Fishing in Virginia*
     » *Their Manner of Making Boats*
     » *The Broiling of Their Fish Over the Flame*
     » *A Werowan or Great Lorde of Virginia*

5. Artifacts: blue beads, reed (raffia also works well), bones, leather strips, etc.

LESSON PLAN

Note: This lesson uses a similar clue sheet as that in Lesson 1. You might consider using the clue sheets to have students compare and contrast the Inca, Powhatan, and Aztec civilizations in the Americas.

Lesson Hook: Display a picture of an archaeology dig. Ask students to brainstorm what they know about the job of an archaeologist from movies, television, or books. Discuss their responses and clarify an archaeologist's role if needed.

The Organizing Question: Explain the following task to students:

Your help is needed with a very important historical project. You and your classmates have been hired as an archaeology team to help determine what the Powhatan culture was like in the 16th century. Your task is to analyze the clues around the room in order to answer the organizing question: *What was life like in a 16th-century Powhatan village in the Eastern Woodlands of North America?*

Examine the Sources: *Cooperative Learning*—Divide the class into groups of 3–4 students, assigning each group member a role of Recorder, Reporter, Sketch Artist, and/or Project Manager. Discuss the duties of each role (see p. 219). Modify these roles and responsibilities as needed for the size of your groups and student needs.

Gallery Walk—Distribute Handout 14.2: Clue Sheet: Life in the 16th-Century Powhatan Culture in North America. Model analyzing one of the images at the stations with students so that they can see how to collect the evidence on the clue sheet. Allow students time to view the images and artifacts, to take notes on their clue sheets, and to discuss the findings with their team.

Make a Hypothesis: Explain to the archaeology teams that they will make a hypothesis about the Powhatan culture and use the chart paper and markers to provide a visual depiction of their hypothesis. Teams should be prepared to explain their hypothesis and visual depiction using evidence from the clues around the room. After students have been given adequate time, have groups present their posters to the class. Depending on the thoroughness and content accuracy of the presentations, end this lesson with a discussion of misconceptions, what content might have been missing from the clues, and ways to find more information to answer the organizing question.

If time permits, have students answer these questions individually as a formative assessment for the lesson:
- What are four details about Powhatan culture that you learned from this archaeology project?
- How was your hypothesis supported by the evidence or clues?
- How do you think this activity was similar to the job of a real archaeologist?
- How well did each group member perform the role he or she was assigned?

HANDOUT 14.2

CLUE SHEET: LIFE IN THE 16TH-CENTURY POWHATAN CULTURE IN NORTH AMERICA

Directions: Using the clues around the room, collect evidence and take notes on the things you notice about life in the Powhatan culture in the 16th century. Then, organize your notes using the categories. You may not have something in every box. Use the evidence to form a hypothesis answering the question: *What was life like in a 16th-century Powhatan village in the Eastern Woodlands of North America?*

NOTES/IDEAS/QUESTIONS
GOVERNMENT
ROLES OF MEN OR WOMEN
GEOGRAPHY OF THE AREA
ACHIEVEMENTS OF THE POWHATANS

HANDOUT 14.2, CONTINUED

TRADE
WARFARE
FOOD
RELIGIOUS BELIEFS

1. Our hypothesis is:

2. The evidence to support this hypothesis is:

3. Questions we still have about the Powhatans:

HANDOUT 14.3

EXCERPTS FROM GABRIEL ARCHER'S "A BRIEF DESCRIPTION OF THE PEOPLE" (1607)

There is a king in this land called Great Pawatah, under whose dominion are at least 20ty several kingdoms, yet each king potent as a prince in his own territory. These have their subjects at so quick command as a beck brings obedience, even to the restitution of stolen goods, which by their natural inclination they are loth to leave.

They go all naked save their privities, yet in cool weather they wear deerskins with the hair on the loose. Some have leather stockings up to their twists and sandals on their feet.

Their hair is black generally, which they wear long on the left side, tied up on a knot, about which knot the kings and best among them have a kind of coronet of deer's hair colored red. Some have chains of long link'd copper about their necks, and some chains of pearl. The common sort stick long feathers in this knot. I found not a gray eye among them all. Their skin is tawny, not so born but with dyeing and painting themselves, in which they delight greatly.

The women are like the men, only this difference: Their hair growth long all over their heads, save clip'd somewhat short afore. These do all the labor, and the men hunt and go at their pleasure.

They live commonly by the waterside in little cottages made of canes and reeds, covered with the bark of trees. They dwell as I guess by families of kindred and alliance, some 40ty or 50ty in a hatto, or small village, which towns are not past a mile or half a mile asunder in most places.

They live upon sodden wheat, beans, and peas for the most part. Also they kill deer, take fish in their weirs, and kill fowl abundance. They eat often and that liberally.

They are proper lusty, straight men, very strong, run exceeding swiftly; their fight is always in the wood with bow and arrows, and a short wooden sword. The celerity they use in skirmish is admirable. The king directs the battle and is always in front.

Their manner of entertainment is upon mats on the ground under some tree, where they sit themselves alone in the middle of the mat, and two mats on each side, on which their people sit; then right against him (making a square form) sat we always. When they came to their mat they have an usher goes before them, and the rest as he sits down give a long shout.

They sacrifice tobacco to the sun, [a] fair picture, or a harmful thing (as a sword or a piece) also; they sprinkle some into the water in the morning before they wash.

They have many wives, to whom, as I could perceive, they keep constant. The Great King Pawatah had most wives. These they abide not to be touch'd before their face.

The women are very cleanly in making their bread and preparing meat. I found they account after death to go into another world, pointing eastward to the element. And when they saw us at prayer they observed us with great silence and respect, especially those to whom I had imparted the meaning of our reverence.

To conclude, they are a very witty and ingenious people, apt both to understand and speak our language, so that I hope in God, as He hath miraculously preserved us hither from all dangers, both of sea and land and their fury, so He will make us authors of His holy will in converting them to our true Christian faith by His own inspiring grace and knowledge of His deity.

CHAPTER 15
GLOBAL EXPLORATION AND EXPANSION

By prevailing over all obstacles and distractions, one may unfailingly arrive at his chosen goal or destination.

—Christopher Columbus

HISTORICAL CONTEXT: WHAT DO I NEED TO KNOW?

The Age of Exploration is often seen as the story of Europeans moving out into the Atlantic World, with Columbus "discovering" the Americas and initiating contact with Native Americans. However, the story is a bit more complex, and the Age of Exploration more properly includes Chinese, African, and European movements in the Atlantic and Indian Oceans along the coast of India and Africa, as well as into the Caribbean and the Americas. In that sense, then, the term *Age of Exploration* is a bit misleading, implying that exploration began at a certain point. Humans have always explored. Chinese explorers began sailing into the Indian Ocean as early as the second century BCE, expediting the spread of Hinduism and Buddhism into Eastern Asia. Chinese ships carried Tang and Song Dynasty diplomats and traders, facilitating cultural exchange, including the spread of Islam, between the peoples around the Indian Ocean. In the early 15th century, large Chinese fleets undertook what came to be known as the "Ming Treasure Voyages." Starting along already-established trade routes, ships under the command of Admiral Zheng He journeyed from the coast of China around the Arabian Peninsula to the Persian Gulf and down the east coast of Africa. In a series of seven voyages on ships laden with troops and treasure, Zheng projected the power of the Ming Dynasty, destroyed pirate ships, exacted trade, and brought in tribute. The few contemporary records that describe the voyages point to massive fleets of several hundred ships of a size far larger than anything Europe would build for several centuries. When the Hongxi Emperor Zhu Gaochi, who saw the voyages as contrary to Confucian principles, ascended to the throne in 1424, the voyages came to an abrupt stop and China turned to land-based trade.

Concurrently, beginning in the 1300s, a number of interrelated causes led Europeans into the Atlantic in search of trade goods. Marco Polo's *Book of the Marvels of the World* described fabulous wealth ripe for trade in China, while goods brought back by the Crusaders had given Europeans a taste of luxury items, such as spices, silk, and porcelain. Those goods increased in price, as trade routes to Asia passed through the Mediterranean and then overland across the Middle East before crossing into Asia, requiring tribute to local Muslim rulers as well as every small kingdom along the way. In the meantime, the Reconquista, or the Portuguese fight to remove Muslims from that section of the Iberian Peninsula, came to a successful conclusion in 1385. Facing west into the Atlantic, the tiny kingdom looked for a route around what was initially thought to be a large island to its south—Africa. News and rumors of Emperor Musa I of Mali's pilgrimage to Mecca across Africa excited European dreams of wealth there, but winds and ocean currents generally pressed the small vessels back to the coast. The development of a deep-draft, two-sailed ship that could take advantage of wind changes and could sail more easily against the prevailing wind allowed the Portuguese to develop a sea route around Africa to Asia.

When Spain concluded its own Reconquista in 1492, Muslims still controlled the openings to the land route to Asia, while the Portuguese controlled the southern route around Africa. Taking the advice of the Genoese sailor Christopher Columbus—who had offered his services in turn to the English, Portuguese, and Italians—the Spanish monarchs Ferdinand and Isabella funded a voyage to Asia following a westerly route. Columbus, of course, encountered the Americas, setting off what is called the *Columbian Exchange*—a transfer of people, plants, goods, and diseases that continues to this day.

During its exploration of Africa, the Portuguese traded for everything from gold to cloth to spices. As time went on, however, trade in human capital—slaves—became more economically important. Unable to conquer large areas of Africa, nations such as Portugal, the Netherlands, Spain, and England worked closely with various coastal kingdoms that procured slaves. In the first several decades, African nations sold to Europeans those Africans who had been enslaved as a byproduct of war, economic hardship, or in the course of normal trade. As Europeans supplied advanced weapons, coastal kingdoms began to make war against interior peoples specifically to in order to satisfy an ever-increasing demand. Pressure from these wars slowly changed the balance of power to favor those kingdoms willing to trade African slaves for guns and other finished European goods, giving birth to what is often called the *Triangular Trade*.

STANDARDS ADDRESSED IN THE CHAPTER

NCHS World History Content Standards, Grades 5–12:
- **Era 6—Standard 1A:** The student understands the origins and consequences of European overseas expansion in the 15th and 16th centuries.
- **Era 6—Standard 5A:** The student understands the development of European maritime power in Asia.
- **Era 6—Standard 5B:** The student understands the transformations in India, China, and Japan in an era of expanding European commercial power.

CCSS for Literacy in History/Social Studies, Grades 6–8 and 9–10:
- **6–8:** Cite specific textual evidence to support analysis of primary and secondary sources; Determine the central ideas or information of a primary or secondary source; Integrate visual information (e.g., in charts, graphs, photographs, videos, or maps) with the other information in print and digital texts.
- **9–10:** Cite specific textual evidence to support analysis of primary and secondary sources; Determine the central ideas or information of a primary or secondary source; Compare and contrast treatments of the same topic in several primary and secondary sources.

LESSON 1

ORGANIZING QUESTION

What were the purposes of Zheng He's voyages during the Ming era?

STRATEGIES USED

Gallery Walk, Student Research, 5W Review (Who? What? When? Where? Why?)

MATERIALS NEEDED

1. Handout 15.1: Clue Sheet: Zheng He's Voyages During the Ming Era
2. The following images, numbered and displayed in stations around the room for a gallery walk:
   ✓ Painting: Shen Du's *Tribute Giraffe With Attendant* (1414), available at https://en.wikipedia.org/wiki/Ming_treasure_voyages#/media/File:Tribute_Giraffe_with_Attendant.jpg
   ✓ Print: *Chinese Woodblock Print, Representing Zheng He's Ships* (ca. 1600), available at https://en.wikipedia.org/wiki/Ming_treasure_voyages#/media/File:ZhengHeShips.gif
   ✓ Drawing: Zheng He's ocean travel chart from Mao Yuanyi's *WuBeiZhi* (1628), available at https://en.wikipedia.org/wiki/Mao_Kun_map#/media/File:WuBeiZhi.jpg
   ✓ Map: *Port Cities on the Maritime Silk Route Featured on the Voyages of Zheng He*, available at https://en.wikipedia.org/wiki/Silk_Road#/media/File:Zheng_He.png
   ✓ Photograph: Full-size model of a Chinese treasure ship, available at https://en.wikipedia.org/wiki/Chinese_treasure_ship#/media/File:Nanjing_Treasure_Boat_-_P1070978.JPG
   ✓ Map: *Map of the Geographical Extension of the Ming Dynasty in China, 1400 CE*, available at http://www.nationsonline.org/oneworld/map/Chinese_dynasties/Ming_Dynasty_Map.htm

3. Computers/devices for research
4. Optional website for student research: "The Ming Voyages" by Asia for Educators, available at http://afe.easia.columbia.edu/special/china_1000ce_mingvoyages.htm

LESSON PLAN

Lesson Hook: Display the following quote on the board. Tell students that they will be learning about a famous adventurer and his journeys. Ask students to read the quote and to look for any clues about the person or the adventure he or she might have taken.

We have traversed more than one hundred thousand li [a Chinese unit of length] of immense water spaces and have beheld in the ocean huge waves like mountains rising sky-high. We have set eyes on barbarian regions far away hidden in a blue transparency of light vapours, while our sails, loftily unfurled like clouds, day and night continued their course with starry speed, breasting the savage waves as if we were treading a public thouroughfare. (Hvistendahl, 2008)

Note: Don't tell students about the source (a tablet by Zheng He) until after they give their ideas. Prompt them to explain what predictions they could make about Zheng He just from his quote.

The Organizing Question: Explain to students that they will examine some images and research to find more information about Zheng He and his adventures in order to answer the organizing question: *What were the purposes of Zheng He's voyages during the Ming era?*

Examine the Sources: *Gallery Walk*—Distribute Handout 15.1: Clue Sheet: Zheng He's Voyages During the Ming Era. Divide students into six groups and assign them to a station around the room to begin their gallery walk. Explain that they will work with their groups to analyze clues at each station and record what they notice on their clue sheet. Allow students 2–3 minutes at each clue and then have them return to their seats to write two hypothesis statements that answer the organizing question. Allow some groups to share their hypotheses and write them on the board.

Student Research and 5W Review (Who? What? When? Where? Why?)—Next tell students that they are going to do a mini-research task called "5W Review." Assign each of the groups one of the voyages of Zheng He. Share websites and resources with students to help focus their search. Explain that they should look for the basic 5W questions for their voyage:

- Who was involved?
- What was it?
- When did it happen?
- Where did the voyagers go?
- Why was it important?

Give students a few minutes to find the information and allow each group to share their answers. Prompt them to write down important facts on the back of their clue sheet and to listen for similarities among the voyages.

Make a Hypothesis: Once all groups have reported their 5W findings, ask students to look again at their initial hypothesis statements and see if they want to revise them now that they have gathered new information. Give them a few minutes to make revisions and share with the class. End the lesson by having students discuss the organizing question together, giving multiple examples of evidence from both the gallery walk clues and their research findings.

HANDOUT 15.1

CLUE SHEET: ZHENG HE'S VOYAGES DURING THE MING ERA

Directions: Examine the evidence or clues posted around the room. Write down what details you notice and what each clue might tell you about the organizing question. Your group will use this information to make hypotheses that answer this organizing question.

ORGANIZING QUESTION: What were the purposes of Zheng He's voyages during the Ming era?

	What details can you learn from this clue?	What does this clue tell you about the organizing question?
Clue #1 _____		
Clue #2 _____		
Clue #3 _____		
Clue #4 _____		
Clue #5 _____		
Clue #6 _____		

Based on the clues/evidence you examined, what are your hypotheses about the organizing question?

LESSON 2

ORGANIZING QUESTION

What happened when Columbus and the Taino first encountered each other?

STRATEGIES USED

Picture Prediction, Annotating Text

MATERIALS NEEDED

1. Painting: John Vanderlyn's *Landing of Columbus*, available at http://www.aoc.gov/capitol-hill/historic-rotunda-paintings/landing-columbus
2. Book: Jane Yolen's *Encounter* (teacher copy)
3. Student access to journal entries from Christopher Columbus's *Personal Narrative of the First Voyage of Columbus to America*, available at https://archive.org/details/personalnarrativ00colu
   ✓ Group 1: October 11 (pp. 34–37)
   ✓ Group 2: October 13 (pp. 37–39)
   ✓ Group 3: October 14 (pp. 39–41)
   ✓ Group 4: October 17 (pp. 48–51)

LESSON PLAN

Lesson Hook: *Picture Prediction*—Show *Landing of Columbus* from the U.S. Capitol Rotunda to the class. Ask students to examine the painting and respond to these two questions:

- What details do you notice in the painting?
- What might this visual predict about encounters between Columbus and the Taino?

Prompt students to explain their predictions with details and evidence from the painting. Make a list of these predictions on the board.

Then, read *Encounter* by Jane Yolen to the class, showing the visuals in the book while reading. As students are listening, ask them to think about how this perspective compares/contrasts with the painting and share their thoughts.

The Organizing Question: Explain that students will read the journals of Columbus for clues to answer the organizing question: *What happened when Columbus and the Taino first encountered each other?*

Examine the Sources: *Annotating Text*—Explain that students will examine translations of Columbus's journals from his first voyage to the Americas. Before they begin reading, display a map of the voyage, explain the story of Ferdinand and Isabella, and tell students that Columbus referred to himself as "The Admiral" in these entries. Divide the class into four groups and instruct them to read a single day's entry from the journal (as described in the Materials Needed section).

As students read their assigned journal entry, have them look for and write down examples of events that occurred in these first encounters between Columbus and the native people.

Make a Hypothesis: Using details from the journal entries, have each group write a hypothesis that answers the organizing question and share the hypothesis and evidence with the class. Encourage students to compare and contrast the events in Columbus's journals with the predictions they made from the *Landing of Columbus* painting and the Taino perspective described in *Encounter*.

LESSON 3

ORGANIZING QUESTION

How did the Columbian Exchange affect both the "Old" and "New" Worlds?

Note: This organizing question has been provided as a sample, but with the Question Formulation Technique (QFT; Rothstein & Santana, 2011), students will generate their own questions that will guide the lesson. If the QFT strategy is new to you, visit the Right Question Institute's website (http://rightquestion. org) for more details, sample lessons, and resources.

STRATEGIES USED

Question Formulation Technique, Student Research

MATERIALS NEEDED

1. Handout 5.1: Question Formulation Technique (QFT)
2. Painting: Diego Rivera's *Colonial Domination*, available at https://www. granger.com/results.asp?image=0007706
3. World history textbooks or computers/devices for research
4. Optional secondary sources:
   ✓ Johann Grolle and Spiegel's "'The Columbian Exchange': How Discovering the Americas Transform the World," available at https://abcnews.go.com/International/columbian-exchange-discovering-americas-transformed-world/story?id=20321543
   ✓ "The Effects of the Columbian Exchange," available at https://aptv. pbslearningmedia.org/resource/midlit11.soc.wh.columbianex/ the-effects-of-the-columbian-exchange

LESSON PLAN

Lesson Hook: *Question Formulation Technique*—Introduce students to the Question Focus (QFocus) for this Question Formulation Technique lesson (Rothstein & Santana, 2011). A QFocus is any type of prompt or stimulus used to encourage students to generate questions. For this lesson, show Diego Rivera's *Colonial Domination* on a screen and have students analyze with a partner. Remind students of the rules for producing questions (see Handout 5.1). Display the painting and give students 1–2 minutes to write down as many questions as possible in their notes.

The Organizing Question: Once students have generated questions for the painting, explain that they are going to work together to categorize and prioritize their questions with groups, choose their best questions, and examine sources for answers to their questions.

Examine the Sources: Before students examine sources for information on the Columbian Exchange, have them complete the QFT process. Divide the class into groups of 3–4 students for the rest of the lesson.

- *Improving the questions*: Ask students to spend a few minutes sharing their own questions with others in their group. They should then label the questions as closed (C) or open (O), discuss the advantages and disadvantages of each type of question, and practice changing some questions from one type to another.
- *Prioritizing questions*: Ask students to come to a consensus in their groups on the three most important questions and write them on a sheet of paper in order to focus the research.
- *Next steps/student research*: Ask groups to develop a plan for how they will answer the questions and what sources they might use. Allow groups time to use textbooks, computers, or another resource to research answers to their own important questions. When students are finished finding text-based answers to their questions, allow groups to share their questions and the answers they found with the whole class. Ask students to write down any questions and answers that were different from their group's so they learn more information about the effects of the Columbian Exchange.

Make a Hypothesis: After all groups have shared their questions and answers, ask students to write a response to the organizing question for this lesson (or you may choose one of the student-generated questions). Ask them to cite evidence in their answer from their own research and the findings of other groups. You may choose to end this lesson with a discussion that returns to Rivera's *Colonial Domination* instead of having students write their responses to the organizing question.

LESSON 4

ORGANIZING QUESTION

How did slaves experience the Middle Passage to the Americas?

STRATEGIES USED

Freewriting, Gallery Walk, Partner Read, Annotating Text

MATERIALS NEEDED

1. Handout 15.2: Excerpts From Olaudah Equiano's *The Interesting Narrative of the Life of Olaudah Equiano, or Gustavus Vassa, the African Written by Himself* (1789)
2. Handout 15.3: Excerpts From Alexander Falconbridge's *Account of the Slave Trade From the Coast of Africa* (1792)
3. The following images displayed at stations around the room with a sheet of chart paper beside each image:
   ✓ Sketch: *Captive Africans Taken to Slave Ship, Nigeria, 1850s,* available at http://www.slaveryimages.org/s/slaveryimages/item/2059
   ✓ Painting: Pretexat Oursel's *Top Deck of French Slave Ship,* available at http://www.slaveryimages.org/s/slaveryimages/item/2549
   ✓ Sketch: Richard Drake's *Scene in the Hold of the "Blood-Stained Gloria"—Middle Passage,* available at http://www.slaveryimages.org/s/slaveryimages/item/2555
   ✓ Painting: Francis Meynell's *Hold of Brazilian Slave Ship,* available at http://www.slaveryimages.org/s/slaveryimages/item/3003
   ✓ Sketch: *Stowage of the British Slave Ship Brookes Under the Regulated Slave Trade,* available at http://www.slaveryimages.org/s/slaveryimages/item/2553

4. Highlighters (one per student)

LESSON PLAN

Lesson Hook: *Freewriting*—Because this lesson contains difficult content for students, allow them a few minutes to freewrite in their notes about what they remember about slavery from previous classes and what questions they wonder about based on their background knowledge.

The Organizing Question: Explain that students will examine several images and read two first-person accounts for clues to answer the organizing question: *How did slaves experience the Middle Passage to the Americas?*

Examine the Sources: *Gallery Walk*—Begin this part of the lesson by explaining the Middle Passage and showing the routes on a map. Tell students that they will participate in a gallery walk and examine images to predict some details about what life was like for slaves during the Middle Passage. Have students choose a partner. Assign the pairs to a station to start the gallery walk. Their task is to examine the image first, then write on the chart paper what they notice and what they think it tells them about the Middle Passage. Have students rotate clockwise, adding their comments and responding to others' written ideas. When they have returned to the image where they started, have them read all of the responses and report to the class what they think the image tells them. As a class, make a list of what questions they have about the images in the gallery walk.

Partner Read and Annotating Text—Explain to students they will examine two first-person accounts of the Middle Passage from a slave and a doctor. Divide the class in half and give one half Equiano's text (Handout 15.2) and the other half Falconbridge's text (Handout 15.3). Allow students to partner with someone who has the same text. As they are reading, have them look for answers to the questions charted on the board and the lesson's organizing question. As they find clues to any of these questions, have them highlight them in the text. Encourage them to read one section at a time, stop and discuss it, and then write main ideas or questions they have in the margins beside that section. As partner groups finish reading and analyzing their text, have them find two people who read the other text and form a group of four. Their task is to explain their sources and to share the main ideas and clues they located.

Make a Hypothesis: After students share both texts, have them work as a group to create a hypothesis that answers the organizing question. Require them to use both first-person accounts and the images in the gallery walk as evidence to support their hypothesis. Allow groups to share hypotheses with the class and evaluate how well other groups use evidence as support.

HANDOUT 15.2

EXCERPTS FROM OLAUDAH EQUIANO'S

THE INTERESTING NARRATIVE OF THE LIFE OF OLAUDAH EQUIANO, OR GUSTAVUS VASSA, THE AFRICAN WRITTEN BY HIMSELF (1789)

The first object which saluted my eyes when I arrived on the coast was the sea, and a slave ship, which was then riding at anchor, and waiting for its cargo. These filled me with astonishment, which was soon converted into terror when I was carried on board. I was immediately handled and tossed up to see if I were sound by some of the crew; and I was now persuaded that I had gotten into a world of bad spirits, and that they were going to kill me. Their complexions too differing so much from ours, their long hair, and the language they spoke, (which was very different from any I had ever heard) united to confirm me in this belief. Indeed such were the horrors of my views and fears at the moment, that, if ten thousand worlds had been my own, I would have freely parted with them all to have exchanged my condition with that of the meanest slave in my own country.

When I looked round the ship too and saw a large furnace or copper boiling, and a multitude of black people of every description chained together, every one of their countenances expressing dejection and sorrow, I no longer doubted of my fate; and, quite overpowered with horror and anguish, I fell motionless on the deck and fainted. When I recovered a little I found some black people about me, who I believed were some of those who brought me on board, and had been receiving their pay; they talked to me in order to cheer me, but all in vain. I asked them if we were not to be eaten by those white men with horrible looks, red faces, and loose hair. They told me I was not; and one of the crew brought me a small portion of spirituous liquor in a wine glass; but, being afraid of him, I would not take it out of his hand. One of the blacks therefore took it from him and gave it to me, and I took a little down my palate, which, instead of reviving me, as they thought it would, threw me into the greatest consternation at the strange feeling it produced, having never tasted any such liquor before.

Soon after this the blacks who brought me on board went off, and left me abandoned to despair. I now saw myself deprived of all chance of returning to my native country, or even the least glimpse of hope of gaining the shore, which I now considered as friendly; and I even wished for my former slavery in preference to my present situation, which was filled with horrors of every kind, still heightened by my ignorance of what I was to undergo. I was not long suffered to indulge my grief; I was soon put down under the decks, and there I received such a salutation in my nostrils as I had never experienced in my life: so that, with the loathsomeness of the stench, and crying together, I became so sick and low that I was not able to eat, nor had I the least desire to taste any thing. I now wished for the last friend, death, to relieve me; but soon, to my grief, two of the white men offered me eatables; and, on my refusing to eat, one of them held me fast by the hands, and laid me across I think the windlass, and tied my feet, while the other flogged me severely. I had never experienced any thing of this kind before; and although, not being used to the water, I naturally feared that element the first time I saw it, yet nevertheless, could I have got over the nettings, I would have jumped over the side, but I could not; and, besides, the crew used to watch us very closely who were not chained down to the decks, lest we

HANDOUT 15.2, CONTINUED

should leap into the water: and I have seen some of these poor African prisoners most severely cut for attempting to do so, and hourly whipped for not eating. This indeed was often the case with myself.

In a little time after, amongst the poor chained men, I found some of my own nation, which in a small degree gave ease to my mind. I inquired of these what was to be done with us; they gave me to understand we were to be carried to these white people's country to work for them. I then was a little revived, and thought, if it were no worse than working, my situation was not so desperate: but still I feared I should be put to death, the white people looked and acted, as I thought, in so savage a manner; for I had never seen among any people such instances of brutal cruelty; and this not only shewn towards us blacks, but also to some of the whites themselves. One white man in particular I saw, when we were permitted to be on deck, flogged so unmercifully with a large rope near the foremast, that he died in consequence of it; and they tossed him over the side as they would have done a brute.

This made me fear these people the more; and I expected nothing less than to be treated in the same manner. I could not help expressing my fears and apprehensions to some of my countrymen: I asked them if these people had no country, but lived in this hollow place (the ship): they told me they did not, but came from a distant one The stench of the hold while we were on the coast was so intolerably loathsome, that it was dangerous to remain there for any time, and some of us had been permitted to stay on the deck for the fresh air; but now that the whole ship's cargo were confined together, it became absolutely pestilential. The closeness of the place, and the heat of the climate, added to the number in the ship, which was so crowded that each had scarcely room to turn himself, almost suffocated us. This produced copious perspirations, so that the air soon became unfit for respiration, from a variety of loathsome smells, and brought on a sickness among the slaves, of which many died, thus falling victims to the improvident avarice, as I may call it, of their purchasers.

This wretched situation was again aggravated by the galling of the chains, now become insupportable; and the filth of the necessary tubs, into which the children often fell, and were almost suffocated. The shrieks of the women, and the groans of the dying, rendered the whole a scene of horror almost inconceivable. One day they had taken a number of fishes; and when they had killed and satisfied themselves with as many as they thought fit, to our astonishment who were on the deck, rather than give any of them to us to eat as we expected, they tossed the remaining fish into the sea again, although we begged and prayed for some as well as we could, but in vain; and some of my countrymen, being pressed by hunger, took an opportunity, when they thought no one saw them, of trying to get a little privately; but they were discovered, and the attempt procured them some very severe floggings.

One day, when we had a smooth sea and moderate wind, two of my wearied countrymen who were chained together (I was near them at the time), preferring death to such a life of misery, somehow made through the nettings and jumped into the sea: immediately another quite dejected fellow, who, on account of his illness, was suffered to be out of irons, also followed their example; and I believe many more would very soon have done the same if they had not been prevented by the ship's crew, who were instantly alarmed. Those of us that were the most active were in a moment put down under the deck, and there was such a noise and confusion amongst the people of the ship as I never heard before, to stop her, and get the boat out to go after the slaves. However two of the wretches were drowned, but they got the other, and afterwards flogged him unmercifully for thus attempting to prefer death to slavery. In this manner we continued to undergo more hardships than I can now relate, hardships which are inseparable from this accursed trade. Many a time we were near suffocation from the want of fresh air, which we were often without for whole days together. This, and the stench of the necessary tubs, carried off many.

At last we came in sight of the island of Barbadoes, at which the whites on board gave a great shout, and made many signs of joy to us. We did not know what to think of this; but as the vessel drew nearer we plainly saw the harbour, and other ships of different kinds and sizes; and we soon anchored amongst them off Bridge Town. Many merchants and planters now came on board, though it was in the evening. They put us in separate parcels, and examined us attentively. They also made us jump, and pointed to the land, signifying we were to go there. We thought by this we should be eaten by these ugly men, as they appeared to us; and, when soon after we were all put down under the deck again, there was much dread and trembling among us, and nothing but bitter cries to be heard all the night from these apprehensions, insomuch that at last the white people got some old slaves from the land to pacify us. They told us we were not to be eaten, but to work, and were soon to go on land, where we should see many of our country people. This report eased us much; and sure enough, soon after we were landed, there came to us Africans of all languages.

We were conducted immediately to the merchant's yard, where we were all pent up together like so many sheep in a fold, without regard to sex or age. As every object was new to me every thing I saw filled me with surprise. What struck me first was that the houses were built with stories, and in every other respect different from those in Africa: but I was still more astonished on seeing people on horseback. We were not many days in the merchant's custody before we were sold after their usual manner, which is this:—On a signal given,(as the beat of a drum) the buyers rush at once into the yard where the slaves are confined, and make choice of that parcel they like best. The noise and clamour with which this is attended, and the eagerness visible in the countenances of the buyers, serve not a little to increase the apprehensions of the terrified Africans, who may well be supposed to consider them as the ministers of that destruction to which they think themselves devoted. In this manner, without scruple, are relations and friends separated, most of them never to see each other again.

HANDOUT 15.3

EXCERPTS FROM ALEXANDER FALCONBRIDGE'S
ACCOUNT OF THE SLAVE TRADE FROM THE COAST OF AFRICA (1792)

About eight o'clock in the morning the negroes are generally brought upon deck. Their irons being examined, a long chain, which is locked to a ring-bolt, fixed in the deck, is run through the rings of the shackles of the men, and then locked to another ring-bolt, fixed also in the deck. By this means fifty or sixty, and sometimes more, are fastened to one chain, in order to prevent them from rising, or endeavoring to escape. If the weather proves favorable, they are permitted to remain in that situation till four or five in the afternoon, when they are disengaged from the chain, and sent down.

The diet of the negroes, while on board, consists chiefly of horse-beans, boiled to the consistency of a pulp, of boiled yams and rice, and sometimes of a small quantity of beef or pork. The latter are frequently taken from the provisions laid in for the jailers. They sometimes make use of a sauce, composed of palm-oil, mixed with flour, water, and pepper, which the jailers call slabber-sauce. Yams are the favorite food of the Ebo, or Bight negroes, and rice or corn, of those from the Gold and Windward Coasts each preferring the produce of their native soil. . . .

They are commonly fed twice a day, about eight o'clock in the morning and four in the afternoon. In most ships they are only fed with their own food once a day. Their food is served up to them in tubs, about the size of a small water bucket. They are placed round these tubs in companies of ten to each tub, out of which they feed themselves with wooden spoons. . . .

Upon the negroes refusing to take sustenance, I have seen coals of fire, glowing hot, put on a shovel, and placed so near their lips, as to scorch and burn them. And this has been accompanied with threats, of forcing them to swallow the coals, if they any longer persisted in refusing to eat. These means have generally had the desired effect. I have also been credibly informed, that a certain captain in the slave trade, poured melted lead on such of the negroes as obstinately refused their food. . . .

The hardships and inconveniencies suffered by the negroes during the passage, are scarcely to be enumerated or conceived. They are far more violently affected by the sea-sickness, than the Europeans. It frequently terminates in death, especially among the women. But the exclusion of the fresh air is among the most intolerable. For the purpose of admitting this needful refreshment, most of the ships in the slave-trade are provided, between the decks, with five or six airports. On each side of the ship, of about six inches in length, and four in breadth in addition to which, some few ships, but not one in twenty, have what they denominate windsails. But whenever the sea is rough, and the rain heavy, it becomes necessary to shut these, and every other conveyance by which the air is admitted. The fresh air being thus excluded, the negroes rooms very soon grow intolerably hot. The confined air, rendered noxious by the effluvia exhaled from their bodies, and by being repeatedly breathed, soon produces fevers and fluxes, which generally carries off great numbers of them.

REFERENCES

Blasi, D. E., Moran, S., Moisik, S. R., Widmer, P., Dediu, D., & Bickel, B. (2019). Human sound systems are shaped by post-Neolithic changes in bite configuration. *Science, 363*(6432). doi: 10.1126/science.aav3218

Gerwin, D., & Zevin, J. (2011). *Teaching U.S. history as mystery* (2nd ed.). New York, NY: Routledge.

Herczog, M. (2013). The college, career, and civic life (C3) framework for social studies: A watershed moment for social studies. In *Social studies for the next generation: Purposes, practices, and implications of the College, Career, and Civic life (C3) Framework for Social Studies State Standards* (pp. vii–x). Silver Spring, MD: National Council for the Social Studies.

Hvistendahl, M. (2008). Rebuilding a treasure ship. *Archaeology Archive.* Retrieved from https://archive.archaeology.org/0803/abstracts/zhenghe.html

Kirchner, J., & McMichael, A. (2015). *Inquiry-based lessons in U.S. history: Decoding the past.* Waco, TX: Prufrock Press.

National Center for History in the Schools. (1996). *World history content standards for Grades 5–12.* Retrieved from https://phi.history.ucla.edu/nchs/world-history-content-standards

National Council for the Social Studies. (2013). *The College, Career, and Civic Life (C3) Framework for Social Studies State Standards: Guidance for enhancing the rigor of K–12 civics, economics, geography, and history.* Silver Spring, MD: Author.

National Governors Association Center for Best Practices, & Council of Chief State School Officers. (2010). *Common Core State Standards for English Language Arts*. Washington, DC: Author.

Roberts, J. L., & Inman, T. F. (2015). *Strategies for differentiating instruction: Best practices in the classroom* (3rd ed.). Waco, TX: Prufrock Press.

Rothstein, D., & Santana, L. (2011). *Make just one change: Teach students to ask their own questions*. Cambridge, MA: Harvard Education Press.

TimeMaps. (n.d.). *The coming of farming*. Retrieved from https://www.timemaps.com/encyclopedia/farming

Wineburg, S., Martin, D., & Monte-Sano, C. (2013). *Reading like a historian: Teaching literacy in middle and high school history classrooms*. New York, NY: Teachers College Press.

STUDENT HANDOUT RESOURCES

Handout 2.1: Excerpts From "Hymn to the Nile" (ca. 2100 BCE), retrieved from https://en.wikisource.org/wiki/Hymn_to_the_Nile. Used under Creative Commons BY-SA 3.0, https://creativecommons.org/licenses/by-sa/3.0.

Handout 2.2: Excerpts From the Flood Story in *The Epic of Gilgamesh* (ca. 2000 BCE), retrieved from https://en.wikisource.org/wiki/Epic_of_Gilgamesh/William_Muss-Arnolt/Tablet_XI. Used under Creative Commons BY-SA 3.0, https://creativecommons.org/licenses/by-sa/3.0.

Handout 4.1: Excerpts From Book 10 of the *Rigveda* About Puruṣa (ca. > 1100 BCE), retrieved from http://www.sacred-texts.com/hin/rigveda/rv10090.htm. In the public domain.

Handout 4.2: Excerpts From the *Sutta Pitaka* (ca. 400 BCE), retrieved from https://www.accesstoinsight.org/tipitaka/kn/dhp/index.html. Used under Creative Commons BY 4.0, https://creativecommons.org/licenses/by/4.0

Handout 6.1: Excerpts From the Rosetta Stone Decree (196 BCE), retrieved from http://www.reshafim.org.il/ad/egypt/texts/rosettastone.htm. In the public domain.

Handout 6.2: Excerpts From Herodotus's *The Histories* (ca. 440 BCE), retrieved from https://en.wikisource.org/wiki/Herodotus_The_Persian_Wars_%z28Godley%29/Book_III. Used under Creative Commons BY-SA 3.0, https://creativecommons.org/licenses/by-sa/3.0.

Handout 6.3: Excerpts From Pericles's "Funeral Oration" (ca. 400 BCE), retrieved from https://en.wikisource.org/wiki/Pericles%27s_Funeral_Oration_%28Jowett%29. In the public domain.

Handout 7.1: Excerpts From Confucius's *Analects* (ca. 500 BCE), retrieved from https://en.wikisource.org/wiki/Confucian_Analects. In the public domain.

Handout 7.2: Excerpts From the Code of Hammurabi (ca. 1754 BCE), retrieved from http://www.gutenberg.org/ebooks/17150. In the public domain. (*Note*: This eBook is for the use of anyone anywhere at no cost and with almost no restrictions whatsoever. You may copy it, give it away or reuse it under the terms of the Project Gutenberg License included with this eBook or online at www.gutenberg.net.)

Handout 8.1: Excerpts From *The Roman History of Ammianus Marcellinus* (ca. 380), retrieved from http://penelope.uchicago.edu/Thayer/E/Roman/Texts/Ammian/31%2A.html. In the public domain.

Handout 8.2: Priscus at the Court of Attila (ca. 448), retrieved from http://faculty.georgetown.edu/jod/texts/priscus.html. In the public domain.

Handout 9.2: Excerpts From Einhard's *Life of Charlemagne* (ca. 830), retrieved from https://archive.org/details/LifeOfCharlemagne1880/page/n6. In the public domain.

Handout 11.3: Excerpts From *The Travels of Marco Polo* (ca. 1290s), retrieved from https://archive.org/details/marcopolo00polouoft/page/n8. In the public domain.

Handout 12.2: Excerpts From Inazo Nitobe's *Bushido: The Soul of Japan* (1908), retrieved from http://www.gutenberg.org/files/12096. In the public domain. (*Note*: This eBook is for the use of anyone anywhere at no cost and with almost no restrictions whatsoever. You may copy it, give it away or reuse it under the terms of the Project Gutenberg License included with this eBook or online at www.gutenberg.net.)

Handout 13.1: Excerpts From Raymond d'Aguilers's *A History of the Franks, Who Have Taken Jerusalem* (ca. 1100), retrieved from http://www.bu.edu/mzank/Jerusalem/tx/Raymondvictory.htm. In the public domain.

Handout 13.2: Excerpts From Ibn Al-Athir's "The Seizure of Jerusalem" (ca. 1200), retrieved from https://archive.org/stream/IbnAlAthirInCicilianMuslims/The%20Seizure%20of%20Jerusalem%20As%20Told%20By%20Ibn%20Al%20Athir_djvu.txt. In the public domain.

Handout 13.3: Excerpts From the Magna Carta (1215), retrieved from https://en.wikisource.org/wiki/Magna_Carta_(trans._Davis). In the public domain.

Handout 13.4: Excerpts From Giovanni Boccaccio's *Decameron* (ca. 1353), retrieved from http://www.gutenberg.org/ebooks/3726. In the public domain. (*Note*: This eBook is for the use of anyone anywhere at no cost and with almost no restrictions whatsoever. You may copy it, give it away or reuse it under the terms of the Project Gutenberg License included with this eBook or online at www.gutenberg.net.)

Handout 14.3: Excerpts From Gabriel Archer's "A Brief Description of the People" (1607), available in E. W. Haile (Ed.), *Jamestown narratives: Eyewitness accounts of the Virginia Colony, the first decade:* 1607–1617 (pp. 122–124). Champlain, VA: Round House. In the public domain.

Handout 15.2: Excerpts From Olaudah Equiano's *The Interesting Narrative of the Life of Olaudah Equiano, or Gustavus Vassa, the African Written by Himself* (1789), retrieved from http://www.gutenberg.org/files/15399. In the public domain. (*Note*: This eBook is for the use of anyone anywhere at no cost and with almost no restrictions whatsoever. You may copy it, give it away or reuse it under the terms of the Project Gutenberg License included with this eBook or online at www.gutenberg.net.)

Handout 15.3: Excerpts From Alexander Falconbridge's *Account of the Slave Trade From the Coast of Africa* (1792), retrieved from https://archive.org/details/accountofslavetr00falc/page/n1. In the public domain.

ABOUT THE AUTHORS

Jana Kirchner, Ph.D., is an educator with 29 years of experience. She has served as a school district instructional supervisor, an assistant professor at Western Kentucky University, a social studies consultant, and a high school social studies and English teacher. She earned her Ph.D. in educational leadership from the University of Louisville. Kirchner coauthored *Inquiry-Based Lessons in U.S. History: Decoding the Past* with Andrew McMichael and *Parenting Gifted Children 101* with Tracy Inman. She provides professional development on social studies strategies, inquiry, and gifted topics with JK Consulting (http://janakirchner.com).

Andrew McMichael, Ph.D., is the dean of the College of Liberal Arts and Social Sciences and a professor of history at Auburn University at Montgomery. Prior to earning his Ph.D. in American History from Vanderbilt University in 2000, he taught high school and gained teaching experience in kindergarten, third-grade, and fifth-grade classrooms. In the past 15 years, McMichael has visited dozens of elementary school classrooms, assisting teachers with content-based lessons.

COMMON CORE STATE STANDARDS ALIGNMENT

Chapter	Common Core State Standards
Chapter 1	CCSS.ELA-Literacy.RH.6-8.2: Determine the central ideas or information of a primary or secondary source. CCSS.ELA-Literacy.RH.6-8.7: Integrate visual information (e.g., in charts, graphs, photographs, videos, or maps) with other information in print and digital texts. CCSS.ELA-Literacy.RH.9-10.1: Cite specific textual evidence to support analysis of primary and secondary sources, attending to such features as the date and origin of the information. CCSS.ELA-Literacy.RH.9-10.2: Determine the central ideas or information of a primary or secondary source. CCSS.ELA-Literacy.RH.9-10.3: Analyze in detail a series of events described in a text; determine whether earlier events caused later ones or simply preceded them.
Chapter 2	CCSS.ELA-Literacy.RH.6-8.2: Determine the central ideas or information of a primary or secondary source. CCSS.ELA-Literacy.RH.6-8.7: Integrate visual information (e.g., in charts, graphs, photographs, videos, or maps) with other information in print and digital texts. CCSS.ELA-Literacy.RH.9-10.1: Cite specific textual evidence to support analysis of primary and secondary sources, attending to such features as the date and origin of the information. CCSS.ELA-Literacy.RH.9-10.2: Determine the central ideas or information of a primary or secondary source.

Chapter	Common Core State Standards
Chapter 3	CCSS.ELA-Literacy.RH.6-8.2: Determine the central ideas or information of a primary or secondary source. CCSS.ELA-Literacy.RH.6-8.7: Integrate visual information (e.g., in charts, graphs, photographs, videos, or maps) with other information in print and digital texts. CCSS.ELA-Literacy.RH.9-10.1: Cite specific textual evidence to support analysis of primary and secondary sources, attending to such features as the date and origin of the information. CCSS.ELA-Literacy.RH.9-10.2: Determine the central ideas or information of a primary or secondary source.
Chapter 4	CCSS.ELA-Literacy.RH.6-8.1: Cite specific textual evidence to support analysis of primary and secondary sources. CCSS.ELA-Literacy.RH.6-8.2: Determine the central ideas or information of a primary or secondary source. CCSS.ELA-Literacy.RH.6-8.9: Analyze the relationship between a primary and secondary source on the same topic. CCSS.ELA-Literacy.RH.9-10.1: Cite specific textual evidence to support analysis of primary and secondary sources, attending to such features as the date and origin of the information. CCSS.ELA-Literacy.RH.9-10.2: Determine the central ideas or information of a primary or secondary source. CCSS.ELA-Literacy.RH.9-10.9: Compare and contrast treatments of the same topic in several primary and secondary sources.
Chapter 5	CCSS.ELA-Literacy.RH.6-8.1: Cite specific textual evidence to support analysis of primary and secondary sources. CCSS.ELA-Literacy.RH.6-8.2: Determine the central ideas or information of a primary or secondary source. CCSS.ELA-Literacy.RH.6-8.7: Integrate visual information (e.g., in charts, graphs, photographs, videos, or maps) with other information in print and digital texts. CCSS.ELA-Literacy.W.6.7: Conduct short research projects to answer a question, drawing on several sources and refocusing the inquiry when appropriate. CCSS.ELA-Literacy.W.6.9: Draw evidence from literary or informational texts to support analysis, reflection, and research. CCSS.ELA-Literacy.RH.9-10.1: Cite specific textual evidence to support analysis of primary and secondary sources, attending to such features as the date and origin of the information. CCSS.ELA-Literacy.RH.9-10.2: Determine the central ideas or information of a primary or secondary source.

Chapter	Common Core State Standards
Chapter 5, continued	CCSS.ELA-Literacy.W.9-10.7: Conduct short as well as more sustained research projects to answer a question (including a self-generated question) or solve a problem; narrow or broaden the inquiry when appropriate. CCSS.ELA-Literacy.W.9-10.9: Draw evidence from literary or informational texts to support analysis, reflection, and research.
Chapter 6	CCSS.ELA-Literacy.RH.6-8.1: Cite specific textual evidence to support analysis of primary and secondary sources. CCSS.ELA-Literacy.RH.6-8.2: Determine the central ideas or information of a primary or secondary source. CCSS.ELA-Literacy.RH.6-8.4: Determine the meaning of words and phrases as they are used in a text, including vocabulary specific to domains related to history/social studies. CCSS.ELA-Literacy.RH.6-8.6: Identify aspects of a text that reveal an author's point of view or purpose. CCSS.ELA-Literacy.RH.9-10.1: Cite specific textual evidence to support analysis of primary and secondary sources, attending to such features as the date and origin of the information. CCSS.ELA-Literacy.RH.9-10.2: Determine the central ideas or information of a primary or secondary source CCSS.ELA-Literacy.RH.9-10.4: Determine the meaning of words and phrases as they are used in a text, including vocabulary describing political, social, or economic aspects of history/social science. CCSS.ELA-Literacy.RH.9-10.6: Compare the point of view of two or more authors for how they treat the same or similar topics, including which details they include and emphasize in their respective accounts.
Chapter 7	CCSS.ELA-Literacy.RH.6-8.1: Cite specific textual evidence to support analysis of primary and secondary sources. CCSS.ELA-Literacy.RH.6-8.2: Determine the central ideas or information of a primary or secondary source. CCSS.ELA-Literacy.RH.6-8.7: Integrate visual information (e.g., in charts, graphs, photographs, videos, or maps) with other information in print and digital texts. CCSS.ELA-Literacy.W.6.7: Conduct short research projects to answer a question, drawing on several sources and refocusing the inquiry when appropriate. CCSS.ELA-Literacy.W.6.9: Draw evidence from literary or informational texts to support analysis, reflection, and research. CCSS.ELA-Literacy.RH.9-10.1: Cite specific textual evidence to support analysis of primary and secondary sources, attending to such features as the date and origin of the information.

Chapter	Common Core State Standards
Chapter 7, continued	CCSS.ELA-Literacy.RH.9-10.2: Determine the central ideas or information of a primary or secondary source, attending to such features as the date and origin of information. CCSS.ELA-Literacy.W.9-10.7: Conduct short as well as more sustained research projects to answer a question (including a self-generated question) or solve a problem; narrow or broaden the inquiry when appropriate. CCSS.ELA-Literacy.W.9-10.9: Draw evidence from literary or informational texts to support analysis, reflection, and research.
Chapter 8	CCSS.ELA-Literacy.RH.6-8.1: Cite specific textual evidence to support analysis of primary and secondary sources. CCSS.ELA-Literacy.RH.6-8.2: Determine the central ideas or information of a primary or secondary source. CCSS.ELA-Literacy.RH.6-8.7: Integrate visual information (e.g., in charts, graphs, photographs, videos, or maps) with other information in print and digital texts. CCSS.ELA-Literacy.W.6.7: Conduct short research projects to answer a question, drawing on several sources and refocusing the inquiry when appropriate. CCSS.ELA-Literacy.W.6.9: Draw evidence from literary or informational texts to support analysis, reflection, and research. CCSS.ELA-Literacy.RH.9-10.1: Cite specific textual evidence to support analysis of primary and secondary sources, attending to such features as the date and origin of the information. CCSS.ELA-Literacy.RH.9-10.2: Determine the central ideas or information of a primary or secondary source, attending to such features as the date and origin of information. CCSS.ELA-Literacy.W.9-10.7: Conduct short as well as more sustained research projects to answer a question (including a self-generated question) or solve a problem; narrow or broaden the inquiry when appropriate. CCSS.ELA-Literacy.W.9-10.9: Draw evidence from literary or informational texts to support analysis, reflection, and research.
Chapter 9	CCSS.ELA-Literacy.RH.6-8.1: Cite specific textual evidence to support analysis of primary and secondary sources. CCSS.ELA-Literacy.RH.6-8.2: Determine the central ideas or information of a primary or secondary source. CCSS.ELA-Literacy.RH.6-8.7: Integrate visual information (e.g., in charts, graphs, photographs, videos, or maps) with other information in print and digital texts. CCSS.ELA-Literacy.W.6.7: Conduct short research projects to answer a question, drawing on several sources and refocusing the inquiry when appropriate.

Chapter	Common Core State Standards
Chapter 9, continued	CCSS.ELA-Literacy.W.6.9: Draw evidence from literary or informational texts to support analysis, reflection, and research. CCSS.ELA-Literacy.RH.9-10.1: Cite specific textual evidence to support analysis of primary and secondary sources, attending to such features as the date and origin of the information. CCSS.ELA-Literacy.RH.9-10.2: Determine the central ideas or information of a primary or secondary source, attending to such features as the date and origin of information. CCSS.ELA-Literacy.W.9-10.7: Conduct short as well as more sustained research projects to answer a question (including a self-generated question) or solve a problem; narrow or broaden the inquiry when appropriate. CCSS.ELA-Literacy.W.9-10.9: Draw evidence from literary or informational texts to support analysis, reflection, and research.
Chapter 10	CCSS.ELA-Literacy.RH.6-8.1: Cite specific textual evidence to support analysis of primary and secondary sources. CCSS.ELA-Literacy.RH.6-8.2: Determine the central ideas or information of a primary or secondary source. CCSS.ELA-Literacy.RH.6-8.7: Integrate visual information (e.g., in charts, graphs, photographs, videos, or maps) with other information in print and digital texts. CCSS.ELA-Literacy.RH.9-10.1: Cite specific textual evidence to support analysis of primary and secondary sources, attending to such features as the date and origin of the information. CCSS.ELA-Literacy.RH.9-10.2: Determine the central ideas or information of a primary or secondary source, attending to such features as the date and origin of information.
Chapter 11	CCSS.ELA-Literacy.RH.6-8.1: Cite specific textual evidence to support analysis of primary and secondary sources. CCSS.ELA-Literacy.RH.6-8.2: Determine the central ideas or information of a primary or secondary source. CCSS.ELA-Literacy.RH.6-8.7: Integrate visual information (e.g., in charts, graphs, photographs, videos, or maps) with other information in print and digital texts. CCSS.ELA-Literacy.W.6.7: Conduct short research projects to answer a question, drawing on several sources and refocusing the inquiry when appropriate. CCSS.ELA-Literacy.W.6.9: Draw evidence from literary or informational texts to support analysis, reflection, and research. CCSS.ELA-Literacy.RH.9-10.1: Cite specific textual evidence to support analysis of primary and secondary sources, attending to such features as the date and origin of the information.

Chapter	Common Core State Standards
Chapter 11, continued	CCSS.ELA-Literacy.RH.9-10.2: Determine the central ideas or information of a primary or secondary source, attending to such features as the date and origin of information. CCSS.ELA-Literacy.W.9-10.7: Conduct short as well as more sustained research projects to answer a question (including a self-generated question) or solve a problem; narrow or broaden the inquiry when appropriate. CCSS.ELA-Literacy.W.9-10.9: Draw evidence from literary or informational texts to support analysis, reflection, and research.
Chapter 12	CCSS.ELA-Literacy.RH.6-8.1: Cite specific textual evidence to support analysis of primary and secondary sources. CCSS.ELA-Literacy.RH.6-8.2: Determine the central ideas or information of a primary or secondary source. CCSS.ELA-Literacy.RH.6-8.7: Integrate visual information (e.g., in charts, graphs, photographs, videos, or maps) with other information in print and digital texts. CCSS.ELA-Literacy.W.6.7: Conduct short research projects to answer a question, drawing on several sources and refocusing the inquiry when appropriate. CCSS.ELA-Literacy.W.6.9: Draw evidence from literary or informational texts to support analysis, reflection, and research. CCSS.ELA-Literacy.RH.9-10.1: Cite specific textual evidence to support analysis of primary and secondary sources, attending to such features as the date and origin of the information. CCSS.ELA-Literacy.RH.9-10.2: Determine the central ideas or information of a primary or secondary source, attending to such features as the date and origin of information. CCSS.ELA-Literacy.W.9-10.7: Conduct short as well as more sustained research projects to answer a question (including a self-generated question) or solve a problem; narrow or broaden the inquiry when appropriate. CCSS.ELA-Literacy.W.9-10.9: Draw evidence from literary or informational texts to support analysis, reflection, and research.
Chapter 13	CCSS.ELA-Literacy.RH.6-8.1: Cite specific textual evidence to support analysis of primary and secondary sources. CCSS.ELA-Literacy.RH.6-8.2: Determine the central ideas or information of a primary or secondary source. CCSS.ELA-Literacy.RH.6-8.9: Analyze the relationship between a primary and secondary source on the same topic. CCSS.ELA-Literacy.RH.9-10.1: Cite specific textual evidence to support analysis of primary and secondary sources, attending to such features as the date and origin of the information. CCSS.ELA-Literacy.RH.9-10.2: Determine the central ideas or information of a primary or secondary source.

Chapter	Common Core State Standards
Chapter 13, continued	CCSS.ELA-Literacy.RH.9-10.9: Compare and contrast treatments of the same topic in several primary and secondary sources.
Chapter 14	CCSS.ELA-Literacy.RH.6-8.1: Cite specific textual evidence to support analysis of primary and secondary sources. CCSS.ELA-Literacy.RH.6-8.2: Determine the central ideas or information of a primary or secondary source. CCSS.ELA-Literacy.RH.6-8.7: Integrate visual information (e.g., in charts, graphs, photographs, videos, or maps) with other information in print and digital texts. CCSS.ELA-Literacy.RH.9-10.1: Cite specific textual evidence to support analysis of primary and secondary sources, attending to such features as the date and origin of the information. CCSS.ELA-Literacy.RH.9-10.2: Determine the central ideas or information of a primary or secondary source. CCSS.ELA-Literacy.RH.9-10.9: Compare and contrast treatments of the same topic in several primary and secondary sources.
Chapter 15	CCSS.ELA-Literacy.RH.6-8.1: Cite specific textual evidence to support analysis of primary and secondary sources. CCSS.ELA-Literacy.RH.6-8.2: Determine the central ideas or information of a primary or secondary source. CCSS.ELA-Literacy.RH.6-8.7: Integrate visual information (e.g., in charts, graphs, photographs, videos, or maps) with other information in print and digital texts. CCSS.ELA-Literacy.RH.9-10.1: Cite specific textual evidence to support analysis of primary and secondary sources, attending to such features as the date and origin of the information. CCSS.ELA-Literacy.RH.9-10.2: Determine the central ideas or information of a primary or secondary source. CCSS.ELA-Literacy.RH.9-10.9: Compare and contrast treatments of the same topic in several primary and secondary sources.